Fighting Back:
The American Working Class in the 1930s

John Newsinger

About the author

John Newsinger is Professor of History at Bath Spa University. He is the author of ten books including *Orwell's Politics* (Macmillan, 2000), *United Irishman* (Merlin, 2001), *Rebel City: Larkin, Connolly and the Dublin Labour Movement* (Merlin, 2004) and *The Blood Never Dried: A People's History of the British Empire* (Bookmarks, 2006). He is working on a new edition of his *British Counterinsurgency* (Palgrave, 2001) including a new chapter on Afghanistan and Iraq.

Acknowledgements

Thanks to Megan Trudell, John Charlton, Sally Campbell, Mary Phillips, Mark Harvey, Peter Robinson and Ben Windsor for their help at various stages in the production of this book.

Fighting Back

The American Working Class in the 1930s

John Newsinger

Bookmarks Publications

Fighting Back: The American Working Class in the 1930s
—John Newsinger

Published July 2012
Bookmarks Publications Ltd
c/o 1 Bloomsbury Street, London WC1B 3QE
Copyright © John Newsinger

ISBN 978 1 905192 93 9

Printed by Halstan Printing
Typeset by Bookmarks Publications
Cover designed by Ben Windsor

Contents

Introduction 7

1 Open-shop America 10

2 The Great Depression 39

3 The ruling class response 57

4 Roosevelt in power 70

5 1934: the year of the fightback 85

6 The split in the union bureaucracy 105

7 Roosevelt turns left 118

8 1937: the year of the sit-down 142

9 On the attack 162

10 The battle for steel 182

11 On the defensive 206

12 Roosevelt and the left 216

Conclusion 243

Notes 246

Index 275

In memory of Tony Cliff, Paul Foot and Chris Harman

Introduction

On 27 February 1937 young women workers, many of them in their teens, staged a sit-down strike in the Woolworth store in downtown Detroit. They evicted the management and barricaded themselves in, demanding union recognition and a pay rise. The management capitulated on 6 March to stop the dispute spreading. This occupation was one episode in a wave of sit-down strikes that swept across much of industrial America that year. It forced employers who had previously resisted unionisation by every means available, including the use of lethal force, to recognise the unions. And this remarkable victory for American workers was achieved at a time when in Europe the workers seemed in retreat and fascism in the ascendant.

This book is an attempt to chronicle the tremendous struggle that American workers waged in the 1930s at a time when we are ourselves confronted with great social and economic battles and an escalating level of class struggle. The American working class provides us with a lesson in courage, militancy and creativity in the face of huge obstacles. Short of a revolutionary situation, no labour movement in an advanced country has fought for its rights with greater determination. American workers faced the richest and most powerful capitalist class in the world, a capitalist class with a history of ruthless and bloody repression. In the post First World War period and in the 1920s trade unions operated in what William Forbath has described as conditions of "semi-outlawry"[1], the left was regularly subjected to "red scare" tactics and working class militancy was met with armed force. In no other democratic country was the effort to unionise met with such deliberate and calculated violence. Indeed, for trade unionists, the United States was a "police state"—something that has generally been ignored because this was not the work of a state secret police, but of a private secret police. Private detective agencies spied on union activists, operated blacklists, infiltrated trade unions and when required inflicted beatings, murdered union organisers and shot down pickets. This repression produced a weak labour movement that was dominated by a corrupt and reactionary union leadership represented by the American Federation of Labor (AFL). The AFL rejected militancy, was hostile to the left and openly supported the capitalist system. And the United States had another dimension of repression that was peculiar to it: the oppression of black Americans, in both North and South. The trade unions were often accomplices in this, banning black workers from membership and trying to drive them from the workplace. Racism was a cancer infecting the US labour movement.

In 1929 this weak labour movement was overwhelmed by the onset of the Great Depression. This economic catastrophe imposed immense suffering on millions of men, women and children, both middle class and working class. The suffering of the poor, the homeless and the unemployed was exacerbated by the success the capitalist class had had in resisting the introduction of even a vestigial welfare state into the US. And yet, while in Germany the strongest labour movement in the world was to go down to defeat, destroyed by the Nazis, in the US the labour movement was to stage a great historic fightback that was to take the country further to the left than ever before.

Workers began rallying to the unions in 1933, but it was in 1934 that great class battles were to be waged in Toledo, Minneapolis and San Francisco, battles that shifted the balance of class forces across the country. Militancy was shown to win! In these mass strikes working class unrest was given leadership and direction by the forces of the American left. Members of the American Workers Party, the Communist League, the Communist Party, the Socialist Party and others played an indispensable role in these struggles. They argued that rank and file militancy was the way forward, that the workers should rely on themselves and on the solidarity of other workers, that the union leaders were not to be trusted and that Roosevelt and the Democratic Party were not on their side. Hard fought class battles saw the employers in retreat.

The victories of 1934 opened the door to union organisation. The miners' leader, John L Lewis, led a militant breakaway from the AFL to form the Congress of Industrial Organizations (CIO). Lewis was determined to ride the great wave of militancy rather than surrender it to the left. The decisive battle was the great confrontation with the world's largest corporation, General Motors, in 1936-1937. Workers brought the company to a stop by the use of the sit-down tactic, occupying the plants and where necessary defending themselves against police attack. Union victory over GM sparked a tremendous wave of militancy with hundreds of thousands of workers staging sit-downs. Many employers rushed to make concessions before they too were overwhelmed by the wave of militancy. These struggles deserve our attention. They provide both an inspiration and an example.

But the ruling class fought back. The labour movement suffered a serious defeat in the Little Steel strike in the summer of 1937, but what brought the labour offensive to an end was the return of recession. The so-called "Roosevelt depression" was a self-inflicted economic catastrophe that would have been Roosevelt's epitaph but for the Second World War.

What came out of these years of struggle was a considerably strengthened labour movement, but one in which the union leaders had been successful in controlling militancy and maintaining bureaucratic control. What of the left? One of the great tragedies of the international working class movement in the 1930s is the extent to which it came under the influence of Stalin's Comintern. The American left was not exempt from this. One consequence of this was that at a time of unparalleled working class militancy the left failed to establish itself as a force in American politics. This too provides important and instructive lessons for us today.

Chapter One

Open-shop America

In the aftermath of the First World War the American working class suffered a historic defeat. The post-war strike wave, which in 1919 saw 3,630 strikes involving 4,160,000 workers, was beaten back. The decisive moment was the defeat of the great steel workers' strike. A rank and file driven campaign to organise the steel industry was crushed by brutal repression compounded by the fact that the strikers received, at best, only half-hearted support from the AFL. According to strike leader William Z Foster, the resources the AFL devoted to the campaign would have been more appropriate if "we were setting out to organise a bunch of peanut stands, instead of 500,000 almost totally unorganised workers in the steel industry, American finance capital's chief open-shop stronghold". He later described trying to work with the AFL leadership as like "swimming in a sewer".[2]

On 22 September 1919 some 275,000 steel workers responded to the strike call. Within a week the number on strike had risen to 365,000. They confronted the fiercest repression. In his account of the strike Foster described how the Steel Trust:

> went ahead with strikebreaking measures unprecedented in industrial history. It provisioned and fortified its great mills and furnaces, surrounding them with stockades, topped off with heavily charged electric wires, and bristling with machine guns. It assembled whole armies of gunmen. Brute force was to be used in breaking the solidarity of the workers.

Civil liberties and free speech were suspended in the strike districts. As James Crawford, the mayor of Duquesne, eloquently put it, "Jesus Christ himself could not speak in Duquesne for the AF of L." According to Foster, for miles "through the heart of America's steel industry, including the important centres of Monessen, Donora, Clairton, Wilson, Glassport, McKeesport, Duquesne, Homestead, Braddock, Rankin, etc, not a meeting of steel workers could be held". The state police "beat, shot, jailed, or trampled steel workers under their horses' hooves", while company police and deputies indulged in "an orgy of robbery and thievery...they even robbed strikers in broad daylight".[3] The labour journalist Mary Heaton Vorse wrote that it was not a strike; it "was warfare" with the union treated as if it were "a predatory outlaw band".[4] By the time the strike was called off on 8 January 1920, 26 strikers had been killed, hundreds had been injured, shot and beaten, and thousands had been arrested. The attempt to organise America's open-shop bastion had failed and with it the prospect of transforming the AFL into an organisation capable of organising the mass production industries. The defeat handed the initiative to the employers.

Once the unions had been contained, the employers prepared for what has been described as "a war of extermination against organised labour".[5] An open-shop drive, the American Plan, was launched across the country to smash the unions. It was accompanied by a red scare intended to crush the left. The employers took advantage of the sharp recession of 1921-22, when US Gross National Product (GNP) fell by an astonishing 24 percent and unemployment shot up to 5 million (worse than the immediate aftermath of the Wall Street Crash in 1929-30). They cleared out union activists and destroyed union organisation in industry after industry. Whereas in 1920 union membership stood at a peak of 5,110,000, by 1923 it had fallen to 3,592,000.

The defeat of the craft unions in the railroad shopmen's strike of 1922 was the decisive engagement in this phase of the struggle. The strike began on 1 July. Some 400,000 men, who repaired and maintained the trains, walked out. In response the railroad companies between them hired over 50,000 armed guards. One line, the Pennsylvania, with 25,000 men on strike, hired 16,000 guards. These were reinforced by police and troops in an overwhelming display of force. From the very beginning, there was, according to the strike's historian, widespread violence and the conflict "assumed an almost insurrectionist quality that pitted strikers against the full weight of judicial and military might". The first pickets were killed on 8 July (two strikers and the 14 year old son of a striker); they were not the last.

President Harding's administration was divided over how to respond, with some urging that in view of the moderation of the AFL unions a sympathetic stance was in order. In the end the president listened to the open-shop hardliners, Harry Daugherty, his attorney general, and Charles Dawes, his director of the budget. Daugherty was little more than a crooked lawyer, heavily involved in the corruption that was to eventually overwhelm the administration. Dawes was a much more substantial figure, a successful Chicago banker, future vice-president and Nobel Peace Prize winner. His hostility to trade unionism was unrelenting and he had established a vigilante strikebreaking organisation, the Minute Men, back in his home state. At their urging Harding agreed to legal action against the strikers. On 1 September, Judge James Wilkerson granted "one of the most sweeping injunctions in US history". The injunction prohibited picketing, forbade any attempt at persuading scabs not to work ("by letters, printed or other circulars, telegrams, telephones, word of mouth, oral persuasion or suggestions"), banned the unions from communicating with their own members about the strike and prohibited them from using their funds to further the dispute in any way. They were even prohibited from consulting their lawyers. In the face of this legal repression the strike went down to a piecemeal defeat with some lines remaining strikebound into 1924. The unions suffered a devastating defeat.[6]

In a number of districts the railroad companies sponsored vigilante action against the strikers, most seriously in Arkansas. Here, in January 1923, hundreds of armed men led by America's home-grown fascists, the Ku Klux Klan, took over towns on the Missouri and North Arkansas line. They "arrested" strikers and put them on trial, with militants being sentenced to flogging and deportation from the district. In the town of Harrison one union activist, E C Gregory, was lynched for his militancy, hanged from a bridge.[7]

This defeat was far from inevitable. The strikers showed incredible determination but the unions on the operating side of the industry stood by and watched them go down to defeat. There were over 2 million railway workers in the US, and the unions representing the train crews allowed their members to work even though the trains were being maintained and repaired by scabs. And this was despite it being clear that a defeat for the shopmen would be a defeat for railway trade unionism generally. True to the worst AFL traditions, craft unions stood by while other craft unions in the same industry were crushed. The American Federation of Labor showed itself to be, in the words of its critics, "the American Separation of Labor".

The defeat of the railway shopmen's strike convinced the AFL leadership that the only hope for the survival of the trade union movement was to throw themselves on the mercy of the employers. Samuel Gompers, the AFL president, in the words of one labour historian, "acted the beggar, beseeching the employers to give the unions a break". After his death in 1924 his even more appalling successor, William Green, "proved even less militant and more deferential to employers".[8] Union leaders proclaimed their conservatism, hailed the virtues of the capitalist system, and expelled militants and "reds". Indeed, in his last months, Gompers was even prepared to praise Mussolini and Italian fascism in the pages of the AFL journal, the *American Federationist*.[9] The AFL, which had long embraced class collaboration, now found itself proclaiming that cause with growing desperation as employers increasingly sought the destruction of the unions.

Symbolising all this was the expulsion of the veteran militant and socialist William Dunne from the 1923 AFL convention for his membership of the Workers Party (the then incarnation of American Communism). As Dunne told the delegates:

> A labour movement cannot be built by attempting to placate the employers… You are trying to convince the employers that you are just as respectable, just as conservative, just as much interested in maintaining the wage system as the employers themselves.

The vote to expel him was proposed by Philip Murray, vice-president of the United Mine Workers (UMW). It was carried by 27,837 to 18.[10] Another UMW delegate, David McDonald, attending an AFL convention for the first time, remembered in his memoirs his surprise at how right wing the delegates were. They "were every bit as conservative, even reactionary in their thinking as a corporate board of directors".[11]

Dunne was, of course, absolutely right: the labour movement could not be built by placating the employers. Class collaboration requires a collaborator—and American employers in the 1920s were not interested. Union membership continued to fall throughout the decade, reaching a mere 3.2 million in 1929. Whereas in 1920 16.7 percent of

American workers had been union members, by 1929 the figure was only 9.3 percent. The unions retreated into their craft strongholds, although even these were shaken by the open-shop campaign. In 1920 the machinists' union had 282,000 members, but in the face of the employers' offensive this had fallen to 148,000 in 1922 and was down to only 70,000 in 1929. Even that great industrial union the United Mine Workers, which had boasted over half a million members in 1920, had by 1929 been virtually destroyed by "the combination of armed power and starvation", reduced to a membership of 80,000.[12] And in the new mass production industries trade unionism had been almost completely eradicated so that, for example, the Carriage, Wagon and Automobile Workers Union, which had 40,000 members in 1920, had been reduced to a mere 1,500 in 1929, out of a total workforce in the car industry of 450,000.[13] Indeed, according to a study carried out for the National Association of Manufacturers in 1928, the anti-union drive in manufacturing industry had been so successful that 92.6 percent of workers worked in factories that did not recognise trade unions.[14]

Among the few unions that bucked this trend were those in the building trades where, on the back of the 1920s construction boom, union membership actually increased to 900,000 in 1929. This only served to strengthen the forces of conservatism in the AFL. The leader of the United Brotherhood of Carpenters, Bill Hutcheson, a diehard reactionary, became increasingly influential.[15] As Robert Zieger has observed of this period, "never had labour's main bodies been so conservative and so willing to cooperate with the business community". The AFL abandoned "its feeble efforts to organise the unskilled workers who comprised the majority of the workforce" and instead "sought diligently to ingratiate itself with the nation's industrialists".[16]

Assault on the left

The First World War and its aftermath also saw crippling blows being inflicted on the American left. During the war both the reformist Socialist Party (SP) and the syndicalist Industrial Workers of the World (IWW) were victims of severe repression. In September 1917, with the support of the AFL leadership, the IWW headquarters in Chicago and locals across the country were raided by police and federal agents, preparatory to the great show trial that began in May 1918.

After a trial that made it clear that the intention was to destroy the IWW, 101 men were found guilty. They received draconian sentences, with 15 of them getting 20 years, 35 of them ten years, 33 of them five years and 12 one year. There were other show trials in California, Kansas and Nebraska, and across the West criminal syndicalism laws were introduced effectively banning the IWW.[17]

The Socialist Party also came under sustained attack. In 1912 the SP had 118,000 members, had elected 1,200 members to office, including one member of Congress, and in that year its presidential candidate, Eugene Debs, polled 897,000 votes. The party had been damaged by the adoption of an "anti-sabotage" clause at its convention that same year, which condemned direct action in the workplace as a form of struggle. This led to the defection of many IWW members and sympathisers. With the outbreak of war in Europe in 1914, however, its strong anti-war stance saw its support increase. In 1917, at its St Louis convention, the party responded to America's entry into the war with a strong declaration of opposition and with the repeal of the anti-sabotage clause. Whereas in Europe the war pulled reformist parties to the right, in the US the SP moved to the left, provoking severe repression. Censorship of the mail closed down its press, and its leaders and activists became the victims of both legal and extra-legal persecution. Among the many party members jailed was Eugene Debs, sentenced to ten years for an anti-war speech he made in June 1918.

The SP was given a boost by the outbreak of revolution in Europe, but in the aftermath of the war it fell victim to the emergence of American Communism and to the red scare orchestrated by the Wilson administration, in particular by the attorney general, Alexander Mitchell Palmer. It is worth noting that Franklin Roosevelt was a member of Wilson's administration at this time. For the SP the consequences were disastrous. Whereas in 1919 the party had 108,504 members, by 1922 the number had fallen to only 11,277. In Oklahoma, the state where the party had been strongest, its membership had been reduced to 14 in 1924. Despite this collapse, when Debs, still in prison, once again stood for the presidency in 1922 as Prisoner 9653, he received 913,664 votes.[18]

The other victim of the red scare was American Communism. The two rival Communist parties formed in 1919 had a joint membership of some 40,000, but the red scare, with its raids, blacklisting, imprisonment and deportations, had reduced this to less than 10,000 the following year.[19]

The persecution of the left continued throughout the 1920s. Beatings and victimisation, legal harassment and imprisonment remained the routine experience of the left activist, but they never became a national campaign of repression. One noteworthy episode took place in August 1929, when police raided a Communist-organised children's summer camp at Yucaipa in California. Eight of the young people running the camp were arrested and charged with criminal syndicalism, with one of their number, 19 year old Yetta Stromberg, also charged with raising the red flag, a criminal offence in California (and many other states). One defendant, Isadore Berkowitz, hanged himself the day before sentencing. The others were all sentenced to five years imprisonment, except for Stromberg, who received ten years. The convictions were eventually overturned, but this was by no means certain at the time, and the effect of such persecution was considerable.[20] The most celebrated episode of repression in this period was the execution of Nicola Sacco and Bartolomeo Vanzetti, two anarchists accused of robbery and murder, on 23 August 1927. They were put to death because of their politics, despite the weakness of the case against them, and in the face of a great international outcry. Evidence that would not have convicted anyone else served to convict them.[21] The United States was not a congenial environment for anyone on the left, but the left survived, albeit in a climate of fear.

Prosperity and the class struggle

In 1919, as we have seen, there were 3,630 strikes involving over 4 million workers. By 1929 the number of strikers had fallen to 289,000 workers taking part in 900 strikes. In 1928 the number of strikes had been 604, the lowest number since 1884 (when the working class was considerably smaller). For many commentators it seemed that the class war was over, that industrial peace and harmony had been realised, and that the future offered unrivalled prosperity. Indeed, in 1928, Herbert Hoover declared that increasing prosperity had put an end to industrial conflict and that the US was now "nearer to the abolition of poverty, to the abolition of the fear of want than humanity has ever reached before".[22] Certainly, at the time and still today, the benign view of American history is that the rising prosperity that followed the 1921-22 recession provides the explanation for the weakness of the trade unions and for the low level of class struggle. A subsidiary explanation points to the extent to which employers embraced what has been described as "welfare capitalism", that is profit-sharing schemes, contributory pensions, share purchase schemes and company unions. They were supposedly killing the unions by kindness!

It is absolutely true that American capitalism underwent a remarkable expansion in the 1920s that in many ways transformed the country. In 1919 GNP was $84 billion and by 1929 it had risen to $104 billion. To what extent did the working class benefit from this growth? According to George Soule, real wages rose by "approximately 15 percent" between 1922 and 1929.[23] This, of course, raises the question of whether an increase that averages out at 2 percent a year is an adequate explanation for the low level of class struggle and the weakness of the trade unions, indeed for their almost complete absence from the mass production industries. While the figures show that rising real wages were an important reality, there is, in fact, no direct relation between this and the level of class struggle. Indeed, a good case can be made that the economic conditions obtaining in the 1920s were precisely those in which one would have expected the unions to make gains. And, of course, large groups of workers did not benefit at all: between 1923 and 1929 coal miners' wages fell by an average of 14 percent.[24] The collapse in UMW membership was not the result of contented workers deciding they did not need the union because the boss would look after them, but was rather, as we shall see, the result of "the blacklist, the blackjack, the assassin's revolver and other New Testament methods of persuasion".[25]

The rise in real wages was not produced by employer generosity, but by the historic rise in productivity that took place in the 1920s. Between 1919 and 1929 US productivity rose by over 60 percent. Wage rises over the same period were parsimonious when put in this context. As Peter Fearon points out, the benefits from the increase in productivity went overwhelmingly "to shareholders, or other owners, in the form of profit".[26] What made it possible for the capitalist class to reward itself so handsomely was, of course, the weakness of the trade unions. A Brookings Institution study showed that in 1929 the wealthiest 27,500 families had a combined income greater than that of the poorest 11.5 million families. The study estimated that a family income of $2,000 a year was just enough to cover the bare necessities and noted that even at the height of the boom 60 percent of families fell below even this basic level. The 1920s consumer boom rested on those with family incomes over $2,500. Even many of these families were only comfortable on a week by week basis, their prosperity depending on the last wage packet. This group included much of the skilled working class, many of them members of the craft unions that dominated the AFL. This was the reality of 1920s prosperity. The veteran liberal journalist Oscar Garrison Villard described the situation well:

> Vast numbers of Americans were not only living at or below the subsistence level but were steadily sinking in the economic scale...millions upon millions of Americans in the South were worse housed and fed than any peasants in Europe. Harding, Coolidge and Hoover one after another mouthed the old sickening lies about the high American standard of living and prided themselves that we were so far ahead of the rest of the world.[27]

And, of course, Herbert Hoover, who became president in 1929, was absolutely certain "that depression was a thing of the past".[28]

Even more problematic in explaining the low level of class struggle in the 1920s was "welfare capitalism". The significance of these schemes has often been exaggerated; indeed, as one study points out, in 1927 the average company expenditure on such schemes was $27 per employee![29]

While most workers hardly participated in the 1920s prosperity, for the capitalist class the US in this period was a veritable utopia. When Warren Harding became president in 1921, presiding over one of the most corrupt administrations in American history,[30] he proclaimed that he intended to have "less government in business and more business in government". According to one historian, Harding "had no qualification for being president except that he looked like one".[31] This was, of course, one more qualification than George W Bush, but his lack of ability was precisely what was required, so that others could get on with running the country. The most important of these others was Andrew Mellon, the third richest man in the country (after J P Morgan and Henry Ford).[32] He was appointed Secretary of the Treasury, a post he held for the rest of the decade; indeed, it was jokingly said at the time that three presidents had served under him. Harding, after his premature death, was succeeded by another non-entity, Calvin Coolidge, who in 1924 proclaimed that "the business of America is business". Indeed, capitalism was celebrated with an often religious fervour, with Coolidge declaring that "the man who builds a factory builds a temple...the man who works there worships there".[33] It is worth making the point here that the Democratic Party's response to the capitalist triumphalism of the time was to wholeheartedly embrace it. In 1924 the Democrat candidate for the presidency was the Morgan bank's lawyer, John Davis, who urged that "our true policy is to out-Mellon Mellon".[34]

The belief that American capitalism had divine inspiration was not new, and is still a powerful ideological force today, but it was particularly potent in the 1920s. A key figure in championing this belief was Bruce Barton, one of the founders of the American public relations industry. In the 1920s his firm, Barton, Durstine and Osborne, had worked hard at persuading American corporations to present themselves as families rather than as businesses. Barton urged business to show that it was not solely concerned with profit but that it had "a soul". The best way to maximise profit, he argued, was to pretend that this was not your overriding concern. General Motors was one of the converts. Barton was also the author of one of the bestselling books of the 1920s, *The Man Nobody Knows*—a biography of Jesus Christ published in 1925. Here he argued that Jesus was "the founder of modern business". He came from a respectable middle class home, was very much a man's man, was fond of parties, but, most important, he "picked 12 men from the bottom ranks of business and forged them into an organisation that conquered the world". The book sold 250,000 copies in 18 months and was even made into a silent film.[35] This Christian capitalism survived into the 1930s, with God actually being proposed for honorary membership of the National Association of Manufacturers in 1937.

Under the Republicans in the 1920s the US became an increasingly unequal society. According to one historian, between 1920 and 1929 the disposable income for the bottom 93 percent of the population grew by 6 percent, while for the top 7 percent of the population it "nearly doubled". With Mellon at the Treasury, the rich and the super-rich were the beneficiaries of massive tax cuts and rebates. By 1926 someone with an annual income of $1 million or more had had their tax bill reduced by a third. During his time at the Treasury, Mellon dispersed $3.5 billion to the corporations in tax rebates, including millions to his own family businesses. Mellon actually had the Bureau of Internal Revenue provide him with a tax expert to prepare his own returns so that he paid as little as possible. The tax regime was so full of loopholes that many of the rich declined to pay tax altogether. J P "Jack" Morgan, one of the richest men in the country, "some years paid no income tax whatsoever".[36]

Mellon justified his tax policy on the grounds that it would stimulate investment, but as the decade closed it was becoming clear, as David Shannon points out in an observation with a very contemporary ring, that "a large part of the funds that wealthy people saved...went into speculation that created neither more jobs nor real wealth".[37] Things looked good though. At Christmas 1928 the partners in the Morgan bank paid themselves a $1 million bonus each and the head of the bank, Jack Morgan, had work begun on the largest private yacht in the world, the 343 foot Corsair. It "was a floating palace with elevators, beamed ceilings, Indian teak panelling, mahogany armchairs and fireplaces, it required a crew of 50 and cost Jack an estimated $2.5 million".[38] America was a capitalist paradise.

Repression

No working class in any bourgeois democracy has fought for trade union rights with the determination, militancy, inventiveness and courage of the American working class. The reason for the weakness of American trade unions does not lie with any "exceptionalism" on the part of American workers, but rather with the "exceptionalism" of the American capitalist class.[39] In the US employers have resisted trade union organisation with exceptional ruthlessness and determination. As David Robertson has pointed out:

> Comparative statistics, though necessarily rough estimates, suggest that American unionisation rates did not differ substantially from those in Great Britain and Germany around 1900. The gap between the United States and these nations widened between the early 1900s and the 1920s.

The reason for this had nothing to do with prosperity, but instead "reflects the exceptional anti-union counterattack mounted by American employers in the first and third decades of the 20th century".

As Robertson insists, "American employers have opposed trade unions with a vehemence unequalled in any other OECD nations".[40]

According to Patrica Cayo Sexton, American employers waged "a uniquely repressive war on the 'labour-left." This often had the character of a "hot war" involving "violence conducted by employer-inspired vigilantes, mercenaries and various public armed forces". The working class everywhere, she observes:

> has "war stories" to tell, but nowhere has the record been so violent as in the United States... One review of some major US strikes puts the figure at 700 dead and untold thousands seriously injured in labour disputes, but these figures, though impressive, include only strike casualties reported in newspapers between 1877 and 1968, and may therefore grossly understate the casualties.[41]

This last point is certainly correct.

On 23 March 1928 Richard Mellon, the brother of the Secretary of the Treasury, appeared before a congressional committee in Washington. He was asked by Oliver Eaton, the UMW attorney, about the family's extensive Pittsburgh mining holdings, and in particular about the weapons provided for their private police. In the exchange, which became quite famous, when asked about the use of machine guns, Mellon replied, "It is necessary. You could not do without them." Although he quickly tried to withdraw this revealing admission ("I don't know anything about machine guns"), he had nevertheless testified to the fact that many of the most important employers in the US, "the captains of industry", would oppose the efforts by their workers to unionise with machine guns if necessary. They would kill rather than surrender the open shop. This was not the testimony of some renegade backwoods employer, but of one of the pillars of the US business establishment, talking about the family business.[42]

Talk of machine guns in the coalfields was far from idle. The Mellon family had a controlling interest in the Pittsburgh Coal Company, the largest mining company in the country, and had led the way in attempting to destroy the UMW. In May 1924 the company had closed all of its pits, reopening them in August 1925 as open-shop concerns, tearing up agreements with the UMW and cutting wages. This union-busting strategy became known as "the Pittsburgh Plan" and was followed by company after company. The mine owners, as UMW president John L Lewis put it, "manned their properties with armed mine guards, searchlights, barbed wire fences, stockades, and such paraphernalia of war".[43] The miners finally struck in an attempt to save the union in 1927. They found themselves pitted against ruthless employers who were armed to the teeth and had the law 100 percent on their side. Strikers and their families were evicted from their homes, deprived of their civil liberties and sentenced to starvation. Pickets were arrested, beaten and sometimes killed.

Lowell Limpus, a New York journalist who visited western Pennsylvania during the struggle, described the situation:

> We saw thousands of women and children literally starving to death. We found hundreds of destitute families living in crudely constructed bare-board shacks. They had been evicted from their homes by the coal companies. We unearthed a system of despotic tyranny reminiscent of Czar-ridden Siberia at its worst. We found police brutality and industrial slavery.

The UMW, he went on, had been assailed by "the weirdest flock of injunctions that ever emanated from an American Temple of Justice".[44] One of these injunctions, issued on behalf of the Clearfield Coal Company operating at Rossiter, not only barred the union from picketing, holding meetings, using union funds to feed the strikers' families, and in any way whatsoever trying to persuade scabs not to work, but also prohibited the singing of hymns.[45] When Senator Robert Wagner visited Rossiter he declared, "Had I not seen it myself I would not have believed that in the United States there were large areas where civil government was supplanted by a system that can only be compared with ancient feudalism".[46]

Fifty years later, when anthropologist Barry Michrina did field work in the Pennsylvania coalfield, he found retired miners still bitter and angry about the 1927 strike. They remembered living under what amounted to "martial law". One interviewee told him of how the coal companies ruled with "an iron hand and ran the company towns like a concentration camp". There was a 9pm curfew, at which time a whistle would blow. The searchlight would be switched on, and the "Coal and Iron Police would patrol the town on horses. There was no freedom of assembly". A number of interviewees told him of "miners who were mysteriously shot or disappeared in Viola, Nanty Glo and Mentcle".[47]

It is not known how many miners and their family members died during the 1927 strike, but Richard Mellon was obviously not exaggerating when he said that machine guns were necessary to mine coal. Breaking the UMW did not come cheap though. In 1927 the Pittsburgh Coal Company spent $472,000 on company police. With the union crushed, expenditure was cut back to $12,000 in 1928.[48] It is worth noticing that, while the miners and their families suffered the most terrible hardships, Andrew Mellon was able to turn his own investment in the company into an extremely lucrative tax avoidance scam. Valued at over $6 million at their peak in 1930, he sold his holdings to his friend Henry McEldowney's Union Trust Company for only $500,000, thereby realising a tax deductible loss of $5,500,000 to be set against future income. Having successfully worked the scam, he then bought the shares back from his partner in crime for the same price as he sold them.[49] All this was perfectly legal.

The readiness of the American capitalist class to use deadly force against workers struggling to unionise is not given enough weight in most histories of the American working class. It is acknowledged readily enough as a factor in individual incidents such as the Ludlow massacre of 1914 or the Memorial Day massacre of 1937, but its importance as one of the defining characteristics of class struggle in the US is not really recognised. Repression was a vital factor in the defeat of the unions after the First World War.

Some mention must be made of the part played by the courts in this repression. The readiness of the courts to grant injunctions against unions seriously curtailed the right to strike, on occasions removing it altogether. The use of injunctions was so widespread and oppressive that Samuel Gompers, the AFL president and certainly no militant, devoted a chapter of his memoirs to "Injunctions I Have Encountered".[50] As well as a strike involving a confrontation with an employer who might well be armed to the teeth, it also often involved a confrontation with the courts. In the 1920s, according to Forbath, "courts issued more than 2,100 anti-strike decrees, and the proportion of strikes met by injunctions to the total number of strikes reached an extraordinary 25 percent".[51] At this time "almost any strike...was likely to face some sort of court injunction".[52] Some historians have remarked on the incongruity of such a widespread use of injunctions at a time when the level of class struggle was so low. More to the point, the use of injunctions, which was enthusiastically advocated by employers' associations, was one of the factors responsible for the low level of class struggle.

The man regarded as the "Father of the Injunction" was former president William Howard Taft, who had been appointed US Chief Justice by Warren Harding in 1921. He had a long history of hostility to trade unions, briefly interrupted by the war, but resumed immediately afterwards. In 1894, during the Pullman strike, he had shown what his biographer describes as "a shocking hostility" to the strikers. On 6 July he had written, "It will be necessary for the military to kill some of the mob before the trouble can be stayed." The following day he wrote of the need for "much bloodletting", welcoming the fact that "tonight...30 men have been killed by the federal troops". He later realised that the death toll had been exaggerated and on 8 July lamented that the troops "have only killed six of the mob as yet. This is hardly enough to make an impression".[53] His attitudes were much the same when he was appointed chief justice. Under Taft the Supreme Court maintained, indeed strengthened, its pro-business and anti-union stance. One of his first decisions, dealing with a strike for union recognition at the American Steel Foundries, effectively outlawed picketing. In a dispute that had involved no violence, Taft nevertheless declared the very word "picket" to be "sinister" and suggestive of "a militant purpose". Picketing, he found, "is unlawful and cannot be peaceable and may be properly enjoined". All he was prepared to allow was one man standing on each gate.[54] As Taft quite candidly put it with regard to the labour movement, "That faction we have to hit every little while".[55]

The experience of the Amalgamated Clothing Workers (ACW) at the hands of the courts is instructive. During the 1920-21 lockout in New York, when Justice Van Sielen issued an injunction against the union, he took the opportunity to make it absolutely clear that in America the judiciary "must stand at all times as the representatives of capital, the captains of industry", must "protect private property and persons from violence and destruction", and be "strongly opposed to all schemes for the nationalisation of industry". In 1925, during another dispute in New York, a judge banned ACW members from approaching within ten blocks in any direction of the strike-bound International Tailoring Company. The union headquarters just happened to be in

FIGHTING BACK

the proscribed area. And, in 1922 in Philadelphia, Judge Rogers made clear his lack of bias when he declared that, in his opinion, the ACW "should be driven out of existence as a menace to the nation".[56] Even as late as 1937 some sort of record was to be achieved as far as injunctions were concerned when workers at the Calderon restaurant in New Jersey walked out on strike at 11.50am and were served with an injunction effectively proscribing their strike at 11.57am.[57]

Unions were also hobbled by the legal recognition given to "yellow dog" contracts (the name supposedly derives from an employer saying he would rather employ a yellow dog than a union member). In 1917, in the Hitchman Coal and Coke Company v Mitchell judgment, the Supreme Court upheld the legality of contracts whereby workers agreed not to join a union. For a union organiser to ask a worker who had signed such a contract to join a union was illegal. This "court-fashioned outlawry", as Forbath points out, provided "a thin hard coat of legality to the activities of Cossacks, Baldwin-Felts guards and other public and private troops in the coalfields".[58] As David Kennedy puts it, the decision in effect "rendered illegal almost any effort to organise a union without the employer's consent. Employers were to seize on this legal instrument with a vengeance in the 1920s".[59]

Among the UMW organisers imprisoned for contempt in the Hitchman case was Fannie Sellins, whose career provides a useful case study in the role of repression. On 26 August 1919, while picketing the Allegheny Coal and Coke Company mine in Brackenridge, western Pennsylvania, she was shot down in cold blood by company guards. It was probably a deliberate targeted assassination. She was shot twice in the back and once in the head and her skull was crushed with a blow from a club while she lay dying. One of her killers paraded up and down wearing her hat. There were dozens of witnesses to her murder. A hand-picked coroner's jury returned a verdict that her killing was "justifiable and in self-defence" and went on to condemn "Anarchy and Bolshevism".[60] According to Mary Heaton Vorse, during the Great Steel Strike there was a picture "of her bruised face...hung in every organiser's office".[61] The manner of her death tells us something about the nature of class conflict in the US. The low level of class struggle in the 1920s rested on the success employers had in intimidating and victimising militants, rooting out union organisation and crushing strikes. It rested on repression.

America as a secret police state

To be a trade unionist in the US was to be the victim of a secret police regime. This is not generally recognised because, as Heber Blankenhorn pointed out, in America the secret police was privatised: "What espionage there is in Europe is a government monopoly; no other civilised country tolerates large-scale, privately owned labour spying".[62] The scale of the operation was enormous. Much of what we know for certain about this dimension of the class struggle in the US comes from the investigations of the La Follette Committee in the late 1930s (to which we will return), but there is every reason to believe that the situation was much the same in the 1920s.[63] Blankenhorn, who worked for the committee, identified 230 private detective agencies engaged in spying on the unions, providing armed guards and strike-breaking. He estimated the absolute minimum number of undercover agents working in the unions at 40,000. This figure was "based on the fact that there are some 41,000 union locals in the United States and it is estimated that there is at least a spy in every local". Indeed, according to one union official testifying before the committee, "there is no gathering of union members large enough to be called a meeting that is small enough to exclude a spy". The minimum expenditure by business on this private secret police was estimated at $80 million a year, an enormous sum in those days—and this was an extremely conservative estimate, as was acknowledged at the time.[64] The most famous private detective agency was the Pinkertons, founded in the 1850s. According to John Abt, the chief legal counsel for the committee, in a typical city like Indianapolis the Pinkertons alone:

> had operatives in the American Clothing Workers Union, the Street Railway Union, the American Federation of Hosiery Workers, the Brotherhood of Railway Shop Crafts, the Brewery Workers Union, the Gas Station Attendants Union, the Pulp and Paper Mill Workers Union, the Teamsters Union, the United Auto Workers, the Electrical and Radio Workers Union, the Wire and Cable Workers Federal Union, and local unions of clerical workers, glass blowers, grocers, warehouse workers, molders, and stereotypers.

He goes on, "We found spies in every union...including company unions".[65]

General Motors (GM) paid nearly a million dollars in the period from January 1934 through to July 1936 to private detective agencies to spy on its workers. Its agents also kept William Green of the AFL and John L Lewis of the UMW under surveillance. Indeed, GM even hired the Pinkerton Agency to spy on its main detective contractor, the Corporations Auxiliary Company. The powerful Citizens' Alliance of Minneapolis, an open-shop business association, not only employed the Burns Detective Agency, but also maintained its own extensive network of spies and informers through its Special Services Division, which claimed to have an agent in every union local in the city. Trade associations, like the ferociously anti-union National Erectors' Association (NEA), routinely ran spy networks and operated blacklists. According to Walter Drew of the NEA, once a strike started it was very difficult to infiltrate a spy, but if "he is already established on the ground he is in a much better position to anticipate and prevent lawlessness". The NEA employed a number of detective agencies to spy on union activists over the years. On one occasion a union official repaid the compliment, bribing a clerk in the NEA's offices to provide him with a list of spies in the Structural Iron Workers Union: "The list contained 25 or more names, some of them prominent officials".[66] And some companies ran their own secret police, for example, Henry Ford's Service Department, headed up by the notorious Harry Bennett. Not only did Ford employ a small army of thugs to police his factories, but the workforce was also riddled with informers, reporting on such things as the number of times their fellow workers visited the toilet as well as their attitude to trade unions.[67]

For union militants and activists, labour spies were part of everyday experience. During the 1922 "coal war" in Somerset County, western Pennsylvania, Heber Blankenhorn, at the time working as a journalist, observed what he described as "a normalcy of repression". He wrote that "gunmen, in or out of uniform, walked along handling their weapons, suggestively flaunting their authority". But there was also a secret terrorism: "Eviction notices or arrests would light on the heads of men a few hours after a conference which they had thought was secret".[68] Ten years later, in Birmingham, Alabama, Hosea Hudson, a black worker, attempted to organise in the Stockhom Pipe and Fittings plant. Unfortunately, one of their number was a "company stoolpigeon" (they actually held their meetings at his house), who promptly provided management with the names of everyone involved. The company ran its own spy system that "consisted of a bunch of spies, our own fellow workers and shop mates, who were paid $5 every week, based on the report they pushed through the pay window".[69]

When Abraham Muste looked back over his time as a militant union organiser, he remembered that he "soon learned that on any strike committee or union executive board there would be one or more labour spies". Indeed, when he was one of the leaders of the 1919 textile workers' strike in Lawrence, he was taken aside by one of the other strike leaders, John Mach, who, in a rare display of remorse, revealed that he was a private detective. He had established his credentials as a militant by exposing several other spies and, as Muste admits, "knew everything there was to be known about strike affairs and plans". Mach had been urging a militant demonstration in defiance of a police ban which would certainly have led to "a clash...in which somebody would be killed—the police would see to that". This, he told Muste, would provide an excuse for the arrest of the strike leadership for "murder", that is for being responsible for the killing even if it had been the work of a policeman. This had been done in Lawrence before, during the 1912 textile strike, when Joseph Ettor and Arturo Giovannitti of the IWW had been arrested under these exact circumstances and held in prison for a year before being acquitted. Mach told him that, as the strike fund was almost exhausted, he had now been told by his employers to disappear so that they could spread the demoralising rumour that he had run off with the funds. The next day he was gone.[70]

On another occasion, also during the great post-war battles, Clint Golden, a left official in the Machinists in Philadelphia, attempted to smoke out the spy network in the city. He placed a number of adverts seeking to recruit "confidential agents" to spy on the unions in a number of newspapers on behalf of bogus employers' organisations. To his astonishment, he received over 300 replies. Although some of his respondents were just "desperate men out of work", there were also "a large number of active union officers and committeemen, particularly in the Machinists" up for sale. Many of them boasted of their previous work for various private detective agencies, and one, a leading member of Golden's own lodge, "boasted of his subversive role in the 1919 steel strike". Another self-confessed spy was the president of the Philadelphia

Central Labor Union, a key body in the struggles of the time, and another a former organiser for the Machinists, "both exposed as agents on the payroll of strikebreaking agencies".[71]

Let us look at one last example from the steel industry. During the great strike of 1919, according to William Z Foster, the campaign "was saturated with company spies". Indeed, he was warned by a sympathiser that US Steel was actually receiving the minutes of the National Committee for Organising Iron and Steel Workers on a regular basis. He already suspected one committee member of being a spy and he was eventually exposed as such, but that member had never received a copy of the minutes for that very reason. To identify the spy the 45 copies of the minutes that were sent out all had a different spelling of the name of one committee member, Edward Nockels. When his source showed him the copy of the minutes that had been passed to the company, he was able to identify the leak. A secretary at the offices of the International Brotherhood of Blacksmiths was subsequently caught copying the minutes and "unceremoniously fired".[72]

During the 1919 steel strike the Sherman detective agency sent revealing instructions to one of its agents, ordering him to do all he could to whip up ethnic conflict among the strikers:

> We want you to stir up as much bad feeling as you possibly can between the Serbians and the Italians. Spread data that the Italians are going back to work. Call up every question you can in reference to racial hatred between these two nationalities; make them realise to the full extent that far better results would be accomplished if they will go back to work. Urge them to go back to work or the Italians will get their jobs.[73]

All this was, of course, perfectly legal; indeed, private detectives often appeared in court as witnesses against union activists. In "normal times" the company spy kept the blacklist up to date, sometimes occupying a union position himself to keep an eye on things. In times of conflict the spy added to the role of surveillance that of agent provocateur, and sometimes even that of assassin. There was nothing comparable to this outside of the US.

More than a decade later, in the early 1930s, John Gates, a young Communist working as an organiser in the steel towns, found that nothing had changed in the industry:

The mills themselves were like military fortresses, with small private armies of uniformed, armed police to intimidate the workers and block organisation. City and town government, controlled by the steel corporations, ruthlessly suppressed all union activity. For all practical purposes, trade unions were illegal and subversive; organisers were arrested, beaten up and driven out of town; workers suspected of union activity were summarily fired and blacklisted throughout the industry. To ferret out militant workers, the companies employed large numbers of spies.

There was still hanging over the mill towns, "a heavy pall of fear, repression and poverty".[74]

The privatised secret police force that was turned loose on the labour movement did not make struggle impossible; the history of the American working class is testimony to that. But it did make the struggle more difficult and more dangerous. Joining a union in the US in the 1920s and 1930s required considerably more courage and determination than it did in Britain (which was certainly not without its blacklists, company spies and police violence but at a much lower level). The decision to join a union in the US often required an uncommon degree of anger, courage and determination. Once the decision was made, American workers fought all the harder. In the 1920s most workers were not prepared to make that decision. This was to change in the 1930s.

A history of human sacrifice[75]

One dimension of the class struggle is often neglected in histories of the working class—the toll of dead and maimed in industrial "accidents". No advanced bourgeois democracy has a worse record than the US in this regard. From 1880 to 1900 on average 35,000 workers were killed in industrial accidents every year in the US, and another half a million were injured, many of them permanently maimed and crippled. In 1913 there were 23,000 workers killed in industrial accidents, over 4,000 on the railways and 2,600 in the mines. In 1936 there were 16,000 fatalities and in 1937 18,000. Between 1920 and 1928 getting on for 2,500 steel workers were killed in industrial accidents. Quite astonishingly, between 1911 and 1985, 103,000 miners were killed in industrial accidents in the US. This death toll reflected a dreadful lack of concern with human life in the pursuit of profit.[76] A widespread attitude was captured by Dr Alice Hamilton when she investigated lead poisoning in Colorado before the First World War. She asked one apothecary if he had ever encountered a case, and when he said no she "explained that that was incredible, and he said, 'Oh, maybe you are thinking of Wops and Hunkies (Italians and Slavs). I guess there's plenty among them. I thought you meant white men'."[77] The lives of immigrant workers and black workers counted for very little.

The daily toll of dead and maimed was highlighted by spectacular disasters that often cost hundreds of lives: the Monongah coal mine disaster in 1907 in which 362 men were killed, the Cherry coal mine disaster in 1909 that killed 180 men, the Triangle fire in New York in 1911 that killed 146 workers, overwhelmingly young women, many of them jumping to their deaths to escape the flames, and the Speculator copper mine disaster of 1917 that killed 164 miners, with the bodies of many of the dead piled up against safety doors that had been illegally welded shut. The worst industrial disaster in US history, however, is one of the least well known, which is somewhat strange as the company involved was Union Carbide, the company responsible for the 1984 Bhopal disaster in India, which was to cost over 15,000 lives.

In 1929 the New Kanawha Power Company, a subsidiary of Union Carbide, began preparations for the construction of a hydroelectric plant in West Virginia. To power the plant the company intended to divert water from the New and Kanawha rivers by means of a 3.75 mile tunnel cut through a mountain at Hawk's Nest, near the town of Gauley Bridge. The construction of the tunnel was subcontracted to a major construction company, Rhinehart-Dennis, but Union Carbide engineers closely supervised the work. Drilling of the Hawk's Nest tunnel began in June 1930 and was completed ahead of schedule in December 1931. This was achieved only at the expense of an appalling loss of life. As Martin Cherniak puts it, "Labour, unlike time, was a dispensable commodity."

The mountain was 97 to 99 percent pure silica; indeed, it was so pure that it was shipped to another Union Carbide plant for processing. Working conditions were so bad in the tunnel that workers on average only stuck with the job for 15 or 16 weeks. Even this short period was enough to condemn them to death. The management neglected standard safety measures, such as the use of water to suppress dust, and did not issue respirators (only managers had respirators and were told they had to use them). A respirator cost $2.50. The workers worked in dust so thick that visibility was often reduced to a few feet. Although West Virginia mining law required a 30-minute wait after blasting, the workers were sent back into the tunnel immediately, on occasions being driven back in by force, herded by foremen armed with pick handles. At no point was any effort made to measure the level of dust in the tunnel. Company doctors were ordered not to tell the men what was wrong with them when they reported sick. Workers became increasingly short of breath and sometimes just dropped dead from silicosis on the job. They were carried from the tunnel and buried, shovelled into the ground, without any ceremony, sometimes within hours of their death. No autopsies were carried out on these victims. One worker remembered how, when a man became too sick to work:

> The sheriff would come around and run him off the place, off the works. I have seen the sheriff and his men run the workers off their places when they were sick and weak, so weak they could hardly walk. Some of them would have to stand up at the sides of trees to hold themselves up. And the sheriff and his men could plainly see that the men were sick and unable to go, yet they kept making them keep on the move.

Men died in the tunnel, in the hospital or were driven off to die wherever they could find shelter. Men died sheltering "under rocks, and every place else".[78] Perhaps as many as 200 men died miserable deaths on the job, and many more were to die in the succeeding months and years.

While the company employed 4,931 men to work on the tunnel project, the turnover was such that the number at work at any one time was much lower. Altogether some 2,500 actually worked in the tunnel, 500 white workers and 2,000 black workers. According to Michael Cherniak, in what he concedes is a conservative estimate, of these 2,500 men at least 764 were dead from silicosis or related complications within five years. Of the dead, 581 were black.[79] Among the dead were also the foremen who had herded them into the tunnel. One Rhinehart-Dennis official was reported as saying that he knew they were going "to kill those niggers within five years", but he had not

FIGHTING BACK

realised they were going to kill so many of them "so quick". It was, according to Rush Dew Holt, the Democrat Senator for West Virginia, "the most barbaric example of industrial construction that has ever happened in this world". The company, he insisted, "knew what it was going to do to these men" and "openly said that if they killed off those men there were plenty of other men to be had".[80]

It was industrial manslaughter on a massive scale and yet no one was ever called to account. Bribery, intimidation and political influence protected Union Carbide from punishment, while for the workers there was a miserable, appalling death, and for some of their dependents derisory compensation. Such a crime would have been impossible in any other advanced bourgeois democracy. Nowhere else was the balance of class forces so heavily tipped against the working class that an employer could fire dying men, evict them and send them off to die alone, "under a rock", in the wilderness; nowhere else would workers, black and white, be shovelled into the ground within hours of dropping dead on the job. In the US the power of big business was such that an employer with enough political clout could actually get away with mass murder.[81]

Black workers and racism

One point that should be emphasised in any discussion of the American working class is that, however bad the situation was for white workers, it was considerably worse for black workers. Moreover, the racism that often characterised white workers' attitudes not only made them accomplices in the oppression of black workers, but also weakened the position of white workers themselves by dividing the working class. Most AFL unions discriminated against black workers, refusing them membership and opposing their employment, or enrolling them in separate "Jim Crow" locals. White workers' racism often created a situation where a strong union was actually to the detriment of black workers. When a union that barred black workers from membership secured a closed shop, for example, any black workers were sacked. There were notable exceptions to this history of racism, but the harsh fact remains that for most black workers the trade union movement was not seen as a friend.[82]

This was not inevitable. The Knights of Labor in the 1880s had fought against white racism and had built a mass movement that united black and white workers.[83] In the 1910s the IWW had fought to unite white and black workers.[84] Those AFL unions that took a stand for black and white unity were almost invariably the industrial unions, such as the UMW. Indeed, a good case can be made that industrial unions, because of their aspiration to unite all the workers in an industry, had a tendency to unite black and white workers.

What this last section is concerned to explore, however, is the scale of the oppression that black workers were subjected to in the period after the First World War. From 1917 through to 1921 there was a succession of pogroms launched against black communities across the US. It began in July 1917 in East St Louis, where 39 black men, women and children were brutally killed by white mobs.[85] The climax came in the "Red Summer" of 1919, when "within a span of weeks racial violence spread from one city to another, and every city feared its turn was next". There were serious outbreaks in 20 cities, including Washington DC, but the worst outbreak was in Chicago, where officially 23 black people were killed and 15 white people. One important feature of these pogroms was the extent of black resistance. While black men and women had always fought back against their oppressors, "in 1919 the resistance was more often overt and direct, defiant in its willingness to inflict as well as suffer casualties". The official response to these pogroms was, by and large, to treat them as if they were black rebellions that had been successfully repressed. There could be no official recognition of black oppression.[86]

Another horrific outbreak occurred at Tulsa, Oklahoma, at the end of May 1921 when a group of black men gathered at the city jail to prevent a lynching. This defiance precipitated a full-scale pogrom against the Greenwood district, known as "Little Africa", with the intention of driving the black population out. The official figure for the number of people killed was ten white people and 26 black people, but this was merely part of the official cover-up. The bodies of many of the black victims were disposed of in secret with the locations still unknown. Walter White of the National Association for the Advancement of Colored People (NAACP) estimated that between 150 and 200 black people had been killed. His estimate is generally accepted as closer to the truth. The pogrom left 35 city blocks in Greenwood burned out.[87]

Throughout the American South black people were disenfranchised, subjected to Jim Crow laws and held in subjugation. In many rural areas conditions were little better than slavery with black tenant farmers held on the plantations as debt slaves and black convicts rented out to white farmers to do as they liked with. One particularly brutal episode in Georgia in 1921 saw a white farmer, John Williams, fearful of federal peonage charges, murder 11 black prisoners that he had bought, disposing of the bodies and claiming that he had set them free. He drowned most of them, shot one and killed another with an axe. He was sentenced to life imprisonment.[88] The *Liberator* magazine, co-edited by Claude McKay, expressed its surprise at the fact that Williams got even a life sentence in Georgia, but confidently expected that "the next governor will pardon him".[89] Brutality at the hands of white people was a routine experience for Southern black men, women and children.

Charles Lincoln remembered a typical episode from when he was a boy of 14 years working to put himself through school in Alabama in the late 1930s. He had picked 41 pounds of cotton for which the white overseer paid him 25c. His calculation was that he was owed over $3 and when he put this to the overseer, he received a savage beating:

> His first blow to my chin lifted me off the floor and crumpled me at his feet. Then he began to rhythmically stomp my head and kick me in the face and stomach... That lesson in racial etiquette cost me a tooth, a bloated, bloody face, a ruptured stomach, and a mouth full of scar tissue.[90]

He could count himself lucky because if he had been beaten to death it would have signified nothing as far as the authorities in Alabama were concerned.

Lynching, with the connivance of the authorities, was a crucial instrument in the subjugation of the black population. In 1918 60 black people were lynched in the US, the great majority in the South. In 1919 there were 76 lynchings, including of a number of war veterans, in 1920 53, in 1921 59 and in 1922 51. Altogether, between 1918 and 1927 405 black men and 11 black women, three of them pregnant, were lynched. Forty two of them were burned alive. These lynchings were usually public affairs, celebrations of white supremacy for the whole family. They often involved incredible cruelty, with the victims subjected to torture and mutilation before being burned alive or hanged. Body parts were much sought after as mementoes and photographs of the tortured victims were sold as postcards.

In 1918, of the 60 lynchings of black men and women that year (four white men were also lynched), 19 took place in Georgia. Here a particularly brutal white plantation owner was killed by a black "debt slave" he had flogged, provoking what has been described as a "lynching orgy". Over five days 11 black people were killed, including one woman, Mary Turner, who was eight months pregnant. Her husband, Hayes, was one of the men lynched and she made clear her intention to see his killers prosecuted. In retaliation, a white mob that, in the words of one newspaper report, "took exception to her remarks as well as her attitude", lynched her as well. They hanged her upside down, drenched her in petrol and set fire to her, then cut her baby from her body and stamped it to death, before finally emptying their guns into her. "You ought to've heard that nigger wench howl," one of the participants cheerfully told Walter White when he took him to the scene. This did not take place in Auschwitz, but in rural Georgia. The NAACP sent the governor, Hugh Dorsey, the names of the ringleaders, all respectable men, but no effort whatsoever was made to pursue her killers. The police were, however, much more successful in tracking down the man who had actually killed the plantation owner, and he was "legally" hanged in 1919. That same year, once again in Georgia, Eli Cooper was burned alive for trying to organise field workers and urging armed resistance to lynch mobs, and 72 year old Berry Washington was burned at the stake after he shot dead a white man trying to rape a neighbour's daughter.[91]

Black attempts at union organisation met with the most ferocious repression in the South. Here they were seen not just as a threat to the employer or plantation owner, but to white supremacy itself. An attempt at establishing a sharecroppers' union in Phillips County, Arkansas, in September 1919, was treated as a black rebellion. Police, vigilantes and federal troops were unleashed against an unarmed population, imposing a reign of terror, generally known as the "Elaine Massacre", that left an unknown number—certainly hundreds—of black men, women and children dead. According to Walter White, who narrowly escaped lynching himself while investigating the massacre, "I was never able to fix definitely the number of negroes killed, but did gather evidence establishing a total in excess of two hundred." One contemporary white account estimated over 800 dead. A white judge later recalled that the federal troops "must have killed 100 niggers right there". Another witness reported seeing 16 black men hanging from one bridge. The troops, police and vigilantes took body parts from the dead as trophies. Hundreds of prisoners were rounded up. Many of them were tortured and one was doused in petrol and burned alive in order to secure evidence of a black insurrection. Eventually 12 black prisoners were brought to trial and duly sentenced to death, while another 80 received lengthy prison sentences. These convictions were later overturned, but justice was never done in Arkansas. As Walter Pickens, another NAACP investigator, put it, the whole Mississippi River Valley was "an American Congo".[92] At the time of this massacre the Assistant Secretary of the Navy, Franklin Roosevelt, soon to be the Democratic Party candidate for the vice-presidency, wrote to a friend in Arkansas about the riot in Washington DC, "With your experience in handling Africans in Arkansas, I think you had better come up here and take charge of the police force".[93]

One last episode is worth recounting for the light it throws on the plight of Southern black people. In 1927 the great Mississippi flood inundated 27,000 square miles of seven states, with 246 people officially dead and tens of thousands homeless. Herbert Hoover, then the secretary of commerce, was put in charge of the relief effort. Not only were black people the last to be rescued (there were reliable accounts of livestock owned by white people being rescued before black people), but the refugee camps were inevitably organised on Jim Crow lines. In the black camps the refugees were kept under armed guard because many of them were "debt slaves" and it was feared they might take the opportunity to escape. In some camps black refugees "were even forced to wear tags listing the name of the planter they had worked for".[94] On occasions men attempting to escape were publicly flogged. In the white camps the Red Cross provided supplies for free, but in the black camps recipients were charged and their debt was sold on. Black refugees were used as forced labour and on occasions they were even hired out to private employers as if they were convicts. A Colored Advisory Committee, established by Hoover to disprove allegations of mistreatment, nevertheless found that there were refugee camps where black people "were beaten by the soldiers and made to work under guns", that the soldiers had committed "more than one wanton murder" and that "women and girls were outraged by these soldiers". Hoover had this indictment removed from the final report. To all intents and purposes, black refugees were treated as prisoners and were only to be released into the custody of the plantation owners who held their debts. As General Curtis Green of the Mississippi National Guard told Walter White, black refugees were only let go when a plantation manager came along and "picks out his niggers".[95]

Chapter Two

The Great Depression

The Great Depression was a catastrophe. US GNP fell from $104.4 billion in 1929 to $94.4 billion in 1930, a less dramatic fall than in the depression of 1921-1922. On this occasion, however, there was no recovery. In 1931 GNP fell to $87.8 billion, in 1932 to $74.8 billion, and in 1933 to $72.7 billion. The US economy shrank by nearly a third, with manufacturing particularly hard hit, shrinking by an incredible half. Private sector investment in 1929 totalled $35 billion, but by 1932 it was down to only $3.9 billion. Even more startling, whereas total corporate profits before tax in 1929 stood at over $9.5 billion, by 1931 this had become a total corporate loss of $781 million, and by 1932 of over $3 billion. In 1933 things "looked up" with a total corporate profit of $151,000. The scale of the collapse was overwhelming.[96]

For American workers the consequences were disastrous. The unemployment figures (unreliable though they are) tell the story: in 1929 3.2 percent; in 1930 8.7 percent; in 1931 15.9 percent; in 1932 23.6 percent and in 1933 24.9 percent. The real figures were certainly higher than these semi-official figures. The great cities were particularly hard hit, so that in Chicago, for example, in 1932 there were 700,000 people unemployed, "fully 40 percent of its workforce".[97]

By 1931, with US Steel leading the way, employers began imposing wage cuts. According to Lens, those lucky enough to still have jobs "had their pay cut by 20, 30 or more percent, as payrolls dropped by 60 percent in just four years". And the pay of women workers was cut even more drastically than that of men. As Irving Bernstein points out, some of the wage rates "defy belief". He writes of how:

early in 1933 a skilled garment operator was netting 58 cents for a nine hour day. In Texas many domestic servants received $1 a week. Black girls sold their labour on street-corner "slave markets" in the Bronx for 9 cents to 15 cents a day. Industrial homework revived. Women, often with their children, worked on knit goods for 5 cents an hour, for 70 hours a week.[98]

Not only were wages cut, but millions of workers found themselves on short-time. In 1932 US Steel, which had already cut wages and laid off thousands of workers, did not employ anyone full time. White collar workers were not exempt, but also suffered lay-offs and pay cuts. In many cities and towns public sector workers, including teachers and even the police, often went unpaid or were paid in "scrip"—IOUs to be redeemed at a later date. The professions were hard hit, with hundreds of thousands of middle class people losing their savings when the banks failed, having their jobs and businesses swept away, their homes repossessed, and being left broke and homeless. In New York in 1932 Sidney Lens records that there were 109 qualified chemists, members of the respectable middle class, completely destitute, homeless, and another 300 looking for work. He tells of a 44 year old civil engineer arrested for vagrancy, who told the court that he had been sleeping rough "for the past 46 days...in a vacant lot near Flatbush Avenue".[99] In 1930 across the US 150,000 homes were repossessed, in 1931 200,000, and in 1932 250,000. By February 1933 "more than a thousand families a day were being evicted in foreclosure actions".[100] There were an estimated 2 million people homeless, and across America shanty towns, "Hoovervilles", sprang up. Even the super-rich were hurt, so that whereas in 1929 513 people had admitted to annual incomes of over a million dollars, by 1932 the figure was down to 20.[101]

In a country with only a vestigial welfare state[102] the Great Depression was to cause misery on a truly massive scale, with widespread hunger, escalating levels of homelessness and unprecedented poverty. Edmund Wilson described the scene in the summer of 1932:

> There is not a garbage-dump in Chicago which is not diligently haunted by the hungry. Last summer in the hot weather when the smell was sickening and the flies were thick, there were a hundred people a day coming to one of the dumps, falling on the heap of refuse as soon as the truck had pulled out and digging in it with sticks and

hands. They would devour all the pulp that was left on the old slices of watermelon and cantloupe till the rinds were thin as paper; and they would take away and wash and cook discarded onions, turnips, potatoes, cabbage or carrots. Meat is a more difficult matter, but they salvage a good deal of that too.

He remembered how one woman, when she "picked up the meat, she would always take off her glasses so that she couldn't see the maggots".[103] In New York, Louis Adamic reported, "many were actually starving. Children ringing doorbells and asking for food! Unemployed stenographers living on a banana a day!"[104] "Wherever one turned", Sidney Lens recalled, "there was a wasteland of shattered lives".[105] According to *Fortune* magazine, in the terrible winter of 1932, there were 34 million men, women and children in America with no income at all.[106] In the mining districts of Pennsylvania, West Virginia and Kentucky there were towns with over 95 percent unemployment, towns where the utility companies had cut off the water supply because of non-payment, "forcing the jobless to bucket drinking water from the polluted streams".[107]

An unknown number of people, but certainly in the low thousands, actually starved to death in these years. As Ronald Edsforth has pointed out, there are no reliable figures because "elected officials, hospitals, and medical examiners seemed determined to hide the facts about hunger and starvation". In New York the city insisted that only two people had died of starvation in 1931, but when an investigator, Eleanor Flexner, looked at the records for just two hospitals, she found 95 deaths from starvation and believed that there were many more people whose cause of death had been recorded as one of the complications resulting from starvation in order to keep the figures down. In Albany in New York State, Edsforth records a ten year old child collapsing and dying from starvation at her school desk.[108] In Detroit in 1931 a doctor at one of the city's hospitals reported that on average four people a day were being admitted "too far gone from starvation for their lives to be saved". Their cause of death was always recorded as "pneumonia or some other complication".[109] John Anderson, who was later to become a union organiser, remembered how during "the summer and fall of 1932 I almost starved...quite often one learned of the bodies of men and women being found in box cars and other places... They died of cold, malnutrition, and lack of medical attention".[110] In West Virginia the journalist Henry Francis described the starving and sick children of the unemployed that he saw as "marked for death, marked by the hundreds".[111]

The paradox of people starving to death in what was still the richest country in the world and where the rich continued to live lives of unprecedented luxury was bought out by the veteran socialist Oscar Ameringer, when addressing a Senate Committee in February 1932. He told them of his trip across America. In Seattle he had seen "numbers of women searching for scraps of food in the refuse piles in the principal market of that city", while in Montana farmers had complained to him "of thousands of bushels of wheat left uncut on account of its low price that hardly paid for the harvesting". In Oregon he had seen "thousands of bushels of apples rotting in the orchards", while in the cities "there are millions of children who, on account of the poverty of their parents, will not eat one apple this winter". He told them of how in Oregon sheep were being slaughtered and their carcasses left to rot, while he had seen "men picking for meat scraps in the garbage cans in the cities of New York and Chicago".[112]

One last point needs making here: however bad it was for white working class men and women, it was worse for black people. In Chicago, where black people were 4 percent of the population, they made up 16 percent of the unemployed, and in Baltimore, where they were 17 percent of the population, they made up 31.5 percent of the unemployed.[113] Another study showed that across 106 American cities "the proportion of Negroes unemployed was from 30 to 60 percent greater than for whites".[114]

Unemployed resistance

When he accepted nomination as the Democratic Party's presidential candidate on 2 July 1932, Franklin Roosevelt went out of his way to comment on what he claimed was "the great social phenomenon of this depression"—that people were suffering passively, without making any trouble. The Depression, he went on, "has produced but a few of the disorderly manifestations that too often attend upon such times". Indeed, "the greatest tribute that I can pay to my countrymen", he proclaimed, was that "in these days of crushing want there persists an orderly and hopeful spirit on the part of millions of people who have suffered so much... Wild radicalism has made few converts." He returned to this comforting theme during the election campaign itself (3 October 1932) when he spoke in Boston. The American people, he told his audience, "stand peacefully, even when they stand in a breadline".[115] This was at a time of increasing social unrest and disorder. Even William Green of the AFL felt obliged to warn the ruling class that they could only drive the workers "so far before they will turn on them and destroy them... Revolutions grow out of the depth of hunger".[116]

Of course, for someone from Roosevelt's ruling class background, the idea of the unemployed suffering passively was immensely comforting. As for it being "hope" that kept people passive, it was in fact despair that had that effect. Hope produced agitation, discontent, anger, and resistance, all of which Roosevelt feared. Indeed, as we shall see, his political trajectory in the 1930s was driven by the need to provide an alternative to the potential for radicalisation that the Great Depression posed. There was no rise of mass Fascist or Communist movements in the US and the American Republic was not to go the way of the Weimar Republic.[117] But while the suffering of the early 1930s did not produce revolution, it did provoke resistance.

Despair was not conducive to resistance. Mauritz Hallgren, an independent Marxist commentator, made the point at the time in his *Seeds of Revolt*, published in 1933. Revolution, he wrote, did not "spring spontaneously out of hunger". As he insisted, "Extreme want and hunger are much more likely to produce humiliation, degradation of the spirit, shame and fear, rather than the violence, formidable courage, and will to power which are so necessary for a successful revolution." Nevertheless, he insisted, contra Roosevelt, there was increasing resistance in the US. Indeed, there were "more disturbances and disorders from 1929 to 1933 than in any other comparable period in the history of the country". Violence was not initiated by the unemployed, however, but was almost always initiated by the police. That these protests did not amount to any sort of concerted generalised challenge to the system was a consequence of the weakness of the left.

Hallgren provides a useful catalogue of the disturbances that had taken place, and it is worth reproducing a selection of them, focusing on 1931, 1932 and 1933:

SAN JOSE, California, 5 August 1931. San Jose is practically under martial law in consequence of disorders arising from the cannery strike. Following the first minor clash between police and strikers, 11 strikers were arrested. About 1,500 strikers and sympathisers then rushed the jail in the City Hall to rescue the prisoners, and were driven back by tear bombs and fire hose.

CLEVELAND, 5 October 1931. A howling, booing mob of Communists marched to the City Hall tonight in a rainstorm and engaged in scores of fist fights with the police. While more than 2,000 of them jostled the police on the steps of City Hall, 600 more stormed into the council chamber and held the meeting for 30 minutes.

NEW YORK, 21 April 1932. Wild rioting ended a Communist unemployment demonstration at City Hall this afternoon when a group of radicals rushed a police cordon around City Hall Park and mounted and foot patrolmen waded into the crowd, swinging sticks and fists. Two patrolmen and four demonstrators were painfully injured.

PHILADELPHIA, 30 April 1932. More than 20 persons were injured today when police broke up a proposed march on City Hall as it was started from two mobilisation points. A dozen marches were arrested, 15 were treated or held at hospitals for observation and five policemen were injured sufficiently to require hospital treatment.

WHITE PLAINS, New York, 3 August 1932. An attempt by more than 100 unemployed men and women to hold a mass meeting here in defiance of the refusal of Police Chief William Miller to permit a public demonstration in the city streets was broken up by 50 policemen after an exchange of blows that lodged two unemployed men in the hospital. Six persons were arrested.

DETROIT, 26 August 1932. Police were keeping a watchful eye today on the 5100 block on Springwells Avenue where a clash between 1,000 civilians and 300 police as the aftermath of a frustrated eviction resulted in injuries to ten persons yesterday.

SOUTH RIVER, New Jersey, 19 September 1932. Twenty state troopers swooped down on this Middlesex County borough shortly before midnight tonight and, using clubs instead of firearms dispersed an angry mob of 3,000 men and women who had held 40 private detectives from Newark and all 14 members of South River police force virtual captives in the Borough Hall for nearly six hours... In this afternoon's clash, one boy was killed, another boy and one of the private detectives were wounded by bullets, and five more deputies and a policeman injured with brickbats hurled by the mob.

CLEVELAND, 21 November 1932. A dozen men and women were trampled and bruised and two men arrested late today when a squad of mounted policemen rode through a gathering they estimated at 300 persons attempting to storm their way to Mayor Roy T Miller's office.

NEW YORK, 21 January 1933. Several hundred jobless surrounded a restaurant just off Union Square today demanding they be fed without charge. Their demands were presented by a delegation of five which attacked the restaurant manager when he refused their request. Police riot squads arrived to find the manager stabbed and hundreds milling outside the restaurant entrance.

SEATTLE, 16 February 1933. A two day siege of the County-City Building, occupied by an army of about 5,000 unemployed, was ended early tonight, deputy sheriffs and police evicting the demonstrators after nearly two hours of effort.

Hallgren provides a particularly grim account of the situation in Chicago where he thought "the suffering among the jobless" was worse than any other city he had visited. By 1933 "street disturbances and food riots had become daily occurrences" with the unemployed fighting back against one of the most brutal police forces in the country (a point we shall return to on a number of occasions). On 25 January on the South Side "two policemen were beaten unconscious during a riot"; on 27 January "Captain James L Mooney was felled with an iron bar, and six other police officers were seriously injured"; and on 28 January "another and more ominous disturbance took place on upper Michigan Avenue". The situation was getting out of control. Hallgren believed at this time that some sort of "revolutionary crisis is inevitable".[118] Chicago's mayor, Anton Cermak, had already warned that the federal government "had a basic choice...between sending relief and sending troops".[119]

The Communists and the Third Period

The weakness of the American left was one of the crucial reasons why resistance was not more widespread. The left had been severely battered during the red scare, coming out of the experience weak and divided. The reformist Socialist Party was a shadow of its former self, often serving as little more than a convenience for union bureaucrats battling the revolutionary left, especially in the clothing industry. As for the Communist Party (CP), it was a revolutionary organisation with hardly any roots in the class, crippled by factionalism and in the process of being transformed into a Stalinist organisation whose first loyalty was to the Soviet Union. In 1928 the party had faithfully adopted the Communist International's "Third Period" turn, expelling a reluctant leadership, led by Jay Lovestone, in the process.[120] The Third Period turn committed the CP to the belief that revolution was imminent, that the working class already had or was about to achieve revolutionary consciousness, and that the main obstacles to victory were the reformist parties, the trade unions and other far left parties. The turn committed the party to "dual unionism", the establishment of revolutionary trade unions in opposition to the AFL. And it involved the embrace of a crazed sectarianism that labelled the AFL "fascist" and other organisations on the left as either "social fascist" or "left social fascist". As Irving Howe and Lewis Coser point out in their history of the CP, the Third Period served as "the ideological teething ring" on which the party's new Stalinist leadership proved themselves. It was responsible for creating "an utterly poisonous atmosphere" on the left.[121] The only redeeming features of the politics of the Third Period were the militancy and determination with which CP members threw themselves into organising the unemployed and into actively, indeed ferociously, combating racism, fighting for the rights of black workers in a way that had never been seen in the US before.

In 1932 the CP published a comprehensive statement of the Third Period turn as it applied to the US, William Z Foster's *Toward Soviet America*. Foster, as we have already seen, was a veteran union organiser. He had joined the party in late 1921. He was to be the CP's candidate for president in 1932, running against both Hoover and Roosevelt. The book was, according to Foster, a response to "a great and growing mass demand in this country to know just what is the Communist Party and its programme". It provided an indictment of the capitalist system in crisis, celebrated the achievements of the Soviet Union and warned of the danger of fascism. What particularly distinguished the volume was its revelation that the AFL unions were not just led by reactionaries, committed to class collaboration on almost any terms, but that they were being "fascized". Indeed, "the process of fascization is far advanced" with the top leadership, "the Greens, Wolls, Lewises...already practically open-fascist". Similarly, the Socialist Party was in the process of "fascization", while those to the left of the SP, the Trotskyists, the Musteites, the Lovestoneites and the IWW, were "the most insidious and dangerous to the workers". These were the "left social fascists", an especial danger because their allotted role in the preservation of capitalism was to mislead those workers who were in the process of being radicalised and to keep them from coming under the influence of the Communist Party. The way forward, Foster told his readers, without any ambiguity whatsoever, was through revolution and civil war leading to the establishment of a Soviet America under the leadership of the Communist Party. Once the revolution had triumphed, all other political parties would be "liquidated", leaving "the Communist Party functioning alone as the party of the toiling masses".[122]

At the time this volume was published, with its assumption of mass revolutionary class consciousness and imminent revolution, the CP had, according to Foster himself, "approximately 15,000 members". It had a fantastically high turnover. In 1930 6,000 people joined the party but membership only increased by 1,000 and in 1931 12,000 people joined but membership only went up by some 4,000.[123] In the 1932 presidential election he was to receive a meagre 102,221 votes. Nothing better demonstrates the way in which the Third Period turn had been imposed on American Communists by Moscow than this discrepancy between the theory and the facts on the ground. In Weimar Germany, where the Communist Party was a mass party, the Third Period turn was to have catastrophic consequences, dividing the working class and helping Hitler into power. In the US the Third Period merely served to cripple the often heroic efforts of self-sacrificing revolutionaries at building resistance. As Howe and Coser put it, in Germany the Third Period "meant high tragedy", whereas in the US it too "often resulted in low comedy".[124]

Bringing misery out of hiding

Small though it was, the CP put a tremendous effort into organising among the unemployed. Many of its members were themselves unemployed.[125] It organised Unemployed Councils that fought for relief, resisted evictions and established gas and electricity squads to switch these utilities back on when the companies switched them off. It organised occupations of relief offices and protest marches that often involved violent clashes with the police.[126] According to Len De Caux, in the early 1930s CP members were:

> the most fully employed persons I met during the depression... They worked ten to 12 hours a day...maybe 16 if you counted yakking time. Most got no pay. A few full-timers had theoretical salaries, more theory than salary... They were in on every protest I saw or heard of. If they didn't start things themselves, they were Johnnies-on-the-spot. The anti-eviction fights were their babies, or adopted babies. They brought demanding crowds to the relief offices. They organised block committees, mass meetings, demonstrations... The communists brought misery out of hiding in the workers' neighbourhoods. They paraded it with angry demands... They raised particular hell.[127]

On 6 March 1930 the Communists organised nationwide protests against unemployment, part of an international protest, that they claimed mobilised over a million people in the US. One historian has argued that 500,000 is a much more realistic figure, but this is still a remarkable achievement for such a small party. The largest of the day's protests was in New York, where some 100,000 people assembled in Union Square, demanding the right to march down Broadway. The city's Democrat mayor, Jimmy Walker, a corrupt playboy politician, refused and put thousands of police on the streets to prevent it. As Foster recalled:

> Union Square on March 6th was an unforgettable sight. The workers were massed in the Square, and all the side streets were crowded. The unemployed had come together to demand the right to live. The police and firemen were in the Square in great force and thousands more were stationed in nearby buildings as reinforcements. On roofs surrounding the Square were machine guns.

Foster protested at the time that "the Queen of Romania, sundry military butchers, and many capitalist organisations had been allowed to parade freely, but now the class that built Broadway was being denied the right to walk along it". When the demonstrators attempted to march, they were attacked by the police, both mounted and on foot, and the fire hoses were turned on them. The police cleared the streets, clubbing to the ground those men and women too slow to flee. In the aftermath of the demonstration four of the organisers were imprisoned, with Foster, Robert Minor and Israel Amter serving six months and Harry Raymond ten months.[128]

There were massive demonstrations in Detroit (100,000), Boston (50,000), Chicago (30,000), Philadelphia (30,000), Cleveland (25,000) and another 30 cities. In Los Angeles, Peggy Dennis remembered how:

> Ten thousand men, women and children tried to march to City Hall, their banners demanding bread or jobs. Machine guns were targeted on them from roof tops. One thousand police on foot, horseback and in patrol cars clubbed, tear-gassed and horse-bumped them into side streets. Falling, fighting, marching, singing, shouting, the demonstrators inched their way through side streets and over barricades... We counted our injured by the hundreds. We checked the jails hourly for those arrested. We tracked down two children arrested for the crime of having stuck their tongues out.

In the fighting her husband, Gene, "had been beaten into unconsciousness" and dragged by his feet "to a patrol cart and to jail".[129] The official position in Los Angeles was made clear by the police commissioner who announced that "Communists have no constitutional rights" and that "the more the police beat them up and wreck their headquarters the better".[130]

The Communist achievement is all the more impressive when one considers the routine repression that they were subjected to. In Chicago, for example, the police raided one neighbourhood meeting in the run-up to the 6 March protest and arrested 14 activists. They were handed over to the tender mercies of the city's "Red Squad". Steve Nelson, one of those arrested, was strapped to a chair, worked over with a baton, and then kicked unconscious. When he rejoined his comrades, "Harold Williams was stretched out, his torn pants revealing an enormous rupture and B D Amos had his front teeth knocked out. Joe Dallet was bleeding from his mouth and had a gash on his cheek... Fourteen year old Fred Fine was slapped around and called 'you dirty little Jew bastard'." Two of their number were untouched: "This, we figured, was done deliberately so as to throw suspicion on their integrity".[131] In much of the US at this time a systematic working over of prisoners was the norm. The so-called "third degree", more properly the use of torture to extract information and confessions, was widespread, indeed routine, in many police departments, Chicago being the most notorious.[132] Despite this harassment, the party still put out 200,000 leaflets and 50,000 stickers, and got 30,000 people, black and white, out on the streets on 6 March. Soon afterwards the party moved Steve Nelson out of Chicago because it was feared that the police intended to kill him.

According to another Communist veteran, John Williamson:

> Nowhere was police terror so bad as in Chicago during those years. Corrupt to the core and in alliance with gangsters, the police arrested hundreds of workers at meetings, demonstrations and strikes and beat them into insensibility in the local police stations.[133]

This capacity for violent repression was fully demonstrated on 31 August 1931, when a large crowd of black workers, led by the Communists, assembled to oppose the eviction of 72 year old Diana Gross. In a scuffle with police two protesters were shot dead and later that day the body of a third was found, having been tortured and shot in the head. The Communist Party responded to this attack by distributing 50,000 leaflets with the slogan "DEMAND DEATH PENALTY FOR THE MURDERERS OF THE WORKERS", and organised a massive funeral for the three men, with 60,000 people, including 20,000 white people, following the coffins.[134] The three men "became the symbol of the city's unemployed masses".[135] This sort of incident was not confined to Chicago, however. Just over a month later in Cleveland, on 6 October, the police fired on a crowd trying to prevent an eviction, killing two black protesters, and, once again "thousands buried the dead at the Woodhill Cemetery".[136]

The most serious incident in the Communist campaign against unemployment occurred on 7 March 1932, when party members led a "hunger march" of some 3,000 people to the Ford River Rouge plant in Dearborn, a suburb of Detroit. The march was halted by the Dearborn police, effectively an auxiliary of the company, who refused entry to the township. When the marchers defied them, they began firing tear gas, but were forced to retreat towards the plant. Here they were joined by members of Ford's Service Department, the company's notorious private police force, and together they opened fire on the demonstration.

A press photographer at the scene estimated that hundreds of shots were fired. Four workers were killed, among them 19 year old Joe York, the leader of the Detroit Young Communist League (YCL), and many more were wounded. One of the wounded, Curtis Williams, a black worker, later died in hospital. The authorities responded to the massacre with a crackdown on the left, with widespread raids and arrests.[137] Inside the Rouge plant itself, according to the labour lawyer Maurice Sugar, "Ford discharged several thousand workers...where there was the slightest suspicion that any of the workers were even sympathetic with the hunger marchers there were discharges—so many and so indiscriminate it was obvious the policy was to discharge a hundred in order to get the one they suspected".[138]

The company claimed that it had foiled a Russian-backed Communist plot to seize the Rouge plant. This was all the more ironic because at the very moment that American Communists were being shot down outside the plant, inside there were Russian Communist officials and technicians "receiving instructions in Ford methods of production. This was part of a highly lucrative contract Ford had signed with the Communist regime".[139] According to Maurice Sugar, the Russians "must have seen the clash, including the shooting".[140] Inevitably, the interests of the Stalinist state prevailed over any sentimental notions of solidarity with the hunger marchers.

While these bloody confrontations inevitably stand out, one has to remember that party members were engaged in organising protests, raising demands and mobilising people on a daily basis. Their efforts produced real improvements for hundreds of thousands of people and they punched far above their weight. When Mauritz Hallgren travelled across the country, time after time social workers told him "that without street demonstrations and hunger marches of the Unemployed Councils no relief whatever would have been provided in some communities, while in others even less help than that which has been extended would have been forthcoming".[141] One particularly innovative campaign that the CP launched was aimed at defending homeowners against "a wave of foreclosures and subsequent evictions". They established the Small Home and Landowners Federation. As John Williamson points out, people "who only a few months before had been decrying the 'rowdiness' and 'violence' of the unemployed" now "fought police and sheriff's deputies and built barricades".[142]

Al Richmond, who as a 17 year old had taken part in the 6 March 1930 demonstration in New York, provides a useful account of the party's mobilising methods, as he learned them from George Mink. He was by now working on the New York waterfront, where relief was provided by the Seamen's Church Institute. He asked Mink what sort of demands they should raise:

> The first thing you do is fight for two meals and when you get two meals you fight for three meals and when you get three meals you fight about the menu; if they give you stew you want roast beef and if you get beef you want steak and if you get steak you want choice on the menu. Remember you cannot demand too much because the workers created it all and until the workers take it all they are not demanding enough.[143]

"The most deep and devilish of American oppressions"

The Communist Party took a strong and determined stand against racism, against what Len De Caux described as "the most deep and devilish of American oppressions".[144] During the Third Period it put forward the demand for black self-determination in the Southern Black Belt, a demand that attracted little popular support. More important was its organising work among black workers and its opposition to white racism. Angelo Herndon, a young black worker, was won over to the party when he heard William Dunne deal with a heckler who asked him if he would let his daughter "marry a nigger". Dunne replied:

> Listen, mister, my daughter will marry any man she likes whether White, Negro or Chinese. That will be her affair, not mine. But one thing you can rest assured of: I would rather that she jump into a lake than to marry such a yellow-bellied Negro-hater like you.

Later in June 1932 Herndon was to organise a protest demonstration against cuts in relief in Atlanta, Georgia. Over 1,000 people, black and white, took part. As Herndon subsequently observed, any united action by black and white workers inevitably "caused alarm and consternation" in the South. The authorities were alarmed enough to make concessions, but soon afterwards Herndon was arrested for organising the demonstration and charged with "inciting insurrection", a capital offence. At his trial he was accused by the prosecution of wanting to set up "a nigger Soviet republic" and the jury was urged "to send this damnable anarchistic Bolsheviki to death by electrocution, and God will be satisfied that justice had been done". The jury could not agree on a death sentence, and so instead he was sentenced to 20 years on the chain gang. The Communist Party campaigned and fought for his release through the International Labor Defense (ILD). His case became a national issue, and he was eventually freed by the Supreme Court in 1935.[145]

The episode that did most to identify the Communist Party with the cause of black liberation, however, was the campaign to save the "Scottsboro Boys". On 26 March 1931 nine young black men and boys (Willie Robertson, Olen Montgomery, Eugene Williams, Roy Wright, Charlie Weems, Ozie Powell, Clarence Norris, Hayward Patterson and Andy Wright), aged from 19 down to 12 years, were accused of raping two young white women. Despite the fact that medical examination clearly showed that neither woman had been raped, eight of "the boys" were sentenced to death after a derisory trial. In the case of the youngest, 12 year old Roy Wright, a mistrial was declared when the jury insisted on the death penalty even though the prosecution had not asked for it. Although clearly innocent, "the boys" were only saved from Alabama justice by the intervention of the ILD. Even so fierce a critic of the Communist Party as Sidney Hook acknowledged that "one indisputable achievement" of the CP was that "its organisational efforts saved the lives of the defendants in the Scottsboro case".[146] While their lives were saved, getting them released was another matter, even after one of the two women, Ruby Bates, admitted she had lied and joined the campaign to secure their release. As one prosecuting attorney put it, Alabama justice was not for sale to "Jew money from New York".[147] Only after the most protracted legal battles were they to be released: Willie Robertson, Olen Montgomery, Eugene Williams and Roy Wright in 1937, Charlie Weems in 1943, Ozie Powell and Clarence Norris in 1948 and Andy Wright in 1950. Hayward Patterson escaped from prison in 1948 and the governor of Michigan refused to extradite him back to Alabama. Considering the horrors of the Alabama prison system, the injustice done to these young men defies belief. It was the Dreyfus affair nine times over. Admission of a black man's innocence in a rape case involving a white woman was seen as fundamentally threatening white supremacy. This was what the legal battle was all about.[148]

The Scottsboro affair serves to highlight the racist terror that prevailed in the South. On 4 August 1931 there was a horrific murder of two white women and the wounding of a third by a black gunman outside Birmingham, Alabama. The white response to this was, in the words of Angelo Herndon, "a reign of terror against all Negroes". There was a widespread belief, propagated by the press, that Communist propaganda advocating racial equality had inspired the crime, and Herndon was one of those arrested and given "the third degree". "The jails were choked with hundreds of Negroes", he wrote, including "every man active in union work". Over the course of the month "70 Negroes of both sexes paid with their lives". What we have here is an unchronicled, unrecorded pogrom. Eventually a culprit was found, Willie Patterson, identified by the surviving victim and brought to trial. Once again the ILD took up the case. Even though the authorities privately acknowledged that the young woman had made a mistake and that he was innocent (according to Herndon, at the time of the murders "he occupied a bed in the tuberculosis ward of the city hospital, whose records corroborated this alibi"), he was found guilty and sentenced to death. His death sentence was commuted to life imprisonment, which in the Alabama judicial system amounted to acknowledgement of his innocence, and he died in prison in 1940.[149]

Elsewhere in Alabama the knowledge that the ILD would come to the assistance of the victims of racial injustice led to resort to lynch law. On 14 June 1933 three black men were arrested for the rape and murder of a white woman in Tuscaloosa. The lawyers provided by the ILD barely escaped lynching themselves, but the three defendants were not so lucky. They were handed over to a lynch mob to be "beaten, burned and riddled with bullets". Incredibly, one of them survived. Only weeks later an 84 year old black invalid, Dennis Cross, was accused of rape, a charge that the Tuscaloosa police dismissed as unfounded. Nevertheless, on 24 September 1933 he was dragged from his bed and lynched. According to the ILD altogether that year there were 47 lynchings.[150] Alabama at this time was one of the few states that imposed the death penalty for robbery. When two black men, Isaac Mims and Percy Irvin, "broke and hungry, stole 50 cents", the state of Alabama put them to death by electrocution.[151] This was judicial lynching.

The Communist Party led the way in fighting this oppression, and although its campaigning was often marred by its sectarianism, nevertheless it took a courageous and uncompromising stand. In 1932, when Foster stood as the party's candidate for the presidency, his running mate for the vice-presidency was James Ford, a black man. Roosevelt's running mate was John Nance Garner, a reactionary white supremacist from Texas.

A balance sheet

How to assess the Communist Party's performance during these early years of the Great Depression? The CP was already completely subordinate to the Stalin regime in the Soviet Union with regard to its general strategic line. During the Third Period this meant that it took an uncompromising revolutionary stand. This stand was compromised, however, by the lack of democracy within the party, by its belief that revolution was imminent despite all the evidence to the contrary, by its vicious sectarianism, and by its subordination to Moscow that prevented these mistakes being remedied. Party membership rose from some 7,500 in 1930 to over 23,000 in 1934, certainly a success, but hardly an indication of imminent revolution. What enabled it to hold to this belief was the fact that the party maintained some 600 full-time staff and organisers.[152] These men and women were completely committed to championing the party line as laid down by the Comintern. Dissent was punished by expulsion. The belief in imminent revolution meant that the party behaved as if the working class was on the offensive, was becoming a revolutionary force, challenging for state power. In reality, the workers were clearly on the defensive. Certainly the Communist Party played an important and often heroic role in many of the defensive struggles that took place, but its revolutionary fervour actually cost it members (the party had a very high turnover of members) as reality failed to live up to expectations. As Howe and Coser put it, the party's "policy of adventurism and hysteria...exhausted many of its most valuable members".[153]

Sidney Lens, a young Trotskyist at the time and certainly no friend to the CP, nevertheless acknowledged that, whatever one thought of their political line, individual party members, "faced hardships, beatings and the threat of jail with great courage... From 1929 to 1932, 23 men and women were shot in strikes and unemployment demonstrations led by Communists".[154]

More damaging was their ferocious, sometimes violent, hostility towards the rest of the left. The Socialist Party was active in organising the unemployed, and there were a number of other smaller organisations actively involved in the struggle. According to the CP these people were not just wrong—they were consciously aiding the fascist cause; indeed, they were actually varieties of fascism and had to be destroyed. Meetings were broken up and newspaper sellers attacked. At the first public meeting organised by the American Trotskyists after their expulsion from the CP, Max Shachtman recalled how the doors "were forced open by a crowd of a hundred party officials and members, armed with lead pipes, blackjacks, clubs, knives and similar persuasive arguments".[155]

To protect their meetings from Communist attack, the Trotskyists, the IWW and the anarchists in New York, out of necessity, formed a "mutual protective alliance".[156] This sectarian violence climaxed on 16 February 1934, when the Socialist Party held a broadly based rally at Madison Square Garden to protest against the military assault launched against workers in Austria by the Dolfuss regime. Over 15,000 people came "to pay homage to the socialist workers of the Karl Marx Hof in Vienna, who had given their lives to forestall fascism in Austria". The rally was deliberately broken up by hundreds of Communists, "armed with the usual bats and brass knuckles", who succeeded in making "a shambles of the affair".[157] As far as the party leadership were concerned, the left social fascists had been dealt a serious blow and the revolution brought nearer. In fact, the party had dealt itself a damaging self-inflicted wound.

Chapter Three

The ruling class response

The Hoover administration set its face against the provision of federal relief for millions of Americans thrown out of work, homeless, working short time or for starvation wages. These people were to be provided for by charity. The provision of unemployment benefit was out of the question, because it would undermine the moral character of the poor and hungry. There were, of course, to be no such concerns with regard to the character of the rich, who were to receive every assistance that the administration could think of. Initially Hoover hoped that the Depression would be short-lived and that the economy would correct itself through Andrew Mellon's mantra of "Liquidate labour, liquidate stocks, liquidate the farmers, liquidate real estate".[158] There would be immense hardship for millions of people, but sooner rather than later the system would correct itself. It has to be said that some of the rich did their best to help pull the country out of the Depression by bravely continuing their conspicuous consumption. Alfred Sloan, the multimillionaire president of General Motors, for example, bought a 236-foot yacht for $42 million, demonstrating, as his biographer ironically puts it, "his commitment to fighting the economic slowdown through continued consumer spending".[159]

The protracted nature of the crisis eventually forced the administration into action. In January 1932 Hoover established one of the most important of the organisations that was to see American capitalism through the Depression years, the Reconstruction Finance Corporation (RFC). Charles Dawes, a banker, was installed as its first president and began disbursing huge loans to business and finance. Dawes, an arch-reactionary, was a determined opponent of any federal relief for the unemployed, but had no such problem with giving business such a helping hand, including businesses in which he personally had an interest. He resigned as RFC president in June 1932, just before the organisation loaned the Central Republic Bank of Chicago, popularly known as "the Dawes Bank", $90 million. This was, as James Stuart Olson observes, "a political disaster for Hoover".[160] As far as most Americans were concerned, Dawes, a man steadfastly opposed to giving any help to the unemployed, had "received at a clip a public dole of $90 million".[161] The situation was made all the worse for the administration because at the same time the mayor of Chicago, Anton Cermak, had appealed to the RFC for a loan of $70 million to pay the wages of city employees, many of whom had gone months without pay, and had been turned down. Senator Robert Wagner spoke for most people when he asked why it was that when bankers asked for bailouts, no one preached to them rugged individualism, but when millions of Americans, "foot-weary and heart-sick, cry out in despair, 'Give us work', we suddenly are overwhelmed with devotion for the preservation of self-reliance".[162]

It is worth noticing that once Roosevelt took office in 1933, the RFC was to actually expand its activities, providing massive amounts of financial assistance for American business and finance. Roosevelt appointed the Texan banker Jesse Jones as RFC president, and as he testifies, the RFC became one of the unnoticed pillars of the New Deal. The RFC grew, in Jones's words, to become "America's largest corporation and the world's biggest and most varied banking organisation".[163] The RFC was to loan $4 billion to US banks and over $1 billion to the railways in the course of the 1930s, something often passed over in histories of the Great Depression. According to one account, the RFC was to distribute to business and finance "as much money as all Roosevelt's work relief programmes".[164] Jesse Jones himself, certainly no liberal, was to observe the irony of business leaders condemning the New Deal while taking huge handouts from the state. In his memoirs he recalled a function where a succession of business leaders attacked the Roosevelt administration, and as each one spoke, he wrote down on his menu how much he had loaned him from the RFC.[165]

The Depression doomed Hoover. His administration was increasingly seen as being only concerned for the rich and caring nothing for the poor, the unemployed and the homeless. What came to symbolise this lack of concern was his treatment of the Bonus Army protest in July 1932. Some 10,000 unemployed First World War veterans from all over the country had set up camp in Washington. They were demanding that a promised bonus due to be paid in 1945 be paid now. Hoover's opposition to paying the bonus had already cost him his Secretary of the Treasury, Andrew Mellon, when its supporters in Congress, led by Wright Patman, moved to impeach him. Patman, a Texan populist, denounced Mellon in the most ferocious terms. He complained that the country was suffering from:

> an overdose of Mellonism. Predatory wealth will remain in control of our government as long as Andrew Mellon is Secretary of the Treasury. He is the worst enemy of the wage-earners, farmers and veterans... He always places property rights above human rights.[166]

The threat of a Congressional investigation into Mellon's tax affairs forced his resignation in February 1932, and Hoover sent him out of the country as ambassador in London. Patman described this appointment as tantamount to a "presidential pardon".[167]

Once the bonus had been denied, Hoover ordered the expulsion of the veterans from Washington. The army was sent in and acted as if they were suppressing a revolutionary insurrection. Tanks were deployed. In the ensuing clashes the police killed two protesters and the army burned down their encampment, tear-gassed them and drove them out at bayonet point. In the melee a seven year old boy was bayoneted in the leg, a veteran had an ear cut off by a sabre and a baby was killed by the effects of the tear gas. All in all, a glorious victory! General Douglas MacArthur subsequently claimed that he had prevented an uprising, that the bonus marchers had been "animated by the essence of revolution", that they were "a bad-looking mob" and that if the president had not acted when he did he "would have been faced with a grave situation which would have caused a real battle". They were beginning "a reign of terror...which may have led to a system of Caponeism, and I believe later to insurgency and insurrection".[168] To most Americans it was a particularly dramatic demonstration of Hoover's callous disregard for the unemployed. By now the administration that was regarded as solely concerned with the interests of the rich and with looking after the banks was completely discredited. As Roosevelt remarked to one of his supporters, the bonus episode "will elect me".[169]

Let us leave the last word on Hoover to the Pennsylvanian coal miners who erected a monument to him over a filled-in privy. It bore the inscription:

Here lies Hoover,
Damn his soul,
Buried in a honey-hole.
Let him lay here till the end,
Poor man's enemy
Rich man's friend.[170]

Roosevelt and American capitalism

The man who was to stand against Hoover in the 1932 presidential election was a most unlikely radical. Franklin Delano Roosevelt was a child of privilege, born into the US ruling class. His father was a banker, who had retired to live the life of a country squire, and his mother was a substantial heiress, whose father had made a fortune in the Chinese opium trade, one of the worst crimes of the 19th century. The family "lived abroad almost as much as they did at home", and by the time he was 15, young Franklin had visited Europe eight times. He went to a private school, Groton, "the most exclusive school in America", and then on to Harvard. From quite early on Franklin decided on a political career that would, he confidently expected, end in the White House. He always seems to have thought that his upper class background entitled him to "the glittering prizes" and, of course, his uncle, Theodore, had already led the way. He was and always remained, in Richard Hofstadter's telling phrase, "a patrician opportunist". His marriage to Eleanor Roosevelt, a cousin, "was one of the brilliant social events of the 1905 season".[171] This was a man born to rule.

In 1910 Roosevelt was elected to the New York State Senate on the Democratic ticket. Although he stood as a "progressive", his progressivism seems to have amounted to little more than opposition to the hold of New York City's corrupt Tammany political machine on the State Democratic Party. He showed little or no interest in social reform. Most telling in this respect was his response, or rather the lack of it, to the 1911 Triangle factory fire that cost the lives of 146 workers, overwhelmingly young immigrant women, many of whom jumped to their deaths to escape the flames. The fire raised a storm of protest and Frank Freidel, one of Roosevelt's biographers, could scarcely conceal his surprise that "his copious correspondence does not even mention the Triangle fire". At the time Roosevelt showed no sympathy for the labour movement, supporting judicial decisions that were intended to cripple the unions, "taking for granted the use of force to suppress disturbances during strikes", and, more generally, he had no time for "the idea of giving labour the weapons with which to obtain its own concessions".[172] He did not support the 54 Hour Bill, limiting the working hours of women and children, when it came before the State Senate in 1911; indeed, he did not even bother to turn up for the crucial vote. What is interesting is that once Roosevelt embraced reform at the end of the 1920s, he and his supporters were to begin rewriting his biography, eventually claiming that he was one of the architects of the bill.[173]

In 1913 Roosevelt was appointed Assistant Secretary to the Navy in Woodrow Wilson's administration. He was an advocate of a strong navy, capable of projecting US power globally, and had close links with the Navy League, a powerful pressure group, financed by steel, shipping and banking interests. Roosevelt was to support US intervention in the Caribbean and in 1914 was an enthusiastic advocate of the invasion of Mexico. "Sooner or later", he proclaimed, "the United States must go down there and clean up the Mexican political mess. The best time is right now." He even suggested that he might "follow in the footsteps of TR and form a regiment of rough riders". Roosevelt was wholeheartedly behind US involvement in the First World War and the subsequent attempts to overthrow the Bolsheviks in Russia. In 1919 he advocated keeping wartime conscription as a protection against Bolshevism.[174] The Wilson administration was strongly white supremacist and introduced segregation for the first time throughout federal government departments. Roosevelt was involved in its introduction in the Navy Department. At the time he seems to have regarded white supremacy and segregation as uncontroversial. Indeed, throughout his life, Roosevelt could not resist "jokes about how some 'darky' contracted venereal disease" and he continued to use "the word 'nigger' casually in private conversation and correspondence".[175]

Roosevelt supported the repression of the American left, both during and after the war. Indeed, the architect of the post-war red scare,

Attorney General Alexander Mitchell Palmer, was a personal friend. His political career was well on track when he secured the Democrat vice-presidential nomination in 1920, serving as running mate to James Cox. During the campaign he visited Centralia, the scene of an attack by vigilantes led by the American Legion on the IWW offices and of the subsequent brutal lynching of Wesley Everest, an IWW member.[176] Roosevelt described his visit as "a pilgrimage to the very graves of the martyred members of the American Legion who gave their lives in the sacred cause of Americanism". They had, he went on, aroused the American people to the need for "ridding the land of the alien anarchist, the criminal syndicalist and all similar anti-Americans". On another occasion during the campaign he boasted that he had written Haiti's constitution when assistant secretary to the navy, "and if I do say so, I think it is a pretty good constitution". He had, he told reporters, been involved "with the running of a couple of little republics" during his time in the Navy Department.[177]

The Democrats went down to a crushing defeat in 1920 and Warren Harding became president. How did Roosevelt adjust to the 1920s? In the words of one biographer:

> he adjusted to the business decade with ease. He became a business-man. Shortly after his defeat in the fall of 1920 he took a job as vice-president of a large surety bonding firm, the Fidelity and Deposit Company of Maryland, in charge of its New York office at $25,000 a year, and he returned to the practice of law. During the next eight years he took part in a variety of business ventures.[178]

He accumulated, in the course of the 1920s, directorships in 11 companies, and Herbert Hoover, a man for whom he had considerable admiration (Roosevelt had urged that Hoover should be the Democrat candidate for the presidency in 1920), was instrumental in his installation as president of the American Construction Council, a major trade association, representing the building industry. In 1921 his income was $48,542 (which today would be worth around $580,000), rising by 1925 to $53,766 (which today would be around $645,000). And in 1927 he inherited $100,000 from his half-brother.[179] The Roosevelt family fortune was in the hands of his mother, although she was always prepared to help out if he was a bit short. Needless to say, he had nothing in common with the American working class.

FIGHTING BACK

Roosevelt's business career was, however, just so much marking time. His real interest remained politics. His apparently effortless political advance was brought to an abrupt halt when he contracted polio, leaving him unable to walk. His illness prevented him from seeking the 1924 Democrat nomination for the presidency. The battle to overcome his disability certainly proved his strength of character. He learned to walk short distances with assistance and to stand in public, although in private he used a wheelchair. During this period Roosevelt developed a great affection for the South, becoming a part-time resident in Georgia, after his purchase for $200,000 of the Warm Springs resort in 1926. He even toyed with the idea of standing as governor of that state. Not until 1928, however, did he once again stand for office. That year Al Smith, the governor of New York State, was nominated as the Democrat presidential candidate and he persuaded Roosevelt to stand as governor in his place. In the event, Roosevelt was to be elected while Smith went down to a crushing defeat at the hands of Herbert Hoover. It is worth noticing here that Smith ran as a conservative, with his campaign managed by John Raskob, a reactionary businessman, who actually listed his occupation in *Who's Who* as "capitalist". Raskob was a senior executive at DuPont and General Motors and, in a decision rich in symbolism, the presidential campaign was managed from the GM building in New York.[180]

What can we say of Roosevelt's politics at this time? In the 1920s, in all essentials, he accepted the world the Republicans had made. There was nothing to suggest the later reformism of the New Deal. One particularly significant episode, when he first became governor of New York State, was the way he quite cheerfully blocked proposals for banking reform.[181] What was to change him was the collapse of that world in 1929. Roosevelt was to show that he was prepared to be "radical" if that was what was necessary to save American capitalism.

The 1932 election

As governor of New York State, Roosevelt's response to the onset of the Great Depression was resolutely conservative. Indeed, in the summer of 1930 at a conference of state governors he criticised Hoover from the right, for doing too much, "for pouring money into public works and, generally, for departing from laissez faire".[182] This very much reflected the dominant view within the Democratic Party leadership, which was staunchly conservative. John Davis, the party's presidential candidate in 1924, roundly condemned Hoover in 1931 for "following the road to socialism".[183] The protracted nature of the crisis, the increasing levels of poverty, hunger and distress, and the growing threat to public order, however, were to lead Roosevelt to shift ground. As Kenneth Davis observes, in the worsening situation, "Roosevelt's conservative ideological aversion to providing state government relief to individual persons was overcome". Confronted "with the prospect of freezing cold and gnawing hunger for tens of thousands of his fellow citizens during the coming winter months, he now saw no alternative to the state's providing as much 'useful work' as possible to those in desperate need".[184] His conscience was helped to this conclusion:

> when a group of unemployed came to Albany on a hunger march and tried to enter the legislative chamber. The state police drove the marchers away after a 45-minute battle, but shortly thereafter the legislature passed the Wicks Law under which relief activities began in November 1931.[185]

Roosevelt established the Temporary Emergency Relief Administration (TERA), which over the winter of 1931-1932 provided relief for some 160,000 people. This, however, "hardly dented the distress the sinking economy was visiting upon New York", where 1.5 million were unemployed that winter.[186] Roosevelt concluded that federal intervention was necessary, that, far from doing too much, Hoover was doing too little.

Roosevelt's nomination as Democrat candidate for the presidency in 1932 was not the result of any grassroots insurgency. There were powerful figures in the party who regarded Roosevelt as too liberal, but Roosevelt himself had the support of a group of respectable and not so respectable businessmen that included Herbert Lehman, Henry Morgenthau, Joseph Kennedy and others. In the end his nomination was secured, not by any reformist upsurge, but by deals and manoeuvres. Roosevelt took care not to alienate the corrupt big city machines. Indeed, as governor of New York, he had stood by while the Tammany leadership in New York City enriched itself through the most blatant graft, while the unemployed collapsed from hunger on the streets. He only finally took action against Mayor Walker when his hand was absolutely forced.[187] Of considerable importance was the support of the Louisiana senator Huey Long. But when he finally secured the nomination, it was by means of a secret deal with William Randolph Hearst, the Rupert Murdoch of the time, brokered by a crooked businessman, Joseph Kennedy, on his behalf. Hearst's price was the nomination of his man, John Nance Garner, a Texan conservative, for the vice-presidency.[188]

At the convention the issue that caused the most excitement was not any "New Deal" but the repeal of prohibition. As Oswald Garrison Villard complained, "the question of beer and booze outranked everything else".[189] Ending prohibition was especially popular with Democratic Party conservatives because taxing alcohol was seen as a way of shifting more of the burden of taxation onto the working and middle classes. Among those finalising the platform, at Roosevelt's invitation, was the architect of the post-war red scare, Alexander Mitchell Palmer. Roosevelt had no intention of mounting any sort of radical challenge to Hoover. As Garner told him, in order to defeat the completely discredited Hoover, "all you have to do is stay alive until election day".[190]

The election campaign saw Roosevelt attacking Hoover from both the left and the right. Indeed, his speeches "so often veered either right or left and contained so many generalities that it would have been hard to have predicted from them what the New Deal might be".[191] As Frances Perkins, soon to become Roosevelt's secretary of labour, observed, Roosevelt was "no political or economic radical" and he took "the status quo in the economic system for granted". He was "the rich man's friend, the poor man's brother". As for his promised New Deal, it "was not a plan with form and content. It was a happy phrase he had coined during the campaign and its value was psychological. It made people feel better".[192] One of his biographers makes the point that Roosevelt's campaign involved "no call to action, no summons to a crusade... On the whole, he was remarkably temperate; there was little passion".[193] In a careful discussion of the campaign, M S Venkataramani has concluded:

> Hoover and Roosevelt did not differ basically in their approach to the problem posed by the Depression. Both outlined cautious and conservative proposals which differed little in ideology or fundamentals

but only in emphasis. They envisaged governmental action to provide unemployment relief only as a last resort. Both hailed charity as an American way of dealing with want... Neither Hoover nor Roosevelt placed before the electorate any comprehensive programme for putting the unemployed back to work.[194]

Roosevelt made no great rallying cry for change, relying instead on disgust with Hoover to elect him.

During the campaign his speeches ranged from attacks on the super-rich to pledges to cut government expenditure. On 20 August in Columbus, Ohio, he condemned the fact that two thirds of American industry was concentrated in a few hundred corporations, and actually managed "by no more than five individuals". He believed in "the sacredness of private property", but not "concentrated economic power in a few hands". And on 2 October in Detroit he condemned the theory "that if we make the rich richer, somehow they will let part of the prosperity trickle down to the rest of us". Instead he proclaimed "the philosophy of social justice" and called for "the reduction of poverty". On other occasions, however, he played the conservative. On 29 September in Sioux City, Iowa, he condemned the Hoover administration for being "the greatest spending administration in peace times in all our history". On 19 October, in a speech written by the conservative financier Bernard Baruch, he told an audience in Pittsburgh that just as a family had to live within its income, so had a nation. Consequently he went on to condemn "federal extravagance" and to make it clear that "I regard reduction in federal spending as one of the most important issues of the coming campaign".[195] Some accounts suggest this was just a sop to the conservatives within the Democratic Party, but in fact the evidence is overwhelming that Roosevelt was himself a fiscal conservative at heart. When those liberals in the Roosevelt camp complained that Baruch's policies would produce rioting in the streets, the financier replied that "there is always tear gas to take care of that". As for Roosevelt himself, he told Rexford Tugwell that Baruch had to be placated because he "owned—he used that word—60 congressmen".[196]

The Hoover administration was swept away in the 1932 presidential election with Roosevelt receiving 22.8 million votes to Hoover's 15.8 million.[197] While this was certainly an electoral landslide, the turnout was only 52.5 percent, and a great many of the poor and unemployed were disenfranchised, especially if they were poor, unemployed and black. Meanwhile the crisis worsened. Tugwell later wrote that when the Roosevelt administration eventually took office in March 1933, they "were confronted with a choice between an orderly revolution—a peaceful and rapid departure from the past concepts—and a violent and disorderly overthrow of the whole capitalist structure".[198]

A textbook protest

The temper of the times is captured by one particular protest, that of the Chicago schoolteachers. In nearly every state educational provision had been seriously cut back as a response to the Depression, with some 200,000 teachers losing their jobs. By 1932 many schools had closed altogether because of cutbacks. In Georgia, the worst hit state, over 1,300 schools had closed, leaving 170,000 children without schooling and their teachers without jobs. Georgia teachers' pay was already in arrears to the tune of $7 million. Across the country teachers' pay was cut and in arrears, and in some places teachers were working for food and board. As Robert Brown points out, in many places by 1933:

> instructional positions were awarded to the lowest bidder—with some bids as low as $45 a year. Some teachers took jobs for room and board, often in a teacherage—a kind of secular convent found primarily in sparsely populated states of the Pacific Northwest, but also in such states as New Jersey and Pennsylvania—where drinking, smoking, dancing and courting were expressly forbidden and regular church attendance was a standing house rule.[199]

In a number of states teachers had gone on strike, demanding to be paid.[200]

In Chicago teachers had responded to the onset of the Depression by establishing a fund to provide free meals for the children of the unemployed. In 1931 the teachers themselves contributed $112,000 to this fund. The following years teachers' pay began to fall in arrears.[201] By March 1933 they were owed eight months salary. The Chicago school board began paying in scrip, in IOUs that supposedly could be redeemed at a bank, but often only at a reduced value. Then, as part of a campaign to force draconian cuts on the city, the banks began refusing to redeem the scrip. Teachers were fainting from malnutrition in school and one teacher was among those who died from starvation. As Elsa Ponselle, then a young schoolteacher, later recalled, they were expected "to starve to death quietly and with refinement. Some of us weren't that much interested in being refined and professional... We marched".[202] A rank and file organisation, the Volunteer Emergency Committee (VEC), led by a gym teacher, John Fewkes, organised a fightback.

On 5 April 1933 some 50,000 school students went on strike and demonstrated in support of their teachers. On 15 April parents and teachers demonstrated. Then, on 24 April, the teachers took to the streets on their own, intent on a protest that would get the authorities' attention. Led by Fewkes, some 5,000 teachers, mostly women, assembled for a march on city hall. Before the march stewards were handed sealed envelopes only to be opened once the march got under way. They contained a change of plan. At a given signal, the march split into five columns that rushed the city's five main banks and occupied them. At the First National, hundreds of teachers chanted, "Pay us! Pay us!" The bank's chairman, Charles Dawes, came down to the lobby to speak to them. Dawes, as we have seen, was a key member of the US ruling class. He was a former vice-president, the architect of the 1924 Dawes Plan for which he had received the Nobel Peace Prize, and, of course, his bank had been bailed out to the tune of $90 million by the RFC. He was jeered and heckled by the teachers who demanded to know why Hoover gave money to the banks but left them to starve. Dawes told them "to go to hell" whereupon "teachers threw ink on the walls, tipped over desks and broke windows".[203]

Two days later, on 26 April, the teachers held another demonstration. They assembled carrying textbooks, the tools of their trade. This time a heavy police guard protected the five banks they had occupied earlier, so instead they rushed the Chicago Title and Trust bank. When mounted police moved in they were pelted with textbooks. Every window in the bank was broken as police and teachers fought each other. In his account of the protest William Manchester describes how the police "clubbed the unpaid teachers...two of them holding one middle-aged woman while a third smashed her face".[204] Police reinforcements were rushed to the scene, whereupon other teachers once again stormed Dawes First National. They were able "to smash their way into the bank. Scores more crashed through the building's plate glass windows".[205]

Confronted with starving teachers fighting the police on the streets of Chicago, the newly inaugurated President Roosevelt intervened behind the scenes. Acting through the RFC, Roosevelt put pressure on the city's banks to make funds available to pay the teachers. When the payments were made, "more than 5,000 teachers formed lines around the old bank building in North Wells Street where the checks were handed out. Some had been in line all night".[206]

The battle for education in Chicago was not over. The Democratic Party machine in the city was corrupt through and through. When Mayor Cermak was assassinated on 6 March 1933 (he was shot dead in an attack in which Roosevelt was believed to be the intended victim),[207] he was found to have a safe deposit box with $1,466,250 in it, with "the sources of the cash never identified".[208] His successor as mayor, Edward Kelly, continued to preside "over an organisation saturated with graft and corruption". When the press revealed that between 1927 and 1929 Kelly had an unexplained income of $450,000, he absolutely refused to reveal where it came from.[209] He proceeded to emasculate the city's education system. Kelly, a Democrat, pushed through massive cuts, firing 1,400 teachers (one in ten), lengthening the teaching day, increasing class sizes and cutting pay by 23.5 percent. Teachers' pay in Chicago was not to return to its 1929 level until 1947. While teachers were savaged, the schools' maintenance budget was actually increased. This was because it was a vital source of patronage for the Democratic Party machine. There were on the books, for example, 500 more school janitors than there were schools, many of them earning more than school principals for jobs that only existed on paper, "no-show" jobs as they were called.[210] Roosevelt was urged a number of times to clean up Chicago, but the Kelly machine was an ally and delivered the votes, and so was left undisturbed.

Chapter Four

Roosevelt in power

The months between Roosevelt's election victory in November 1932 and his inauguration as president in March 1933 were, according to one historian, "the most harrowing four months of the Depression".[211] The economic situation continued to deteriorate, while popular unrest grew, with hostility to the rich and powerful, especially bankers, or "banksters" as they were popularly known, becoming increasingly fierce. Indeed, there was "a breakdown of social order in the winter of 1932-33".[212] The stakes could not have been higher. When Roosevelt took office, according to Arthur Schlesinger, it "was a matter of seeing whether a representative democracy could conquer economic collapse...staving off violence, even (at least some thought) revolution".[213] And yet Roosevelt had been elected with a clear mandate to cut federal spending and, urged on by his director of the Budget Bureau, the arch-reactionary Lewis Douglas, a man described as having "a heart of stone", he was to stick to this commitment.[214]

In a remarkable display of fiscal conservatism, Roosevelt forced through his Economy Bill in the face of fierce opposition from many Democrats in Congress (in the House of Representatives 92 Democrats voted against the measure and 69 Republicans voted for it). One progressive Republican, Bronson Cutting, described the bill as "the most indefensible piece of legislation ever passed by Congress".[215] Roosevelt, however, made it clear that he regarded it as a crucial measure that would indicate the direction he intended to take. It was intended to be the first measure passed by the new administration, but the banking collapse forced it into second place. The measure cut the pay of federal employees by up to 15 percent, reduced veterans' benefits and pensions (some lost all their benefits) and cut military spending. It also authorised the sacking of married women in federal employment if their husbands also worked for the government.[216] Roosevelt, as Rexford Tugwell insisted, "felt just as much convinced that imbalanced budgets were sinful as Hoover had been". Indeed, at this time "Roosevelt was far nearer to Hoover than either realised, or than historians have realised since". The difference between the two men, as far as Tugwell was concerned, was that Roosevelt was at least able to eventually "recognise necessity".[217] For the time being though, as one historian has argued, the Economy Act put Roosevelt's programme "something to the right of the Hoover programme".[218] As Julian Zelizer has pointed out, "fiscal conservatism constituted a key component of the New Deal" and, as far as Roosevelt was concerned, was always an aspiration, even when not politically possible. Among those supporting the cuts in government spending was William Green of the AFL.[219]

The cuts in veterans' benefits and pensions inevitably provoked another bonus march that assembled outside Washington in May. On this occasion the army put up tents for them and they were visited by Eleanor Roosevelt, the president's wife. Instead of ordering their dispersal by force, Roosevelt instead offered to create 25,000 places for veterans in the Civilian Conservation Corps that he was establishing. They were shipped off to build bridges in the Florida Keys, over 1,000 miles away. This is remembered as one of Roosevelt's early triumphs, showing the difference between his caring administration and that of Hoover. What it actually demonstrates is the way that the historical record has been too often written to show Roosevelt in the best possible light. On 2 September 1935 a hurricane devastated the Keys and destroyed the veterans' camps. No attempt was made to evacuate them though there had been plenty of warning. Their camps were at sea level and consisted of no more than tents and shacks without any hurricane shelters. Officially, 256 people were killed, but the real figure was much higher, certainly over 400. Among the dead were over 250 veterans.[220] The administration rushed to exonerate itself from any blame for the disaster. A preliminary report prepared by John Abt (who admitted that "we hadn't gathered much evidence and couldn't say we conducted a serious investigation") was issued as the official report, absolving the administration from any responsibility. As Abt later recalled, this was "an episode of my life I look back on without pride".[221] The disaster provoked one of Ernest Hemingway's finest pieces of prose, the ferocious

"Who Killed The Vets?", that appeared in the journal *New Masses* in September 1935. He charged the administration with manslaughter.[222]

The desperate circumstances that gripped the country in 1933 forced Roosevelt, however reluctantly, to embrace emergency measures to relieve the unemployed. He reluctantly recognised that the system was breaking and that something had to be done. James Farley described a conversation he witnessed between Roosevelt and two of the country's leading steel bosses, Charles Schwab of Bethlehem Steel and Myron Taylor of US Steel. Schwab assured Roosevelt that:

> his company was doing very well in caring for its employees and that no complaint was justified on that score. Schwab's attitude annoyed Roosevelt who pointed out that according to reports reaching the White House many of the unemployed steel workers were living in coke ovens while the company was paying bonuses running as high as $1,000,000 annually to some of its officials. He very properly took the position that policies of that sort brought discredit upon big business and that if business itself did nothing to correct such conditions, the government would be compelled to step in.[223]

This callous and heartless complacency on the part of big business was putting capitalism itself at risk. As Roosevelt himself put it on another occasion, if the hands-off, laissez-faire approach "hadn't proved to be bankrupt, Herbert Hoover would be sitting here right now".[224]

Moreover, popular anger was fuelled by the revelations that emerged from the hearings of the Senate Banking and Currency Committee. The committee's chief counsel, Ferdinand Pecora, began the hearings in February 1933 and proceeded to reveal a catalogue of greed, hypocrisy and fraud that embraced the whole of Wall Street. Charles Mitchell, the chairman of the National City Bank, was shown to have sold shares to his wife for a loss of $2.5 million, which he then claimed against his income tax. After 30 days he was free to buy them back at the price at which he had sold them. This scam was widely practised. Jack Morgan "did not pay a dollar of income tax to the United States government for the years 1930, 1931, 1932. Neither did any of his partners—with the exception of a few who paid small amounts". Pecora revealed that the Morgan bank had a "preferred list" of individuals to whom it sold shares cheap so that they could realise an immediate profit. The sums involved were not small. Richard Whitney, the president of the New York Stock Exchange, for example, bought Allegheny shares at $20 and promptly sold them for $225,000 profit. On the "preferred list" were numerous senior politicians, including William Woodin, Roosevelt's Secretary of the Treasury, and John Raskob, the Democratic Party national chairman. This was not corrupt, insisted Morgan; it was just helping out friends.[225]

Morgan had initially welcomed Roosevelt's election, because at least he "was approaching his problems in the spirit of getting something done...it is quite possible that some of his cures may be the wrong ones, but on the whole things were so bad that almost any cure may do some good". He took great exception, however, to the impertinence of that "dirty little wop", Pecora.[226] He attempted to have him removed, but without success.[227] Roosevelt was only too aware of the outrage the hearings had whipped up and had no intention of damaging himself by standing in their way. For Morgan, the final indignity was when he became the victim of a publicity stunt for a circus. When he appeared before the committee in May 1933 a young woman, Lya Graf, only just over two feet tall, sat on his lap with the cameras recording his embarrassment.[228] Sitting next to Morgan was the bank's counsel, John Davis, the 1924 Democrat presidential candidate.

The Morgan bank had expected Roosevelt to appoint one of their board, Russell Leffingwell, to his Treasury team, but the outcry against the financial establishment was such that Roosevelt dropped the idea. Interestingly, the Pecora hearings actually made a substantial profit for the administration: they cost $250,000 but led to tax bills and penalties exceeding $2 million imposed on those who appeared. And millions more were paid over by "frightened individuals who amended their tax returns voluntarily".[229] The hearings resulted in the passage of the Securities Exchange Act, establishing the Securities and Exchange Commission. Pecora, who had unfinished business with Wall Street, hoped that he would be appointed chair of this regulatory body. Typically, Roosevelt appointed instead a crooked businessman and Democrat insider, Joseph Kennedy.[230] His generosity towards fraudsters who happened to be political allies was demonstrated even more dramatically by the administration's suppression of reports into the crooked dealings of Wisconsin banker Leo Crowley. Instead of sending him to jail, Roosevelt appointed him head of the Federal Deposit Insurance Company.[231]

Relief and the NIRA

With another winter of starvation, hardship and growing disorder looming, Roosevelt, according to Michael Katz, "put the national government directly and massively into the business of relief", although as Katz insists, "he did so unwillingly". In May 1933 the Federal Emergency Relief Administration (FERA) was established, modelled on the agency that Roosevelt had established when governor of New York State. By April 1934 there were over 4.5 million families and single people receiving relief from FERA. The administration also established the Civilian Conservation Corps (CCC) to provide work for young people. By August 1935 half a million people were employed on conservation work in 2,600 camps. And there was the Civil Works Administration (CWA) established in November 1933 and by early the following year providing work for some 4 million people. By February 1934, according to Katz, "the FERA, the CWA, and the CCC assisted about 8 million households with 28 million people or 22.2 percent of the American population".[232] Even so, there were millions left out in the cold. The CWA turned away 7 million applicants for relief work and in Chicago there were 300,000 applicants for 49,000 CWA jobs to be allocated by lottery.[233] The administration's relief effort is perhaps best put in perspective by the fact that between 1933 and 1940 some $16 billion was spent on relief, which averages out at about 4.5 percent of GDP a year. In retrospect, this was hardly generous, yet alone revolutionary.[234] Nevertheless, it did enough to take the edge off popular unrest throughout the winter, to alleviate some of the suffering and hardship, and to contain the left.

The measure that emerged as the cornerstone of the first New Deal, of Roosevelt's first attempt at saving US capitalism, was the National Industrial Recovery Act (NIRA). Congress passed this measure on 16 June 1933. The act was a victory for those in the administration and for many prominent businessmen who saw federally-sponsored cartelisation of the economy as the way out of the Depression. It provided state encouragement for the organisation of firms and businesses into trade associations that were charged with the regulation of their particular industry. Those firms that joined were exempt from anti-trust legislation and were charged with producing "codes of fair practice" to regulate prices, output, wages and working conditions across their industry. These associations were inevitably dominated by the bigger firms. As one contemporary critic observed:

> The government was underwriting monopoly more flagrantly than it had ever done before. In most instances the codes were merely the existing agreements of the monopolistic trade associations, with the government underwriting and agreeing to enforce them; in some cases they were precise copies of those agreements.

The Roosevelt administration had adopted a corporatist strategy "to restore industrial stability by guaranteeing the status quo of worker and employer, one in possession of little, the other in possession of much".[235] According to the Socialist Party leader, Norman Thomas, Roosevelt had introduced a version of "state capitalism...that is a degree of government ownership and a much greater degree of government regulation of economic enterprises for the sake of bolstering the profit system".[236] There was nothing left wing about this strategy. The NIRA was intended to restore the fortunes of US capitalism by increasing profits.

The NIRA did include what Sidney Lens has described as "a sop to the working class"—Section 7a.[237] This stated that "employees shall have the right to organise and bargain collectively through representatives of their own choosing".[238] Roosevelt did not intend this to do anything more than prop up the ailing AFL, but it had an electrifying impact on the working class. Years of defeat boiled up in anger and rage. Even with between 12 and 17 million unemployed, the working class seized on the opportunity to fight back that Roosevelt had inadvertently presented. Roosevelt, or so it seemed, had guaranteed the right to join a union.

This was not what the administration had intended. According to Rexford Tugwell, "Roosevelt was not really sympathetic to organised labour".[239] And, as John L Lewis later recalled, this supposed "friend of organised labour repeatedly fought in the most underhanded way against the inclusion of Section 7a". Lewis made clear that after this he "never trusted Roosevelt fully".[240] What was intended as an empty gesture, however, sparked an explosion of working class unrest. Underpinning this explosion was the widespread belief in 1933 that the economic collapse had reached bottom. Now was the right time to fight back. As the AFL reported, there was "a virtual uprising of workers for union membership". In factory after factory the workers were holding mass meetings and then "sent word they wanted to be organised".[241] The open shop was under attack.

While the AFL was really little more than a bystander to this revolt, the industrial unions, most notably the UMW, stepped in to give it an official lead. John L Lewis sent organisers into the coalfields proclaiming that the president wanted the miners to join the union. According to one historian of the UMW, in the history of the American labour movement "there has never been any other organising campaign carried out so quickly with enrolment of so many members as the 1933 UMW drive".[242] Indeed, according to John Brophy, there was actually no need to campaign: "an organiser had only to see that he had a good supply of application blanks and a place to file them, and the rank and file did the rest".[243]

Even in the fiercely anti-union South, where the UMW had gone down in bloody defeat in the early 1920s, the union steamrollered over company opposition. One organiser, Jesse Aquino, at the first meeting he held in McDowell County, West Virginia, had a pistol stuck in his back by a company guard while he was speaking. He carried on regardless and the guard slipped away as the men signed up with the union. On the way to his next meeting, his car was machine-gunned, but the momentum was unstoppable.[244] Another organiser, Van Bittner, later recalled that "the greatest meeting of my life" was when he spoke to miners assembled in the Charleston Armory in July 1933. Many had travelled overnight from as far away as the Hazzard coalfield in Kentucky. He told them that "you men of McDowell, Logan, Mingo, the Winding Gulf and Kanawha field—you are now free citizens of the United States".[245] This was not unionisation in the conventional sense—this was liberation. Tens of thousands of men defied company guards (many of them known killers) and spies to overthrow a tyranny that had ground them down without mercy for years. The campaign broke the back of the mine owners' resistance and over a 12-month period the UMW increased its membership from some 80,000 to over 500,000. The transformation was most dramatic in the South. In June 1933 the UMW had only seven members in West Virginia; a year later it had 100,000. In Alabama where membership had been around 200, a year later it was over 20,000.[246] Where the coal companies continued to hold out, in the so-called "captive mines" owned by the steel companies and in parts of the South, there were bitter strikes.

The clothing unions, the International Ladies Garment Workers Union (ILGWU) and the Amalgamated Clothing Workers (ACW) also launched organising drives to take advantage of Section 7a. In New York the ILGWU had fewer than 10,000 members, but its strike call on 16 August saw over 70,000 workers walk out, forcing the employers to surrender four days later. This was "as memorable a victory...as the famous Uprising of the Twenty Thousand in the same trade in 1909".[247] The ILGWU increased its national membership from 50,000 to over 200,000 by the spring of 1934, while the ACW, which had been reduced to some 7,000 members, increased to over 130,000. Edward Levinson provides a useful account of the 1933 uprising:

> Between 60,000 and 70,000 joined the unions in the Akron rubber plants and adjacent industries; almost 200 local unions with 100,000 members sprang up in auto; the membership of Amalgamated Iron, Steel and Tin Workers increased to 90,000; the metal workers climbed from less than 5,000 to 40,000; union recruits in aluminium totalled 15,000; the lumberjacks and sawmill workers of the Northwest came together 90,000 strong; in the cement industry, 20,000 workers joined; 385,000 workers in the South and North flocked to the standard of the unions.[248]

Most of the workers who organised in 1933 did so outside of these recruitment drives by the industrial unions. In workplace after workplace workers organised themselves, either establishing independent unions or turning to the AFL. Here they encountered the limitations of craft unionism. First of all, many craft union leaders regarded unskilled workers with open contempt and dismissed them as either unorganisable or too militant. Daniel Tobin of the Teamsters was not alone when he dismissed the men and women rallying to the union cause in 1933 as so much "rubbish".[249] The AFL itself responded to the wave of organising by putting the new members in unorganised industries into Federal Labor Unions (FLUs), which were affiliated directly to the federation. By October 1933 there were 3,573 of these federal locals. The intention was always that once they were established, the craft unions would take possession of those members who fell within their jurisdiction and generally the FLUs would subsequently wither away. They were often weak and exposed, poorly supported, and many were to fall prey to the employers' repression.

The wave of organising was inevitably accompanied by strike action. In July 1933 there were nearly 300 strikes across the country and the following month nearly 400. By the end of 1933 there had been more strikes than in any year since 1921. For most workers the decision to confront the boss was momentous. As John Anderson remembered:

Taking up a picket sign and walking the picket line was a difficult emotional experience for workers in 1933. Few of us had ever seen a picket line much less walked in one. The fears of physical injury or even death in those days were deterrents to workers joining the picket line or engaging in other strike activity.[250]

These were not unrealistic concerns. The great rank and file revolt of 1933 met with fierce resistance, with the Roosevelt administration only paying lip service to the protection of workers' rights, while the AFL leadership stood by helpless. According to the American Civil Liberties Union (ACLU), the months from July 1933 until the end of the year saw "widespread violations of workers' rights by injunctions, troops, private police, deputy sheriffs, labour spies and vigilantes".[251] By the end of the year at least 15 workers had been "killed by police, company guards or vigilantes".[252]

Under the NRA

The National Industrial Recovery Act established the National Recovery Administration (NRA) to put its provisions into effect. Roosevelt appointed General Hugh Johnson, a protégé of Bernard Baruch, the multi-millionaire bastion of the Democratic Party's right wing, to head it. As far as Johnson was concerned, the NRA would get government and business working together to pull the country out of the Depression. There was really no place in his thinking for the trade unions. He quickly made it clear that the largely spontaneous organising drive that had erupted did not have government support, and that "this administration is not going to be used as a means of organising industry". At the AFL convention in October 1933 he told delegates "that unions were no longer needed and that strikes had become superfluous since the president had created new mediation machinery under the NRA". Indeed, he warned that under present circumstances "you cannot tolerate strikes". Roosevelt wholeheartedly endorsed this view.

As far as he was concerned, the creation of the National Labor Board (NLB) to mediate between workers and employers removed any need for strike action. He warned the unions at the same convention that "just as in 1917, horses that kick over the traces will have to be put in the corral".[253]

What the unions found in practice was that Johnson made no attempt, beyond half-hearted exhortation, to enforce the labour provisions of the codes agreed under the NIRA. And he opposed any attempts by the unions to force employers to adhere to them. Employers completely ignored the codes in respect to pay, conditions and union recognition. Johnson stood by while there was wholesale victimisation of union members and, with Roosevelt's agreement, sanctioned the formation of company unions as meeting the terms of Section 7a. Under the auspices of the NRA, over a million workers found themselves enrolled in company unions. Johnson even succeeded in provoking his own NRA staff into strike action when he sacked one of them for his union activity, and a picket line was set up outside the NRA headquarters.[254] Roosevelt's own attitude to the unions at this time was perhaps best demonstrated when he appointed the fiercely anti-union Pierre du Pont, one of the richest and most powerful industrialists in the country, to the NLB.[255] Mauritz Hallgren summed up Roosevelt's attitude at this time in his 1935 biography of the man:

> [He only paid] lip service to the rights of the workers...not once had he lifted a finger of his own accord to give meaning to labour's "charter of rights". Not once had he sought to safeguard the principle of collective bargaining when it was opposed by any employer or group of employers.

He had only been able to maintain even the appearance of impartiality by letting his subordinates "bear the immediate responsibility for the execution of his labour policies".[256]

How did the AFL leadership respond? William Green, the AFL president, was not a fighter. His proudest boast was "that he was the leader of the largest Baptist bible class in Coshocton".[257] When he toured the South in 1930, supposedly spearheading an organisation drive, he made no effort to rally the workers to the union cause. Instead he attempted to convince the most reactionary employers in the country that the AFL was good for business, that it was a bastion against Communism, and that it would help raise productivity. He told employers:

> There is no sword in our scabbard. There is no weapon in our hand. We come not with the mailed fist, but with the open hand.[258]

This is, needless to say, not a recommended negotiating strategy. Green promised a business luncheon in Memphis that "American labour will never seek to capture the government as British labour had done". As one Memphis newspaper pointed out, Green:

> might have been taken for the president of a bank, the president of a railroad, a United States Senator or a great corporation lawyer... He is the kind of person who deplores strikes and walkouts... The policies he advocated might have come with great propriety from the president of the American Bankers' association.[259]

The British socialist academic Harold Laski, who had taught in America, described Green as someone who "if he was praised by J P Morgan, he would cry with pleasure".[260]

The intransigence of Southern employers was to be amply demonstrated with the coming of the NRA in 1933. Green was informed in August that there was not a single textile mill in the South "living up to the code signed by the president". Indeed, those workers who had joined the United Textile Workers (UTW) in their thousands were being victimised, the agreed rates of pay were being ignored or evaded and, at the same time, the pace of work was being relentlessly intensified. On one occasion an employer in Arkansas sacked 194 workers when he could not discover which one of them had complained to the NRA that he was only paying $6 a week instead of the agreed minimum of $12. The NRA did nothing to protect these workers. The AFL opposed industrial action in these cases, urging instead that the workers should put their faith in Roosevelt.[261]

Success or failure in the hundreds of strikes that took place in 1933 was largely determined by whether or not the workers listened to the AFL. As James Wechsler observed, in AFL-led strikes, "only the degree of disaster varied".[262] What often proved decisive was the lead given by men and women on the left, whether it was Communists, Socialists, Trotskyists, Musteites, Wobblies or others. Sidney Lens, at the time a young Trotskyist, remembered how, even though few in number, the left had played a vital strategic role in the struggle:

A group of workers enraged over wages or an unresolved grievance would be taken in hand by a leftist fellow worker who just knew what to do under the circumstances, or if not, where to get the best advice. The radicals brought to their task a number of a priori concepts, which were immensely helpful in organising the unorganised. They opposed in principle any collaboration with business. They considered the government an implacable enemy to be fought without restraint. And they were unequivocal about the "labour fakers"—heads of the established unions—whom they thought of as the concubines of the employers and the state, to be opposed with equal vigour.[263]

Among those fighting back were many of the most oppressed workers in America. In California, Communist Party members led a wave of farm workers' strikes that were "without precedent in the history of labour in the United States".[264] At the end of 1932 fruit pickers at Vacaville had gone on strike, but the union had been broken by vigilante action (the strike leaders were flogged, had their heads shaved and red enamel poured over them). Despite this setback, the following April saw the start of a wave of strikes, 37 altogether, involving over 50,000 workers, that swept the state. Leading the way was the Communist-controlled Cannery and Agricultural Workers Industrial Union (CAWIU). Over the course of the year pea, cherry, peach, lettuce, beet, grape and pear pickers struck, culminating in a strike of 18,000 cotton pickers in the San Joaquin Valley in October. The strike lasted 27 days and extended over 100 miles, with truckloads of pickets patrolling the roads to deter scabs. It was, Devra Weber writes, "the largest, longest and most bitter agricultural conflict to that date...a social earthquake".[265]

The strikers were overwhelmingly Mexican, many of them veterans of the Mexican Revolution of 1910. By the time the strike ended three of them had been shot dead. A proposal to wire Roosevelt to ask for federal intervention was defeated at a mass meeting on the grounds that "the son of a bitch" only had to pick up a newspaper to find out what was going on. Indeed, behind the scenes, George Creel, a senior Democratic Party official on the Regional Labor Board, was opposing union recognition and urging that the union leaders be prosecuted for criminal syndicalism. Courage, determination and solidarity produced a 25 percent pay rise, but no union recognition.[266] As Caroline Decker, one of the CP strike leaders, later recalled, the California fruit pickers' strikes provided a model of solidarity, with "Mexicans, whites, coloured workers living, eating, picketing and going to jail together—forgetting racial prejudice".[267]

Two other 1933 strikes in many ways presaged the struggles of the following year: the nut pickers' strike in St Louis and the meat packers' strike in Austin, Minnesota. Both demonstrated the crucial importance of the coming together of working class anger and of strategically placed revolutionaries.

In St Louis more than 1,500 women, mostly black, worked in nutshelling sweatshops. The largest employer was the Funsten Company, which employed both black and white women but kept them segregated. The white women worked shorter hours and were paid more, although everyone's pay was pitifully low. Since 1931 the company had cut piece rates five times, so white women could earn $4 to $6 a week and black women only $3 to $4. There were four Funsten plants in St Louis. The CP-controlled Food Workers Industrial Union began efforts at organising the workers and established a core of supporters at the all-black Eaton Avenue plant. In May the Eaton Avenue workers presented the management with demands for a 50 percent pay rise, equal pay for black and white women and union recognition. When the company refused to negotiate, they walked out, closing the Eaton Avenue plant and marching on the other plants. The strikers were reinforced on the picket line by members of the Unemployed Council. By the end of the second day of the strike there were 800 black women out, and then 200 white women walked out as well. By the end of the week all the Funsten plants were closed and the strike had spread to the Liberty Nut Company and the Central Pecan Company. In the course of the strike over 100 women were arrested and there were some violent clashes on the picket lines. Carrie Smith, one of the strike leaders and a deeply religious woman, addressed a strike meeting while holding a Bible in one hand and a brick in the other. She believed both were necessary if they were to win. After ten days the companies capitulated, conceding all the strikers' demands. Communist Party organisers, in particular William Sentner and Ralph Shaw, played a vital role in the success of the strike, which had "an electrifying effect" on the whole St Louis labour movement.[268]

A similar role was played by socialist and syndicalist activists at the Hormel meat packing plant in Austin. One of the foremen, Frank Ellis, was a former member of the IWW's national executive who "had been thrown into almost every jail from Texas to Minnesota". He had been imprisoned for criminal syndicalism in Nebraska and on one occasion "had been beaten and left for dead by vigilantes". As a foreman, he had given jobs to every good union man he could find, recommending men to other foremen as well. The result was that there were militants in a number of sections, including a group of Trotskyists led by Joe Ollman in the hog kill section. They were biding their time. Their moment came on 13 July in the hog kill section when a foreman was trying to sign workers up for the company pension scheme. The workers stopped work and the company backed down. This small incident was the turning point—the company had been successfully confronted.

Ellis and his supporters began signing up members for a new independent Wobbly-style union, the Independent Union of All Workers (IUAW). The union was built by small-scale confrontations with management that finally resulted in the company recognising the IUAW in September. Hormel refused to increase pay, however, and the union voted to strike on 10 November. Pickets were put on the gates, but the workers decided that more direct action was needed to make sure the plant shut down. Some 400 workers stormed the factory, clearing out any management, company guards and scabs they found. There was, one worker recalled, "a lot of suppressed hatred".[269] Foremen were assaulted, management cars had their windscreens broken and time clocks were smashed. One much-hated foreman made his escape by rowboat across the Cedar River and was loudly cheered when the boat sank halfway. When the sheriff arrived at the plant, strikers bodily picked up his car with him in it, turned it round and sent him away. The plant was in the hands of the workers.

Governor Floyd Olson of the Minnesota Farmer-Labor Party, a reformist politician elected with the support of the labour movement, stepped in to mediate. Although he regularly boasted of his radicalism, Olson told the strikers that they were putting him "on the spot because if I have to choose between my proper duty and my sympathy, I will be obliged to choose duty". With the threat of intervention by the National Guard hanging over them, the strikers returned to work, having won only a partial victory. Once back on the job, however, the union proceeded to batter the management into submission by means of a guerrilla campaign of sectional disputes and stoppages. As Ellis explained:

> Most of our strikes were sit-down, sit down right on the job and not do a damn bit of work until we got it settled. We had a strike every day. Hell, if a fellow farted crooked we would strike about it.

From its base at the Hormel plant, the IUAW proceeded to organise the workers in the rest of Austin and then moved on to the neighbouring towns. By the end of 1935 the union was putting out a weekly newspaper, *The Unionist*, edited by a Trotskyist, Carl Nilson, and delivered free to every to every home in Hormel.[270]

Chapter Five

1934: the year of the fightback

Despite some notable successes, for most workers 1933 ended in demoralisation and defeat. By the end of the year, largely due to the misleadership of the AFL, the working class insurgency had been contained and was being rolled back. In steel, rubber and the car industry the employers had seen off the challenge, leaving wrecked unions and thousands of victimised militants. At best, Bellush writes, "the door to labour's rights was slightly opened".[271] The AFL leadership remained helplessly clutching at Section 7a and looking to an uninterested Roosevelt to rescue them. Instead it was to be rank and file action, independent of the AFL, that would kick down the door in 1934.

There were many strikes in 1934 but three in particular, the Auto-Lite strike in Toledo, the Teamsters' strike in Minneapolis, and the dockers' strike in San Francisco, were to reach almost insurrectionary proportions and completely change the strategic context for the American working class. All three strikes were led by radicals and revolutionaries; all three defied the AFL leadership, confronted the state and were fought with fierce determination. They served notice on the Roosevelt administration that the working class could no longer be ignored.

Toledo

The AFL was completely dominated by the craft unions but it had paid some lip-service to organising workers in the mass production industries. They were recruited, as we have seen, into Federal Labor Unions (FLUs) affiliated directly to the national organisation. By mid-1934 there were 350,000 workers signed up in 1,700 FLUs. The problem was that the AFL gave them no real support even though they were confronting the most anti-union employers. The only advice they got was to trust in the government. Most FLUs were based in individual plants, but in Toledo FLU Local 18384 had organised throughout the city, recruiting members in all the car component firms. Auto-Lite was regarded as the key employer that had to be organised if the Local was to survive.

On 23 February 1934 the Local struck at Auto-Lite, demanding a pay rise and union recognition. Only a minority of the workforce walked out, but enough to cause the company problems. After five days the company conceded a 5 percent pay rise and promised negotiations on recognition. In fact, Auto-Lite prepared for further strikes, taking on extra workers, trying to undermine the union by intimidation and then reneging on the promised negotiations. On 12 April union members walked out once again. Most workers crossed the picket line and the strike looked like ending in a crushing defeat, one of many such setbacks at the time. On this occasion, however, the strikers turned to the American Workers Party (AWP) for help.

The AWP is almost completely forgotten today. It was largely the brainchild of one of the most remarkable men in the history of American radicalism, Abraham Muste.[272] He was a Protestant clergyman, radicalised by his opposition to the First World War, who threw himself into the post-war workers' struggles. He was one of the leaders of the 1919 textile workers' strike in Lawrence and emerged from that conflict as the general-secretary of the radical United Textile Workers. The union was one of the victims of the employers' open-shop offensive, eventually driven out of existence. In late 1921 he became dean of Brookwood Labor College, which under his direction became a centre of radical opposition. He condemned the AFL leadership, which, as he put it, "thinks, feels, talks and acts like businessmen".[273] The college trained union organisers, but trained them to build industrial unions committed to socialist politics. Muste's radicalism led to determined efforts by the AFL president William Green to close the college down.[274] In May 1929 Muste and his supporters established the Conference for Progressive Labor Action (CPLA) to campaign for "progressive" trade unionism and to actively support workers in struggle. In late 1929 the CPLA had organisers working in North Carolina supporting striking mill workers. On 2 October in the town of Marion police opened fire on pickets, shooting 36 men and women, most of them in the back as they ran for their lives. Six of the pickets were killed, one of them, 65 year old George Jonas, shot dead when he was already under arrest and in handcuffs. The president of the Marion Manufacturing Company, B W Baldwin, praised the police as "damned good marksmen". When the workers came to bury their dead, none of the local preachers was prepared to defy the mill owners and officiate, so Muste stepped forward.[275]

The Depression transformed Muste from a radical into a revolutionary and a Marxist. In 1932 the CPLA began organising the unemployed, setting up Unemployed Leagues to fight for relief, resist evictions and support workers on strike. By the end of 1933 the leagues had successfully been established in Ohio (100,000 members) and in Pennsylvania (40,000 members).[276] Encouraged by this, in December 1933 Muste and his supporters established the American Workers Party. The AWP proclaimed itself a revolutionary socialist party. It was anti-Stalinist in politics, but part of that stance involved a rejection of Bolshevism as well. It was one of a number of such organisations internationally that developed in the 1930s, trying to find a radical way between reformism and Stalinism—the Spanish POUM is another example. The AWP attracted a number of Marxist intellectuals, such as Sidney Hook[277] and James Burnham, but its orientation was very much to mass struggle.

In Toledo two AWP members, Sam Pollock and Theodore Selander of the Lucas County Unemployed League, offered to reinforce the picket line with unemployed volunteers. The offer was accepted and the party secretary, Louis Budenz, quickly became a key adviser to the strike committee. According to Muste, Budenz "was a phenomenally effective organiser of strikes and demonstrations...he had no rival in those days as a speaker who could sway masses of workers and bring them out of the mill and mine to the picket line". He made a vital contribution to the struggle.[278]

The decisive moment in the strike came when the company secured a court injunction restricting picketing. Urged on by the AWP, the strikers decided to defy the injunction. The police began making arrests (107 on 15 May) but this only led to the picket numbers growing. The strike increasingly came to be seen as a battle affecting the whole of the Toledo labour movement with workers from other factories joining the strikers and the unemployed on the picket line. On 21

May there were 1,000 pickets, on 22 May 4,000 and on the morning of 23 May 6,000, swelling to 10,000 as the day went on. That afternoon the police once again began making arrests and their brutality provoked resistance:

> The fighting went on from mid-afternoon until midnight. In effect, the great crowd outside imprisoned 1,500 strike-breakers inside the factory. Auto-Lite barricaded its doors and turned off the lights. From the roof and upper-storey windows deputies rained tear gas bombs on the people in the streets below... The crowd replied with a seven-hour barrage of stones and bricks...heaved through the factory windows. Fires broke out in the shipping room and the parking lot...cars were overturned, saturated with gasoline and set on fire. During the evening strikers broke into the factory at three points and there was hand to hand fighting before they were driven out. The area for blocks around was blanketed with tear gas.[279]

The strikers improvised catapults out of inner tubes and bombarded the factory through the night, breaking every window. The next day pickets joked that it really was an "open shop" now.[280]

At dawn on 22 May the National Guard arrived to rescue the besieged scabs who had been trapped in the plant overnight. The workers were in no mood to have the strike broken by part-time troops and the fighting continued. The guardsmen were driven back to the factory gates under a hail of bricks. They responded with bayonet charges and, when this failed, they opened fire. Two pickets, both unemployed, were shot dead. Still the fighting continued. According to the journalist John Spivak the area around the plant had become "a no-man's land". People were ordered from their homes by the troops, streetlights were shot out to keep the area in darkness, and all the time "workers singing and shouting tore up the streets for cobble stones to hurl at the soldiers". He writes of how "the sound of exploding tear gas bombs mingled with the crack of rifles and the sirens of police cars". The Toledo Central Labor Union threatened to call a general strike, with 83 local unions voting in favour. AFL officials "opposed the general strike move, but were swept away in the storm of approval". The AFL was, in Spivak's words, terrified by the "rising fury".[281] The company agreed to shut the plant. The troops were withdrawn and negotiations got under way. On 2 June Local 18384 won recognition. The strikers had not won all their demands, but they had inflicted a complete and unambiguous defeat on Auto-Lite. The open shop was dead.

The strike was, as Muste put it, "an expression of the pent-up suffering of many years".[282] How did William Green of the AFL respond to it? He wrote to the Toledo Central Labor Union condemning the strike as a mistake and making it clear that there should be no thought of a general strike. With the fighting raging in the streets, he wrote to one of his organisers that "I hardly know what to do in this situation at the present moment". As his biographer observes he made himself "both ludicrous and pathetic". Green, he writes, believed "it necessary to oppose workers' interests in the name of industrial peace... In setting himself up as a mediator between labour and capital, Green had, in effect, deserted the strikers".[283] All that can be said in his favour is that his desertion to the other side was no great loss. Instead the strike was won by working class militancy given direction by revolutionary socialists. In the aftermath of the conflict Muste wrote of the "great disillusionment with...the Roosevelt administration" that growing numbers of workers felt. They were recognising that "not Section 7a of the NRA, nor labour boards, nor even the White Father himself can be trusted to give them anything. Their gains have been brought about by their own militant fight for organisation".[284]

Minneapolis

At the end of 1933 Local 574 of the Teamsters union in Minneapolis had 75 members. It had relied for its survival on sweetheart agreements with a handful of coal yards, but in November 1933 it was taken over by a remarkable group of militants. Carl Skogland, Ray Dunne and his brothers, Miles and Grant, and Farrell Dobbs were all members of the Trotskyist Communist League. Inspired by the success of the Hormel strike in nearby Austin (Skogland had actually assisted in the strike), they developed a strategy for organising the trucking industry in the city. They recruited not just the drivers but the indoor warehouse workers as well, transforming the Teamsters in Minneapolis from a craft into an industrial union. This was to be accomplished in defiance of the Citizens' Alliance (CA), one of the most powerful and ruthless open-shop organisations in the US. The CA had nearly 800 business affiliates in 1934. It ran a network of informers and spies, operated blacklists and broke strikes. In 1923 it boasted that "the open shop is more firmly established in private industry than any time in the history of the city".[285] In 1920 there had been 27,000 union members in Minneapolis, but by 1928 the number had been driven down to 14,000, and under the impact of the Depression fell to 7,000 in 1934.[286] The Teamsters had not won a strike in the city since they had been crushed in the great strike of 1916.

The first step in building the union required a victory to show that the employers could actually be beaten. To this end, Skogland set about organising the coal yards, recruiting enough drivers to be able to call a strike on 7 February 1934. Some 700 drivers struck, hitting 67 yards. As Charles Walker admiringly observed:

Preparation had been surprisingly detailed and painstaking. A map of the coal yards of Minneapolis was prepared, and mimeographed instructions were issued to each picket captain before the strike. Within three hours 65 coal yards out of 67 were closed "as tight as a bull's eye in fly time".

The tactic that decided the strike was the brainchild of a "rank and file coal heaver": "the militant use of cruising picket squads".[287] Instead of trying to maintain stationary pickets at 67 yards, the union put its men in cars and trucks and they patrolled the streets looking for scab trucks. They knew the routes, intercepted and stopped scab trucks, dumping their loads into the road. The strike was further aided by sub-zero temperatures, and after three days the employers surrendered. Thousands of drivers joined the union in the wake of its success.

The next step was to organise the trucking industry across the city. This required closing the market district and the union prepared to accomplish this with almost military precision. As Farrell Dobbs wrote in his classic account, *Teamster Rebellion*:

Seldom anywhere...has there been such a well-prepared strike. When the sun rose on May 16, 1934, the headquarters at 1900 Chicago Avenue was a beehive of activity. Union carpenters and plumbers were installing gas stoves, sinks and serving counters in the commissary. The Cooks and Waiters Union sent experts in mass cooking and serving to help organise things and train the volunteer help. Working in two 12-hour shifts, over 100 volunteers served 4,000 to 5,000 people daily.

The union established its own medical centre to treat those injured in the struggle so they could not be arrested at the hospital. It was manned by sympathetic doctors, nurses and volunteers. As for the picketing:

> We had a special staff at our disposal to handle the telephones and operate a shortwave radio used to monitor police calls. Teenage volunteers with motorcycles were organised into an efficient courier service. Scooting around the city under strict orders to stay out of the fighting, they served as the eyes and ears of the picket dispatchers and as a swift means of contact with picket captains.[288]

Once again they relied on "cruising picket squads", operating their own repair shop to keep dozens of cars and trucks on the road. The union headquarters itself was guarded by men equipped with tommy guns to deter vigilante attacks.[289]

To begin with pickets were unarmed and included members of the Women's Auxiliary group, formed of women supporters and strikers' wives. On 19 May, however, pickets were subjected to brutal beatings by police and deputised volunteers that left many seriously injured, including "20 blood-covered women...several with broken legs or unconscious".[290] After this women were withdrawn from picket duty and pickets were armed with clubs. The union was ready to resist any attempt to drive its pickets off the streets, recognising that picketing was the key to winning the dispute. They prepared for confrontation. On 21 May union vehicles driving into the market district went in with more passengers than they came out with. The union hid 600 men in the AFL hall unnoticed by the police. When fighting broke out between pickets and police at the Gamble and Robinson Company, instead of the pickets receiving a beating, 600 men armed with clubs marched to their assistance, taking the police completely by surprise. When the police brought in reinforcements, the union motored in its reserve of 900 men from union headquarters. Police lines were broken by the simple device of driving a truck through them. Over 30 police and deputies were hospitalised in hand to hand fighting. As Dobbs observed, the "union had fought the trained police to a draw, and not a single truck had been moved".[291]

The following day (22 May) another battle took place for control of the market district. The police were reinforced by large numbers of deputies provided by the Citizens' Alliance—some came to do battle in their polo helmets. The Teamsters were reinforced by hundreds of building workers, who had walked out on strike in solidarity. In the ensuing "Battle of Deputies Run" two deputies were killed, one of them, C Arthur Lyman, a leading member of the CA. The forces of law and order were driven from the market district and the pickets were left in control, "directing the traffic".[292]

The employers agreed to negotiations in the aftermath of the battle. These took place under the auspices of Governor Floyd Olson of the Farmer-Labor Party. He was generally regarded as a man to be trusted, and was also known to be a bitter enemy of the Citizens' Alliance (in 1923 he had exposed an attempt by private detectives in the employ of the CA to frame union activists on dynamite charges) and had donated $500 to Local 574's strike fund. But his concern was to end the strike as soon as possible, before it could become an electoral liability, rather than to ensure victory on the union's terms. And he had no wish to strengthen the position of the Trotskyists in the Minneapolis labour movement. In the negotiations the union was led to believe by Olson that the employers had accepted their definition of indoor workers. On this basis it recommended acceptance of the proposed settlement on 25 May.

Local 574 had won a stunning victory over a feared opponent. The union quickly discovered, however, that the May agreement was only a truce—the employers' interpretation of the agreement was different from theirs. Both sides prepared for another confrontation. The second Teamsters' strike began on 17 July. The union had immeasurably strengthened its organisation, recruiting more members and establishing an unemployed auxiliary with 5,000 members. It had started a weekly newspaper, *The Organizer*, edited by Max Shachtman. During the strike it became a daily. This was to prove absolutely vital in order to counter the red scare that the CA ran in the press, aided and abetted by the Teamsters' president, Daniel Tobin.

The strike began and the union's picketing operation swung into action. To begin with, pickets were once again unarmed. This time, however, the police had orders not to allow a rerun of the May strike. On 20 July the police staged an ambush, opening fire with shotguns on a truckload of pickets as they tried to stop a scab truck. When other pickets on foot went to the rescue, they too were shot down. By the time the shooting stopped 69 pickets and bystanders had been shot, with two pickets killed and many more seriously wounded.[293] This deliberate, calculated attack was intended to put an end to picketing. It was hoped that it would allow the employers to break the strike and smash the union. The union's first response was to take steps to prevent its members picketing with guns. Dobbs describes taking firearms off the pickets as "the hardest thing I ever did in my life".[294] A shoot-out with the police would give the authorities just the excuse they needed to destroy the union by open repression. But they continued picketing. Determined not to be shot off the streets, the union kept "cars and trucks trailing scab vehicles, forcing the police to provide large escorts, up to 20 police cars for one scab truck, and therefore severely limited the number of scab trucks they could run".[295]

On 26 July Governor Olson sent 4,000 National Guardsmen into the city and declared martial law. This was justified as necessary to prevent any further loss of life, as necessary to protect the strikers. In fact, Olson intended to force the union into surrender. Olson was pro-union, but they had to be "responsible" unions led by moderates, certainly not led by Trotskyists. The CA's determination to restore the open shop seriously weakened Olson's position and strengthened that of Local 574's leadership. He wanted to impose a compromise on the union, but the CA was insisting that he help them destroy it. The guardsmen set about breaking the strike. They introduced a permit system, licensing trucks to operate so as to maintain essential services (something the union had already been doing), but in reality allowing the employers to restart their deliveries with scab drivers. Within days the employers had thousands of scab trucks running. The Local 574 leadership had to convince its members to confront Olson and take on the National Guard. Olson was trusted as a man who was on the side of the workers, who had taken on big business and beaten it. The CA had done everything it could to prevent his election. Now Ray Dunne had to argue that they must take him on: "Submit to the governor and the strike is lost," he insisted. As Charles Walker points out, he did not use Marxist theory to explain the role of reformism; he simply pointed "to the 6,000 trucks moving in Minneapolis".[296]

The union took the crucial decision to defy the martial law regime and reinstate the cruising picket squads as a guerrilla-style operation. Dobbs describes how it worked:

Since the kind of fight we intended to wage would probably bring further military raids on any suspected centre of picket concentration, we decided to decentralise operations. A series of control points was set up around the town, mainly in friendly filling stations, which cruising squads could enter and leave without attracting attention. Pay phones in the stations and couriers scouting the neighbourhood were used to report scab trucks to picket dispatchers. Cruising squads were then sent to the reported locations to do the necessary and get away in a hurry. Trucks operating with military permits were soon being put out of commission throughout the city. Within a few hours over 500 calls for help were reported to have come into military headquarters. Troops in squad cars responded to the calls usually to find scabs who had been worked over, but no pickets.[297]

Olson responded as predicted with a raid on the union headquarters and the arrest of the union leadership, but the picketing operation continued. The only way he could get it called off was to release the people he had just arrested and force the CA to come to terms with them. His predicament was made worse by growing demands throughout the Minneapolis labour movement for a general strike to protest at the crackdown. While the AFL bureaucrats were heroically resisting this, they could not hold out indefinitely.

Olson was, as the Trotskyist leader James Cannon pointed out, trapped in a contradiction. He was "on the one hand supposedly a representative of the workers; on the other hand, he was the governor of a bourgeois state".[298] He had taken action to break the strike, but there was a limit to how far he could go without losing the support of the working class on whom his electoral survival depended. The union was confident that he would not order pickets to be shot down in cold blood as had been done by the police. Such action would destroy his political career. Having failed to break the union, he turned his attention to the CA. In a gesture of even-handedness, he ordered their headquarters raided by troops. More to the point, on 8 August he met with Roosevelt to discuss the situation. Roosevelt agreed to put pressure on the banks that were the backbone of the CA and were financing the employers' resistance. The federal government's Reconstruction Finance Corporation threatened to withdraw its loans which were saving the banks from bankruptcy and the employers' resistance collapsed.[299]

FIGHTING BACK

Against all the odds, Local 574 had won a decisive victory in one of the best conducted strikes in the history of the American working class.[300]

San Francisco

Before the First World War San Francisco had been one of the best organised cities in the US. This changed in the post-war years when the open-shop drive, spearheaded by the Industrial Association, broke union power. The longshoremen (dockers) were defeated in 1919, with the employers establishing a company union known as the "Blue Union". The employers' success in San Francisco was repeated along the Pacific coast, with the International Longshoremen's Association (ILA) only maintaining a foothold in Tacoma. With the onset of the Depression conditions on the docks worsened. In Seattle between 1929 and 1932 the earnings of regular workers fell by over 50 percent and those of casual workers even more, and a speed-up produced a growing toll of accidents.[301]

In San Francisco a group of left militants, mostly syndicalist in sympathy, many of them former Wobblies, but open to Communist Party influence, had started a rank and file paper, the monthly *Waterfront Worker*, in December 1932. As one of its founders, Mitch Slobodek, put it, "There was an undercurrent of restlessness on the waterfront when we started putting out the paper, but no direction. The paper gave one".[302] In its second issue in January 1933 the paper urged its readers to form "small undercover groups of those whom we know on each dock".[303] They proposed the establishment of a covert network of militants, the nucleus of a union, ready to come out in the open when the time was right. Later in the year, in response to the NIRA, the ILA appointed an organiser in San Francisco, Lee Holman, who began signing up members.

In the early 1930s the CP had been committed to a policy of "dual unionism"—the formation of revolutionary trade unions in opposition to the "fascist" AFL. This policy had failed, despite the often extraordinary heroism of party members, but its failure was not always recognised because the AFL unions were not growing either. In 1933 this began to change, and with the rush of workers into the AFL, many CP members began ignoring the policy in practice. This was the case in San Francisco, where the rank and file group that had developed around the *Waterfront Worker* with CP support, resolved to take over the ILA, democratise it and turn it into a militant fighting organisation.[304] In Seattle and Portland, CP branches stuck to the party line, condemning the ILA as a "social fascist" organisation, and consequently had no influence on events whatsoever.[305]

Towards the end of 1933 more and more dockers joined the ILA and increasingly came into conflict with the Blue Union and the employers. The official ILA position argued by Holman was that they should place their trust in the NRA and at all costs avoid trouble. The militants around the *Waterfront Worker*, led by Harry Bridges, decided to act. In September 1933 on the Matson dock men refused to show their Blue Union cards and four of them were suspended for wearing their ILA buttons. Holman refused to support them, but the militants led a walkout that threatened to spread throughout the port and the employer backed down. The Blue Union was finished. As Bridges put it, that "was the end of the fear and intimidation" and they were now "in business".[306] A small tactical victory had been carefully calculated so as to have a decisive strategic result. For Bridges, "in a small way temporarily a strike is a small revolution".[307]

Still the ILA leadership urged restraint, but the situation was escaping out of their control. Rank and file dockers all along the Pacific coast were taking control of their union. They endorsed a policy based on union-controlled hiring halls that would effectively establish the closed shop and give the union control of who was hired at the docks. At the end of March 1934 Pacific longshoremen voted 6,616 to 699 for strike action if their demands were not met. ILA president Joseph Ryan, the very worst type of AFL bureaucrat, stepped in to suspend the strike when Roosevelt promised mediation. The employers refused to give any ground; indeed, backed up by the Industrial Association, they were preparing to break the threatened strike and smash the union. George Creel of the NRA Regional Council told Washington that the employers had made it clear to him "confidentially that even if they lost 2 to 3 million, it would be worth it to destroy the union".[308] The militants succeeded in having the completely discredited Holman suspended from office, and they elected a strike committee to direct the struggle. The rank and file were in control. On 8 May mass meetings the length of the Pacific coast voted for immediate strike action. Only in Seattle did dockers vote to carry on working, but the Local officers locked the hall doors and kept them discussing the question until 1am, by which time they had the results from all the other ports.[309] When it was clear that every other port was out, the Seattle dockers voted to join the strike. On 9 May 12,000 dockers stopped work.

The walkout was quickly joined by the seamen, coming out in solidarity, but also with their own demands. Crucial, however, was the decision by the San Francisco Teamsters, defying their full-time officials, to boycott the docks. According to Paul Eliel, a spokesman for the employers, had it not been for the Teamsters, "the strike of longshoremen would undoubtedly have collapsed within a week or ten days at most". He bitterly lamented the fact that the Teamsters' leader, Michael Casey, seemed to have completely lost control of his men.[310] Even when the employers got scabs onto the docks to load and unload ships, they could not move goods off the docks because of the Teamsters' decision to respect picket lines. Despite this, every day there were clashes between pickets and police. In Seattle on 12 May scabs were successfully cleared from the docks when the picket was reinforced by 600 men from Tacoma and 150 from Everitt, who overwhelmed the police. The first fatalities occurred in San Pedro on 14 May when police and company guards shot two pickets dead during an attempt to storm a scab compound. The strike remained solid. In Portland many of the police were sympathetic to the strike. According to one of the strike organisers, every week they received the names and addresses of all those who had enlisted as "specials" for strikebreaking duty and many of these men just "happened to run into unfriendly people in the streets". On another occasion when the police were detailed to escort scabs onto the docks, a detective told the union that they would abandon them a block from the gates: "There was quite a lot of monkey business out in the street that morning". Eventually 12 policemen were suspended from duty for their union sympathies.[311]

Joseph Ryan, the ILA president (on occasions he claimed the union initials stood for "I Love America"), intervened to try and bring the strike to an end. His support in the union rested on the New York docks, where the union worked in close collaboration with the employers and organised crime. Indeed, one historian has described the ILA in New York as "a company union run by gangsters".[312] Ryan was not accustomed to the idea of actually having to put agreements to the membership and normally relied on suppressing dissent by strong-arm methods. In all his years as union president (1927 to 1942) there was not one official strike on the New York docks. He proceeded to negotiate a deal over the heads of the strikers, surrendering the union-controlled hiring hall, only to have it repudiated at mass meetings on 28 May. Not used to this sort of rebuff, he had another attempt the following month, trying to split the ports and leave San Francisco isolated. Once again, on 16 June, he was repudiated.[313]

The union leadership's attempt to deliver a sell-out had failed; now the employers determined to open the San Francisco docks by force. The Industrial Association set up a non-union trucking firm with scab drivers who would cross picket lines. On 2 July five trucks with a massive police presence carried goods off the docks to a nearby warehouse. On 3 July a repeat effort led to fierce fighting between pickets and police with the police making free use of clubs and tear gas. The next day, 4 July, was a holiday. On 5 July some 20,000 pickets (dockers, seamen, unemployed workers, Teamsters and others) assembled to stop the trucks. Bridges and his picket captains marshalled their forces to fight a regular battle. By the end of the day two pickets, Howard Sperry and Nick Bordoise, had been shot dead and dozens more were seriously injured, two more were to die from their injuries and a number were permanently disabled.[314] The next day, just as in Minneapolis, the union disarmed pickets who turned up for duty with firearms. The state governor, Roger Lapham, seized on the shootings as an excuse to send in the National Guard.

By now it was clear to more and more workers that what was at stake was not just the longshoremen's cause, but the fate of the San Francisco labour movement. The Industrial Association was clearly intent on keeping San Francisco an open-shop city. On 12 July the Teamsters voted, once again in defiance of their officials, for an indefinite all-out strike. Workers across the city were walking out in sympathy in growing numbers in what one historian has described as "a creeping general strike".[315] The AFL officials on the Central Labor Union reluctantly bowed to the inevitable. One official admitted that it "was an avalanche. I saw it coming so I ran ahead before it crushed me".[316] Frances Perkins reported to Roosevelt that "the officers of the unions have been swept off their feet by the rank and file movement".[317] The CLU called a general strike on 14 July, but managed to beat off attempts to establish a rank and file controlled strike committee. The strike was kept firmly under official control. Indeed, they only called it to head off a developing unofficial general strike that they could not have controlled. Support for the strike was overwhelming.

At government level there was serious discussion about whether or not to send in federal troops to break the general strike. Governor Lapham urged the use of force: "We can cure this thing best by bloodshed. We have got to have bloodshed to stop it. It is the best thing to do".[318] Roosevelt was on holiday, and both acting president Cordell Hull and attorney general Cummings were in favour of the use of force. Secretary of labour Perkins was strongly opposed. She argued that it would mean "regular shooting and a lot of people will drop in the streets". Such bloodletting would cause "frightful resentment", and would do serious damage "politically and morally and for the basic labour-industry and labour-government relationship".[319] Roosevelt backed her judgement, a decision that, in effect, determined the direction of the New Deal. If the administration had sent in the troops, it would have alienated working class support and been forced into a different trajectory. Instead the decision was made to rely on the union leaders to police their members, keeping them aboard as allies, even if it meant making concessions that Roosevelt had little sympathy with.

This did not preclude action against the left. On 17 July there was a well-organised wave of vigilante attacks on left targets in San Francisco and across California. With the police conveniently absent, gangs of armed vigilantes, many of them from the American Legion,[320] wrecked offices and meeting halls and administered beatings. The Communist Party was the favourite target. Once the vigilantes had done their work, the police arrived to arrest the victims. By the end of the day over 450 people had been arrested and charged with vagrancy—with bail set at $1,000 instead of the normal $10.[321] The opportunity was also taken to finally crush the farm workers' union, the CAIWU, whose leadership was arrested, charged with criminal syndicalism and eventually jailed.[322] This carefully organised assault was celebrated in the press as a popular uprising against the reds. Earlier a group of businessmen had got together to discuss having Bridges killed (he had already turned down a $50,000 bribe), but one of their number warned he would go public if they did.[323]

On 20 July the CLU called off the general strike on the grounds that acceptable mediation terms were now on offer. This effectively outmanoeuvred the longshoremen. Even more damaging, the Teamsters voted to end their boycott of the docks. This left the dockers facing a long war of attrition on their own. They voted to accept mediation. Bridges was criticised by some on the left for this but in retrospect it seems he accurately judged the balance of forces. If the dockers stayed out they would be taking on the employers, the Industrial Association and the state. If they returned to work undefeated, they could confront their employers on the job. On strike the balance of forces was against them; back at work it was in their favour. The final settlement gave the dockers a coast-wide contract with a six-hour day and time and a half for overtime. The hiring hall was to be joint union and employer, but the dispatcher was to be appointed by the union. Once back at work, on the job action soon cleared any scabs off the docks, ended the speed-up and established the closed shop.[324] It was a historic victory.[325] The strike was also a pivotal moment for many employers who had been so far going along with the New Deal. They turned against Roosevelt for failing to take federal action against union militancy. The struggle had been a tremendous success for the Communist Party. Whereas at the start of the dockers' strike in San Francisco, the party had had no members on the docks, by the end of the strike it had 25 and the number of seamen in the party had increased to over 50. In the San Francisco area itself overall party membership had increased from 2,100 in May 1934 to 3,000 in August 1934.[326] And this success had been achieved by ignoring the Third Period policy with regard to the unions.

Defeat

The victories in Toledo, Minneapolis and San Francisco dramatically changed the strategic picture as far as the class struggle was concerned. 1934 also saw the first appearance of the sit-down strike with workers occupying the White Motor Company in Cleveland at the start of the year and over 1,000 workers staging a sit-down in the General Tire and Rubber Plant in Akron in June.[327] These remained isolated episodes, although they certainly presaged what was to come. The Roosevelt administration could no longer ignore the working class. And as far as the working class itself was concerned, it had been demonstrated that militant action, amounting on occasions to virtual insurrection, could triumph. Even in conditions of mass unemployment, militancy and solidarity could defeat the most ruthless employers. Instead of the unemployed breaking strikes, thousands of the unemployed reinforced picket lines and fought with the police. In all three strikes the formula for victory was rank and file militancy and radical or revolutionary socialist leadership confronting employers, the union leadership and the state. 1934 was to see another great strike that proved the importance of this formula in a negative sense, in defeat. On 1 September 1934 the United Textile Workers called a national strike, the largest stoppage in US history up to that point. Between 350,000 and 400,000 workers walked out. Three weeks later the strike was called off by the leadership on the basis of "assurances" given by the president personally. It was a crushing defeat.

Textile workers were among the hardest hit by the Depression, with wages driven down and work relentlessly intensified by the "stretch-out". The union had virtually collapsed. In February 1933 it had 15,000 members. Section 7a revolutionised the situation. By September 1933 membership had increased to 40,000, by June 1934 to 250,000 and by August of that year to 340,000. This explosion in membership was driven by rage, but the rage was regarded as a dangerous embarrassment by the union leadership. They looked to Roosevelt and the NRA for justice. As Francis Gorman, one of the UTW's leaders, put it, "We have a friend in the White House".[328] In practice the textile companies completely ignored the codes agreed for the industry and this was effectively connived at by the NRA. Between August 1933 and August 1934 the Textile Labor Relations Board, set up to mediate in disputes, "received 3,920 complaints...and resolved only one wage and hour dispute in a worker's favour".[329] The White House was deluged with letters from desperate mill workers who were convinced that Roosevelt could not know how oppressed and exploited they were or he would surely do something about it. One worker wrote to Roosevelt and described how the "stretch-out" was killing them all "inch by inch".[330] The president did nothing and disappointment led to revolt.

It was only under intense rank and file pressure that the union leadership finally called a strike on 1 September. While the mills in New England and Maine were shut down, the region where the strike would be decided was acknowledged to be in the South, in the Carolina Piedmont. Here the workers formed "flying squadrons"—car and truck convoys of pickets that motored from mill to mill, closing them down. Some involved over 100 vehicles and one "flying squadron" mobilised some 2,000 flying pickets.[331] The tactic met with great success, despite the employers arming themselves to the teeth (one company in Alabama bought four machine guns, spent $1,700 on tear gas and hired private guards who "proceeded to barricade public roads and assault union sympathisers").[332] The authorities responded to the "flying squadrons" with the mobilisation of the National Guard. In Georgia, Governor George Talmadge, a self-proclaimed "friend of the workers", declared martial law, mobilised 4,000 National Guardsmen, and ordered the internment of strikers. An internment camp was opened at Fort McPherson and in all 126 union members were held there, including 16 women.[333]

There were violent clashes. On 6 September in Honea Park, South Carolina, company guards opened fire on a group of about 70 strikers picketing the Chiquola mill and killed seven of them. They were, in the words of one picket, "shot down like dogs".[334] None of the local churches would allow funeral services for the victims, but the union held a memorial service that was attended by 10,000 mourners. The Reverend James Myers, a strong clerical supporter of trade unionism from New York, stepped in, proclaiming the dead men "the instruments of Jesus Christ" and union membership "a test of Christian character". Francis Gorman held up before the mourners the bullet-riddled American flag under which the pickets had assembled.[335] Secretary of labour Perkins described this massacre as "an unfortunate situation".[336] Altogether 15 strikers were to be killed in the three weeks of the dispute. Incredibly, one employers' trade journal actually argued that "a few hundred funerals will have a quieting influence".[337] In the face of this repression the union retreated, suspending the flying squadrons and effectively abandoning any serious attempt to spread the strike. It threw itself on the tender mercies of the Roosevelt administration. Unfortunately, as Kenneth Davis writes, "insofar as it took any action at all in this matter, it was action that strengthened the employers' already mighty hand".[338] Norman Thomas was absolutely scathing about the failure of the White House to condemn the use of the National Guard to break the strike, which, as he pointed out, "in Georgia meant the maintenance of concentration camps in the best Hitler style. In North Carolina it meant a reign of armed terror".[339] All this was the work of Democratic Party governors.

On the basis of Roosevelt's personal assurances, the strike was called off. Francis Gorman proclaimed that it was "one of the most amazing victories ever recorded in the annals of the AF of L". The union newspaper announced proudly that "textile workers at last are free".[340] In fact, the union had surrendered. Roosevelt's assurances were worthless (he counted Southern mill owners among his personal friends) and the employers proceeded with mass sackings and wholesale victimisation. Thousands of workers found themselves sacked, evicted from company housing, denied relief by relief agencies run by men appointed by the "millocracy", and, of course, blacklisted. According to the union 226 mills across the South did not take strikers back. The intention was to strike a blow that would deter attempts at unionisation for a generation. UTW membership collapsed from 340,000 in August 1934 to only 79,000 in the summer of 1935. The significance of this defeat was that it left the South an open-shop stronghold. It was a major strategic setback for the whole for the whole American labour movement.

Was defeat inevitable? Certainly the UTW confronted ruthless employers, armed to the teeth with the full support of the police and the National Guard. The union had few financial resources and it received no help from the AFL. Nevertheless, when the strike was called off, its members were still fighting and still believed they could win. It is worth making the point that while the union surrendered on 21 July, its members in many areas continued fighting. Between the end of the strike and the end of July 1935 there were 94 textile strikes across the South as the workers tried to protect themselves with or without the union.[341] Instead of even a fighting retreat the union leadership chose surrender and proclaimed the disaster a historic victory. When Martha Gellhorn visited the South in November 1934 she found conditions in the mills as "grim as is to be expected". In one mill in Gastonia, North Carolina, she came across three young women hiding in the toilet, lying on the concrete floor with their eyes closed: "They had come in to rest for a few minutes because the eight-hour shift on heavy machines with no breaks was making them faint." The conditions were "heart-breaking and horrifying" and she could only hope that one day "the owners of this place will get shot and lynched".[342]

Looking back on the strike in 1936 Francis Gorman showed that somewhat belatedly he had learned something from the defeat:

Many of us did not understand fully the role of government in a struggle between labour and industry. Many of us did not understand what we do now: that the government protects the strong, not the weak, and that it operates under pressure and yields to that group which is strong enough to assert itself over the other...we know now that we are naive to depend on the forces of government to protect us.[343]

Chapter Six

The split in the union bureaucracy

In 1935 the employers counterattacked and the movement stalled. The number of strikes fell and increasingly they were defensive struggles against a new wave of wage cuts. Strikes were often met with considerable violence.[344] As for the AFL, all they had to show for their organising efforts was a succession of disasters. When the union leaders relied on Roosevelt, the result was defeat. Only rank and file initiative exercised independently of the union bureaucracy offered any hope of success, and even then success was far from assured.

In Terre Haute, Indiana, for example, a bitter strike for union recognition at the Columbian Enamelling and Stamping Company involving some 450 workers organised in FLU No 19694 had begun on 23 March. The company was seen as spearheading a counterattack against the unions so that the strikers received considerable support from other workers, especially from the UMW. On 15 June the company escalated the conflict by bringing in armed guards to protect strike-breakers. The next day hundreds of workers, including many miners, stormed the plant and threw the guards out. The company brought in more guards, armed with shotguns and sub-machineguns on 17 July. In response local unions called a general strike the following day, a "labour holiday" involving some 26,000 workers, and closed the city down. They demanded the withdrawal of the armed guards. At 5pm that day Indiana's Democratic Party governor, Paul McNutt, declared martial law in Terre Haute and surrounding districts and sent in over 1,000 National Guardsmen. The troops broke up the protesting crowds with tear gas and rifle butts, effectively crushing the general strike. McNutt kept martial law in place until February 1936. FLU No 19694 was destroyed by the action of a Democratic Party state administration.[345]

Hundreds of FLU locals collapsed and were disbanded as disillusioned members tore up their union cards and the more militant were victimised and blacklisted. In 1933 Green had reported that the FLUs had some 350,000 members, but by 1935 the figure had fallen to 89,000. In the mass production industries the unions were rolled back. The disaster was particularly serious in the steel industry, where the long-moribund craft union, the Amalgamated Association of Iron, Steel and Tin Workers, had seen its membership rocket to some 200,000 by April 1934. There was a strong rank and file movement pushing for a fight with the employers. The right wing union leadership responded in February 1935 by expelling a majority of the membership from the union, preferring a small, weak and completely ineffectual union to a militant union. When outraged members demonstrated outside the union headquarters, they "found a wall of policemen". Over the course of 1935 the Amalgamated was reduced to a membership of less than 10,000.[346] Only the UMW, the ACW and the ILGWU were continuing to drive organisation forward.

The setback the working class movement suffered was the result both of the manifest inadequacies of the AFL and of the Roosevelt administration's pro-business stand. Working class unrest continued to grow, however, producing two developments that were to transform the situation: a split in the trade union bureaucracy that led to the creation of the Committee for Industrial Organization (CIO) and Roosevelt's decision, in the face of growing unpopularity, to turn to the left.

First, let us look at the trade union bureaucracy. The British Fabian socialists Beatrice and Sidney Webb were among the first commentators to focus on the emergence of the full-time union official and the way in which they had come to constitute a social group separate from the working class. In their 1894 volume, *The History of Trade Unionism*, they had identified this group as "the civil service of the trade union world". According to the Webbs, the full-time official "occupies a unique position. He belongs neither to the middle nor to the working class" and consequently finds himself in a contradictory position, mediating between employers and workers, rather than leading the workers in struggle. The full-time official finds himself identifying less and less with the grievances of the rank and file and more and more looking for compromise. Indeed, struggle increasingly comes to be seen as a threat to the organisation upon which the official's social position depends. In this situation the full-time official finds himself trying to contain, demobilise and circumvent rank and file initiative in the interests of maintaining "good" relations with the employer. Of course, there are employers who are so anti-union that even the most pacific officials can be driven to endorse militancy on occasion. If an attempt is actually made to destroy the union, then it is the full-time officials' jobs that are on the line as well as those of the rank and file, although they will almost invariably be looking for a compromise rather than for the consolidation of rank and file power.[347]

The nature of the trade union bureaucracy in the US was in a number of important respects different from that of full-time officials in Britain. In the early decades of the 20th century American trade unionists encountered a far more hostile environment. Repression left the unions weak and cowed by the 1920s, grateful just to survive and not interested in the fate of the unorganised. Red baiting and repression damaged the socialist tradition among workers, and rendered it completely absent from trade union officialdom. The commitment to reformist politics, to independent working class representation in politics, was very weak in the US compared with Britain and Europe. Indeed, American trade union officials were generally open supporters of the capitalist system and often had business interests themselves. They regarded the unions as businesses and the members as customers of the union rather than actually constituting the union. Democracy was often only nominal and many unions were, in fact, run by official oligarchies that suppressed all opposition. And, of course, there was another characteristic unique to the US—the extent to which organised crime was involved with elements of the trade union bureaucracy.[348]

The trade union bureaucracy that controlled the AFL and its constituent unions was a particularly reactionary body of men that collectively displayed no real concern for the fate of the working class. Of these men, John L Lewis was one of the most reactionary and authoritarian. The British socialist and academic Harold Laski dismissed him as a "typical AF of L thug".[349] But the impact of the Great Depression was to precipitate a split in their ranks. With an already weak trade union movement in apparently terminal decline, sections of the bureaucracy felt their own survival was in peril. Rather than seeing the great explosion of unrest that took place in 1933 and 1934 as a threat, these people saw it as an opportunity to reverse the movement's decline. They also recognised that if they did not give a lead then the left—Communists, Socialists, Trotskyists, Musteites and IWWers— would. A faction within the trade union bureaucracy came to consider AFL conservatism as an obstacle to rebuilding the movement. The man who was to lead the revolt against the AFL was John L Lewis.

John L Lewis

For miners' leader John L Lewis the failure to organise steel was a dagger aimed at the heart of the UMW. As far as he was concerned, the low pay of the steel workers "was a drag on the wage-scale of the United Mine Workers...the mine workers could never really win a just wage until the steel workers were organised and their miserable wages raised to a human decent standard".[350] Moreover, the open-shop steel industry continued to provide an example for the mine owners to emulate when they once again felt strong enough. His union would not be safe until steel was organised, and by 1935 he had concluded that the task was beyond both the Amalgamated Association of Iron, Steel and Tin Workers and the AFL. Indeed, he was increasingly coming to regard the AFL as an obstacle to organisation rather than a help, and he determined to do something about it. In the coming years Lewis was to emerge as the unlikely leader of a national working class insurgency.

At the end of the 1920s Lewis was generally regarded as one of the most reactionary union bureaucrats in the country. The Communist leader William Z Foster, himself a veteran union organiser, described the Lewis regime in the UMW at this time as "a curse to the miners". Once the UMW had been:

> the most progressive organisation in the American labour movement. Under Lewis it has degenerated into one of the most reactionary... union democracy has been destroyed. Lewis, in cooperation with the employers, rules like a despot. Opposition leaders are ruthlessly crushed, expelled and driven from the union and industry. The conventions are a tragic farce. Lewis dominates them with unparalleled corruption and violence.[351]

This was not just a Communist gripe. John Brophy, Lewis's reformist challenger for the union presidency in 1928, complained of how his opponent had become "increasingly ruthless in crushing union democracy". The ballot-rigging that year was "so obvious and flagrant...that the inference that Lewis would not have won without stealing votes is a defensible one".[352] Attempts to challenge the result at the 1927 UMW convention were met, as Foster puts it, with "fraudulent delegations, gangster terrorism and black reaction" that "has never been equalled in the American labour movement". Lewis only held on to office "Mussolini-fashion".[353] One of Lewis's opponents at the convention, the socialist Powers Hapgood, was beaten up in a hotel room, and then, when he had the nerve to still turn up at the convention, was assaulted on the convention floor.[354] At the convention hand-picked delegates voted to ban Communists from union membership, to abandon the union's support for the nationalisation of the mining industry and to give Lewis a 50 percent pay rise.

Lewis continued to rule the UMW by the same autocratic methods in the early years of the Great Depression. By 1932 he had removed the elected officers in 19 out of the union's 29 districts, suspending democracy and installing men loyal to him.[355] This meant that a majority of the union's executive board was actually appointed by Lewis. Opponents were expelled from the union and blacklisted by the mine owners. When they tried to organise independently, Lewis joined with the mine owners to crush them. He even hired private detectives to spy on his opponents.[356] It is important to remember that even when Lewis was to embrace militancy in 1933, he continued to rule the UMW by these same bureaucratic methods, ruthlessly suppressing dissent and democracy.

Throughout the 1920s Lewis situated himself politically on the right, actively supporting the main party of big business, the Republicans. The Democrats were, at this time, hardly an improvement on the Republicans and could be best described as the aspiring party of big business. Lewis cultivated what his biographers describe as "a distinctly haute bourgeois lifestyle". At the end of 1922 he joined the elite Congressional Country Club in Washington, proposed for membership by Herbert Hoover. As far as Lewis was concerned, the union was a business and he was its chief executive, entitled to the same lifestyle as other business leaders. While no one has, so far, been successful in establishing his income (like most other union leaders he had an investment portfolio), he bought his first Cadillac in 1922, sent his son to an expensive private school, employed servants and socialised with the rich and powerful. In 1924 the Harriman banking interest actually put him forward as a potential republican vice-presidential candidate. After the election business interests lobbied President Coolidge to appoint him secretary of labour. When Hoover became president, Lewis was once again unsuccessfully suggested for the position.[357] All this was at a time when the labour movement was being relentlessly rolled back, employers were rampant, the government was openly identified with the interests of big business in a way not to be seen again until the 1980s, and the miners themselves were under sustained attack.

The Great Depression brought about a change in Lewis's outlook. He came to the conclusion that the survival of the labour movement, and of the UMW in particular, required a regulated capitalism that was not at the mercy of unrestrained market forces. What was necessary was a regulated capitalism in which the unions, or, more properly, their leaders, were recognised as partners by both employers and government. He had also come to despise and detest (as had most Americans) financiers and bankers as parasites. For Lewis the best way to bring about a regulated capitalism was to build a strong bureaucratic labour movement, founded on great industrial unions, organising the mass production industries. Such a movement would ally itself with, but not be subordinate to, those in business and politics who had similar objectives. To this end, Lewis was to embrace the New Deal, although he thought it never went far enough and he never trusted Roosevelt. As we have already seen, he took full advantage of the Democrats' ascendancy to launch the greatest union organising drive in the history of the mining industry in 1933.

Lewis never had any illusions in Roosevelt's supposed sympathy for the working man or for the unions. He knew better. As he told Saul Alinsky:

> Roosevelt was not too friendly to Section 7a; and if there was any time when I began to question and wonder and have reservations about the president, it was at that time... I never trusted Roosevelt fully. Never... The great friend of organised labour repeatedly fought in the most underhanded way against the inclusion of Section 7a in the NRA.[358]

He recognised that Roosevelt was a political operator who only respected power—so he was determined to create a trade union movement strong and powerful enough to command Roosevelt's attention. Ideally, such a trade union movement could be built by bureaucratic means from above, with the rank and file firmly under the control of the officials, and with working class militancy tightly harnessed. If this was not possible, however, Lewis was prepared to ride the wave of working class revolt, to identify himself unambiguously with the rank and file, to make their cause his own and, if necessary, to stand alongside them in defying both the employers and the government. Once victory had been secured, however, militancy would have to be restrained and bureaucratic control reasserted and consolidated. He intended to secure a place for the trade unions within capitalism rather than overthrow it.

In the interim Lewis reinvented himself as a militant labour leader, as the spokesman of working class insurgency. He was, as Benjamin Stolberg somewhat begrudgingly put it, "a competent and courageous opportunist".[359] Len De Caux, a Communist who was to work closely with Lewis, observed that he always "carried the minimum of ideological baggage" and that this "gave him an advantage. He could move fast in any direction".[360] Lewis spoke for an insurgent working class, and he spoke with a passion that inspired and thrilled hundreds of thousands. As he told a Congressional Committee with reference to his own union:

> I speak not for the dollars invested... I speak for the human beings who go down into these coal mines and serve the public interest by getting the coal... The men I represent during this 37-year period, have carried from these mines, on stretchers, 79,000 dead.

He had, he told them, stood at a pithead on Christmas Eve with the women and children, waiting "for their dead to be brought up out of that mine".[361]

Lewis made clear his break with AFL moderation in an exchange of correspondence with the AFL president, William Green (or "Sitting Bill" as Lewis derisively called him). He completely rejected what he described as the AFL's "policy of anxious inertia" and was "temperamentally incapable of sitting with you in sackcloth and ashes, endlessly intoning, 'O tempora! O mores!'" Instead he preferred to be "on the side of America's underprivileged and exploited millions".[362]

Establishing the CIO

Lewis and his union allies initially hoped to secure AFL support for an organising drive along industrial lines in the mass production industries. They failed. It was not just a matter of craft versus industrial unionism. Crucial as well was the fact that the AFL rejected militancy, relying instead on being able to convince employers that union organisation would be a good thing for them. If the employer proved reluctant then they relied on the federal government to intervene to secure recognition. When that failed, the rank and file were effectively abandoned, left to be intimidated, victimised and blacklisted. Lewis recognised that companies would have to be battered into accepting such a partnership. This would require militancy, at least in the initial stages. Consequently Lewis embraced the militancy in the 1930s that he had fought so hard against in the 1920s. He also recognised that if the trade union leadership did not give a lead, many workers would turn to the left for assistance, as had already happened in Toledo, Minneapolis, San Francisco and elsewhere. Indeed, he recognised that he needed the help of the left.

Conflict within the AFL came out into the open at the October 1935 convention in Atlantic City. Lewis told delegates that he was enraged by the AFL's failures. There were tens of thousands of steel workers desperate for unionisation, but the discredited and moribund craft union, the Amalgamated Association of Iron, Steel and Tin Workers, had thrown away the opportunity. Indeed, any attempt to organise mass production industries along craft lines was doomed. "Great combinations of capital have assembled great industrial plants... they have assembled to themselves tremendous power and influence", he warned, and the harsh reality was that they were "almost 100 percent effective in opposing organisation of the workers under the policies of the American Federation of Labor". The employers in the mass production industries, he told delegates, "will mow you down like the Italian machine guns will mow down the Ethiopians in the war now going on in that country...they will mow you down and laugh while they are doing it". AFL officials might just as well "sit down in their easy chairs and twiddle their thumbs and take a nap as to conclude that any results will come from that kind of organisation". He warned that "our people" are suffering because of the AFL's failures and asked the delegates how long they thought the UMW would put up with this.[363] The craft unions voted down any change.

On 19 October, the last day of the convention, Lewis very deliberately gave public notice to militants throughout the country that change was coming. During a discussion on the organisation of the rubber industry he picked an argument on the convention floor with Bill Hutcheson, the leader of the carpenters' union and one of the most powerful men in the AFL.[364] After an exchange of insults, Lewis punched Hutcheson in the mouth, knocking him to the ground. Victor Reuther, at that time a socialist militant in the car industry, later recalled that "this bit of melodrama gave new hope to thousands of industrial workers".[365] Later on Lewis was to explain his thinking at the time to Saul Alinsky:

> By 1935 the workers, embittered, frustrated, and filled with a certain degree of hopelessness, began to hate the conservative, short-sighted, ignorant labour leadership of the American Federation of Labor almost as much as they hated their own employers... Bill Hutcheson represented symbolically the kind of leadership in the American Federation of Labor that the workers in this country detested... All I will say is that I never walked across an aisle so slowly and grimly as I did that day... An act of some kind, an act dramatic to the degree that it could inspire and enthuse the workers of this country was necessary. Did I say necessary? It was essential.[366]

The next day Lewis met with his allies and they established the Committee for Industrial Organization (CIO), ostensibly to fight to change policy within the AFL, but more importantly to rally the hundreds of thousands of working men and women waiting for a lead. The trade union bureaucracy was beginning to split down the middle, between those who would fight and those who wouldn't.

The CIO was formally established on 9 November 1935 with Lewis as very much the dominant figure. His chief allies were David Dubinsky of the ILGWU and Sidney Hillman of the ACW. Dubinsky, still a member of the Socialist Party, was a somewhat uncertain ally. He was desperately hoping for a compromise with the AFL and was ferociously anti-Communist, indeed he was described on one occasion as "the ultimate Communist-hater in the labour movement".[367] His hatred of the CP derived from the struggle that had taken place within the ILGWU in the 1920s when the Communists had succeeded in winning over a majority of the union membership and were only prevented from taking control by bureaucratic means. This had left him with a fear of the CP that verged on the paranoid.[368] Sidney Hillman, whose union had been established as a democratic breakaway from an AFL affiliate, had none of Dubinsky's insecurities, and was much more forcefully committed to the cause of industrial unionism and to Roosevelt's New Deal. But Lewis, with all of the UMW's resources at his disposal, was certainly the driving force. He had already decided that a break with the AFL was both inevitable and necessary.

Lewis recognised that in the coming struggle the left would be an essential ally. There were no more dedicated union militants and activists than the Socialists and Communists, men and women who were prepared to risk victimisation and blacklisting, injury and imprisonment, even death. Even though he had spent the 1920s and early 1930s fighting these people, he now extended his hand to them. Lewis installed his former bitter rival, John Brophy, the man from whom he had stolen the 1926 union election, as CIO director. Once again this was a demonstration that the CIO was ready for a fight. Brophy brought in (with Lewis's agreement) two other longstanding opponents of the UMW leader, Adolph Germer and Powers Hapgood. Even more significant, Lewis appointed as the CIO's publicity director Len De Caux, a radical journalist, known to be close to the Communist Party (he was in fact a covert member). And he appointed as legal counsel Lee Pressman, another covert Communist, who was to become his closest adviser. Inevitably the CIO was to soon make overtures to the Communist Party. In November 1936 John Brophy had a secret meeting with Earl Browder, the general secretary of the CP, seeking to enlist his support for the CIO's organising efforts. Browder promised that the party would provide organisers for the struggles ahead.[369] As far as Lewis was concerned, the left was to be enrolled to help build a new bureaucratic labour movement, controlled, as far as possible, from above. He was absolutely committed to class collaboration, but from a position of strength, and he was prepared to support and encourage militancy to get there. As he put it, "Who gets the bird, the hunter or the dog?"[370]

Akron 1936

The CIO was soon put to the test. The first great demonstration of resurgent working class militancy took place in Akron, Ohio, the centre of the rubber industry. The Great Depression had hit the city hard, with the number of workers employed in the rubber factories falling from 58,000 in June 1929 to only 27,000 in March 1933. This was accompanied by wage cuts and speed-up. A rubber worker in 1932-1933 earned less than two thirds what he would have earned in 1928 and worked considerably harder for it as management ruthlessly exploited the presence of thousands of unemployed outside the gate. Here, as in many other places, Section 7a of the NIRA led to an explosion of union organisation. By the end of 1933 some 85 percent of the city's rubber workers had been signed up in the AFL's FLU locals. The following year over a thousand workers at General Tire took part in the first of the great sit-down strikes. 1935, however, saw a collapse in union membership across the city as it became clear that the AFL would not fight. By September of that year all the rubber locals together could only claim 3,100 members. That same month the AFL finally reluctantly agreed to establish the United Rubber Workers. It was Bill Hutcheson's objection to this new union's claim to organise all the workers in the industry, skilled and unskilled, that prompted John L Lewis's assault on the carpenters' leader at the AFL convention.

After the convention Lewis made it absolutely clear that the CIO was going to actively encourage and assist the organisation of workers in mass production, whether the AFL liked it or not. He spoke to thousands of workers at mass meetings across the country, preaching the message of militant industrial organisation, urging them to action. Men and women who had despaired of the AFL began to rally to the cause. Organise and the CIO will support you, Lewis proclaimed. On 19 January 1936 he spoke in Akron to an enthusiastic crowd of rubber workers who had braved appalling weather to come and hear him. Lewis told his audience that while workers and their employers might be partners "in theory...they are enemies in fact". While the rubber industry had "made untold millions...it has been a constant struggle for its workers to live at all". The way forward was to "Organise! Organise! Organise!" This was very different from the platitudes dished up by the likes of William Green. Nine days later there was a spontaneous sit-down strike in the Firestone plant, following the suspension of a union militant, Clayton Dicks. Ruth McKenny provides a graphic description of the moment production halted:

> The noise stopped. The whole room lay in perfect silence. The tirebuild-
> ers stood in long lines... Out of the terrifying quiet came the wondering

voice of a big tirebuilder near the windows: "Jesus Christ, it's like the end of the world". He broke the spell... "By God, We done it!" And the men began to cheer.[371]

The company backed down, reinstated Dicks and paid both him and the strikers half pay for the duration of the dispute. This was a small victory of immense strategic importance. News of the success quickly spread throughout the city. As one union official wrote to Adolph Germer of the CIO, the sit-down at Firestone had "done more to build the trade union movement here than anything we could have even thought of doing".[372] The victory at Firestone encouraged workers at Goodyear to demand the restoration of a pay cut with a sit-down on 31 January. Soon after, on 7 February, workers at the Goodrich plant sat down in a dispute over piece rates. Then, on 14 February, in what was to become known as "the first CIO strike", workers at Goodyear sat down in response to lay-offs.[373] They only briefly occupied the plant before marching out and setting up picket lines. It was, according to historian Robert Zieger, "a revolt-like outpouring, with thousands of Akron workers taking to the streets".[374]

Both union and non-union workers walked out so that "the second day of the strike found the largest rubber factory in the world at a standstill and more than 10,000 in the strikers' ranks". The union encircled the factory with picket posts so as to maintain a 24-hour blockade of its 11-mile perimeter. Each post was equipped with huts to cope with the ferocious Ohio winter with temperatures reaching -9°. When the company obtained an injunction restricting picketing on 22 February, the union responded with a tremendous show of strength. On 23 February when the sheriff attempted to enforce the injunction, he found over 5,000 union members and sympathisers, many armed with clubs and some with guns, blocking his way. He backed down and the factory remained under siege.

Meanwhile the CIO sent organisers—not to sell the strike down the river, AFL-style, but to help it on to victory, very publicly making the strikers' cause the CIO's cause as well. By supporting the strike the CIO organisers (who included militants of the calibre of the Socialist Powers Hapgood and the anarchist Rose Pesotta)[375] were also able to contain the influence of the Musteites in a way that the AFL would never have been able to, preventing the strike from getting out of their control. On 20 March, Goodyear surrendered. Akron, as Edward Levinson wrote, was "set on the road to becoming a fortress of the CIO".[376]

With working class revolt reviving, the CIO established the Steel Workers Organizing Committee (SWOC). Lewis's UMW, through the CIO, was going to organise steel along industrial lines without any care for the concerns of the craft unions. The Amalgamated Association was persuaded to join the SWOC, but Lewis put one of his trusted lieutenants, Philip Murray, in as director. The steel industry was to be organised from the top down into an industrial union modelled on the UMW. This precipitated a crisis in relations with the AFL. On 5 September William Green suspended the ten unions affiliated with the CIO—unions representing 1.2 million workers, that is a third of the AFL's membership. The US trade union movement had split.

Chapter Seven

Roosevelt turns left

What of the man in the White House? Franklin Roosevelt had two over-riding concerns in the 1930s: saving US capitalism and strengthening his presidency. This might seem to contradict his apparent ability to empa-thise with the downtrodden, but when it came to practical politics he would ruthlessly sacrifice their interests if it was to his political advantage.

One of Roosevelt's black admirers, Mary Mcleod Bethune, provides testimony to his ability to show empathy with those who were suffer-ing. She describes a meeting with the president where she told of the hardships and struggles of black people:

> When I had finished, I saw that tears were coursing down President Roosevelt's cheeks. He leaned across the table and grasped my hand in his. "Mrs Bethune," he said, "I am glad I am able to contribute some-thing to make life better for your people. I want to assure you that I will continue to do my best for them in every way." He choked a little. Tears flowed from his eyes.[377]

It is hard to believe that someone so moved by the suffering of black people would actually do so little for them. As Roy Wilkins of the NAACP observed, "FDR was always overrated as a champion of the Negro." Roosevelt had "no compelling inner commitment to their cause". The administration had no programme "for uplifting the coun-try's Negroes from generations of neglect and centuries of servitude". What Wilkins found "extremely disappointing" was Roosevelt's stead-fast refusal to support anti-lynching legislation, and he wrote of "the outrage I felt at FDR's expedient cowardice on this issue".[378]

Two episodes highlighted Roosevelt's determined silence. On 18 October 1933 a mob of some 2,000 to 3,000 white men and women stormed the jail in the Maryland town of Princess Anne. They seized George Armwood, a 28 year old black man who was being held for rape, hanged him and then publicly burned his body. The next day Roosevelt received an honorary degree from Washington College, Maryland, and did not so much as mention the atrocity that had taken place nearby.[379] In October the following year in Florida a young black man, Claude Neal, was accused of the rape and murder of a white woman. He was transported to jail in Alabama, but was then handed over to armed men, who transported him 200 miles back to the town of Marianna where he was to be lynched. The forthcoming lynching was widely advertised. Neal was beaten, castrated and forced to eat his own genitals; his fingers and toes were cut off; he was branded with red hot irons from head to foot, repeatedly part-hanged and then finally shot dead. His body was dragged through the town behind a car, further mutilated in front of a crowd of some 2,000 to 3,000 people, including children, and then strung up on the courthouse plaza. This was accompanied by a general attack on the town's black population with hundreds of men, women and children beaten, homes and businesses burned and people fleeing for safety into the countryside.

The NAACP attempted to have the lynchers prosecuted under the 1931 Lindbergh Kidnap Act, as Neal had been taken across the state line to be lynched. In a historic display of political cowardice, Roosevelt's attorney general, Homer Cummings, decided that as the kidnapping of Claude Neal had not been for profit, no federal offence had been committed. Roosevelt himself still remained silent and refused to support legislation to curb the public torture and murder of black men and women in the South. The furthest he would go was to say that he was "wholly in favour of decent discussion" of the issue.[380] One black newspaper in New York appeared with a big blank space on its front page with the caption, "Here's Mr Roosevelt's message on lynching".[381] His silence was also commented on abroad. In October 1935 the Nazi SS journal, *Das Schwarze Korps*, actually complained that if such lynchings took place in the Third Reich the whole world would have raised its voice in protest, but they could be carried out in the US with barely a murmur.[382] Meanwhile black journalists could not challenge Roosevelt over his attitude towards lynching at White House press conferences because they were barred until 1946!

Nowhere was Roosevelt's failure to intervene on the behalf of the oppressed better demonstrated than by the administration's refusal to come to the aid of the Southern sharecroppers. There were over a million white and 700,000 black tenant farmers in the South, America's peasantry, trapped in lives of often appalling poverty and brutal oppression. And the great majority of sharecroppers were disenfranchised. Not only did the New Deal not do anything to assist these people, but the administration's agricultural policies actually benefited their landlords at their expense. The sharecroppers lived in conditions that shocked every outsider who encountered them. Any attempt at organising to improve their situation met with ferocious repression that was either condoned or supported by the Southern Democratic Party leadership. The Southern Tenant Farmers' Union (STFU) that was established in July 1934 met with a brutal response. The Arkansas legislature actually made it a criminal offence to be in possession of five or more copies of any STFU literature considered to be seditious, with five to 20 years imprisonment as the punishment.[383] When the British socialist and writer Naomi Mitchison visited the South early in 1936 and "got involved with the sharecroppers", she had to confess that:

> I had never met such poverty: the houses built of old pieces of tin and cardboard, the children obviously suffering from pellagra, American children who didn't know a chocolate bar when they saw one; poor whites and poor blacks living equally badly and determined to struggle together for a slightly fairer share of the cake.[384]

Mitchison spoke at meetings of the STFU that, with the help of the Socialist Party, was organising the sharecroppers, both black and white, in Arkansas and neighbouring states.

There was widespread violence against the STFU in early 1935, with homes riddled with gunfire, men, women and children beaten and hundreds of families evicted. The situation was described as resembling a war zone with the roads clogged with refugees driven from their homes.[385] The Socialist Party leader, Norman Thomas, visited Arkansas in March in an attempt to focus national attention and, hopefully, force federal intervention. He found both misery and courage:

> While driving over the plantation roads he witnessed one of many evictions. A white sharecropper's family, household goods and all, were

dumped by the roadside. The man and his wife had tried to arrest a plantation rider who had kidnapped and raped their 14 year old daughter. Instead of arresting the rapist, officials had arrested the father on a trumped-up charge of "stealing two eggs". After he was released from jail, the father, a staunch union man, had been brutally beaten and his family evicted...[386]

This was 20th century feudalism in action. On the last day of his tour Thomas attempted to speak at a meeting of 500 STFU members in the town of Birdsong. The meeting was broken up by armed planters and their riding bosses and Thomas was told that "we don't need no God-damn Yankee bastard to tell us what to do with our niggers".[387] His tour provoked a wave of violent reprisals against the STFU, but no federal intervention. The attitude of the planters was made clear by the secretary of the planters' association, the Reverend Abner Sage, when he told the *New York Times* that it would have been better to have had "a few no-account shiftless people killed at the start" so as to avoid all this trouble, "what with the mistering of the niggers and stirring them up".[388]

Union members displayed the most remarkable courage. A black preacher and sharecropper, A B Brookins, told the STFU convention:

They shot up my house with machine guns, and they made me run away from where I lived at, but they couldn't make me run away from my union... When I lived at Marked Tree, Arkansas, nightriders broke into my house, and they shot a bullet that went through my daughter's hair. But I am not afraid to go on being a union man.[389]

Harry Mitchell, one of the union's leaders, remembered a public meeting at Marked Tree with a Socialist Party speaker from New York. He was worried that "a number of tough-looking white and black men...lined up against the walls" were there to break it up. He was assured that "they were union men with Winchester rifles and shotguns down the legs of their overalls which they would have used to stop any attempt to break up that meeting".[390] Superior force was overwhelmingly on the side of the planters, however.

The following year, on 17 January 1936, some 450 STFU members met at the Methodist church in Providence. The meeting was broken up by armed vigilantes who attacked "the sharecroppers with axe handles and pistol butts...cracked the skulls of screaming women and children, smashed the furniture and broke the windows". One of the gunmen warned Howard Kester, a union leader, that the planters' patience was wearing thin, that "there's going to be another Elaine massacre, only next time we'll kill whites as well as blacks". The threat of another Elaine massacre, the 1919 slaughter of hundreds of black men and women, became so common that people lived in expectation of another such outrage. Indeed, fear of an impending massacre actually prompted a cabinet discussion on 6 March. Calls for a federal investigation into the situation were rejected by Roosevelt at the prompting of Vice-President Garner because of the embarrassment it would cause Southern Democrats, and, in particular, to Joe Robinson, an Arkansas Senator and the powerful majority leader in the Senate. Instead the governor of Arkansas, Junius Futrell, was asked to conduct an investigation. As Norman Thomas pointed out, this was like asking Al Capone to investigate organised crime in Chicago. Privately, Futrell was warned to make sure there was no repeat of the Elaine massacre.[391]

Roosevelt deferred to the reactionary white supremacist Robinson without any apparent qualms. When he visited Arkansas for the state's centennial celebrations he publicly praised the man, while refusing even to meet a delegation from the STFU. Robinson was to be the chairman of the Democratic Party national convention that met over five days in June 1936 and nominated Roosevelt for a second term. As Norman Thomas pointed out, every delegate was aware of the "peonage, terrorism, the flogging of men and women" that went on in Arkansas, and yet they "listened without gasping while Joe Robinson, senator from one of the most backward of our states in social legislation, protector of nightriders and floggers, apostrophised liberty and justice".[392]

The Department of Agriculture under Henry Wallace highlights the New Deal predicament. Howard Kester made the point that when you listened to Wallace, you heard someone with "a genuine sense of justice", but if you looked instead at what he did then you found someone who "turned a deaf ear to hundreds of grievances laid before him".[393] Wallace refused to even meet Norman Thomas and blamed the trouble in Arkansas on outside socialist agitators. He did commission a report by one of his officials, Mary Connors Myers, but when it corroborated STFU allegations he suppressed it. Thomas warned him that the failure of the federal government to intervene had shown the planters that they could "with impunity adopt any illegal methods which they wish to employ".[394] Those officials in the department sympathetic to the sharecroppers were purged.[395]

Such was Roosevelt's commitment to the poor and downtrodden.

Thunder on the left

By early 1935 the Roosevelt administration was in serious trouble. It had betrayed the hopes of the millions who had looked to the president to end the Depression. He had proved to be at best an unreliable friend to the labour movement. More generally, the poor and the unemployed who had looked to him for social justice had been sadly disappointed and were beginning to look elsewhere. The writer H G Wells visited the US in 1935 and observed "widespread discontent" and "an impatient preparedness for sweeping changes". "The masses", he wrote, "were ready and eager for a New Deal; the actual New Deal had not gone far enough and fast enough for them, and that is what the shouting is about." He fully expected that in the not too distant future "they may be demanding not a New Deal but a new sort of game".[396]

Wells was not alone in this reading of the situation. The militant protests in city after city against the cost of meat in the summer of 1935 were a sign of the times. Beginning in Chicago with demonstrations by thousands of housewives, the movement spread to New York. Here the United Council of Working Class Women, led by veteran Communist Clara Lemlich Shavelson,[397] organised a boycott of butcher shops with militant picket lines closing down 4,500 shops and forcing a cut in prices. The movement spread to Los Angeles, Philadelphia, Boston, Paterson, St Louis and Kansas City. At the end of July it erupted in Detroit, where Mary Zuk led thousands of women through the streets, overturning meat trucks and storming warehouses. When the police arrested demonstrators the women blockaded the city jails until they were freed.[398] There was, as Rexford Tugwell put it, "thunder on the left".

The dissatisfaction with the New Deal was first given a political expression by Upton Sinclair's End Poverty In California (EPIC) campaign. Sinclair, a celebrated novelist and lifelong socialist, had resigned from the SP and joined the Democratic Party. As far as he was concerned, the Socialist Party was an electoral dead end and instead he argued that the left should try to make the Democrats the party of reform. He proposed a radical programme that mobilised thousands of supporters, overwhelmingly working class, and successfully captured the Democratic Party nomination for governor. Sinclair looked to Roosevelt for endorsement, even watering down his programme in an attempt to make it acceptable to the White House, but the man who was prepared to embrace reactionary white supremacist Southern Democrats was not prepared to embrace one of America's greatest exponents of social justice. Not only was an endorsement not forthcoming, but the administration stood by while much of the Democratic Party machine in California threw its lot in with the Republicans to defeat the challenge from the left. In a campaign that set new lows for media manipulation, slander, abuse and dishonesty (it has been described as the occasion of the invention of modern American electoral politics), Sinclair went down to defeat. Hollywood joined the campaign against him with the studios threatening to leave California if he was elected, producing fake newsreels to discredit the EPIC campaign and imposing compulsory donations on its workforce (whatever their politics) to pay for them.[399] Sinclair was also bitterly attacked by the Communists, still in the grip of their Third Period turn. They accused him of plunging ahead towards his "fascist goal with great speed".[400]

Sinclair's defeat encouraged the right, both renegade Democrats and Republicans, in the belief that they could defeat Roosevelt. He faced a big business backlash that looked forward to his defeat in 1936. More serious though was the growing electoral challenge from the left. The administration was confronted with a variety of voices of protest that achieved mass appeal. These were not voices from the political left, from the Socialist Party or the Communist Party, but nevertheless, they articulated a growing dissatisfaction with Roosevelt's conservatism, his lack of radical ambition. They did not propose the overthrow of capitalism, but its radical reform, to be accomplished at the expense of the rich and the super-rich. There was the "radio priest", Father Coughlin, who had initially been courted by the White House, but by this time was presenting an anti-business critique of the New Deal's limitations to millions of listeners. There was Doctor Francis Townsend's tremendously popular old age pension programme. Most dangerous as far as the White House was concerned, however, was the threat posed by Huey Long, the senator from Louisiana.[401]

Long had established almost complete control over his home state, where he had broken the power of the traditional elite and installed his own political machine in power. From this base he condemned Roosevelt in the most ferocious terms for having sold out to the bankers and big business, and made no secret of his presidential ambitions. In February 1934 he launched his Share Our Wealth campaign. Long proposed a maximum income of $1 million a year, with his newspaper producing a spoof budget to prove that it was possible to manage on $1 million a year. Personal fortunes over $3 million were to be confiscated. From the revenue this generated he promised to provide every American family with the money for a home, a car and other necessities and luxuries. He promised old age pensions, free university education and generous bonuses for veterans. He would introduce a 30-hour working week with a month's paid holiday a year. Long strenuously denied that he was either a Communist or a Socialist, and strongly supported private enterprise. What he condemned was the concentration of wealth and privilege in a few hands and he championed radical redistribution. Indeed, he argued that the Share Our Wealth programme was "the only defence this country's got against Communism".[402]

Within a month of its being launched, the Share Our Wealth campaign had attracted over 200,000 members and by the end of the year had over 3 million. By the spring of 1935 Share Our Wealth clubs across the country claimed well over 7 million members, organised in 27,431 clubs. Many trade unionists joined and in New York one club chairman, Eugene Daniell, was already well known for having let off tear gas bombs in the New York Stock Exchange.[403] There were even clubs in Canada. Long's message of confiscating the wealth of the super-rich and redistributing it had a powerful impact. He was a compelling public speaker, contrasting his humble beginnings (one of his sisters remarked that the house they were raised in got smaller every time he mentioned it) with "Prince Franklin's" background of wealth and privilege. As far as Long was concerned, Roosevelt had turned out to be just another rich man with too many rich friends, and he was particularly scathing about his "fondness for vacationing aboard Vincent Astor's yacht".[404] In his posthumously published *My First Days in the White House*, President Long appoints Roosevelt secretary of the navy.

Huey Long remains an exceptionally controversial figure. The Communist *Daily Worker* condemned him as "Louisiana's Hitler",[405] but this seriously mistakes him. While Long can certainly be seen as the champion of an authoritarian populism in Louisiana, nationally he was one of a number of "progressive" congressmen, dissatisfied with Roosevelt's conservatism and his friendships with the rich. He was part of a "progressive" bloc in Congress that included both Democrats and Republicans and that historians have neglected, a bloc that included the likes of George Norris, Burton Wheeler, Maury Maverick, Bronson Cutting and others who were certainly not socialists, but were to the left of Roosevelt. Long insisted that "whenever the administration has gone to the left I have voted with it, and whenever it has gone to the right I have voted against it".[406] He was a scourge of the Democrat conservatives. On one occasion he insisted on reading into the Congressional record the names of the great corporations that retained the services of the Arkansas law firm owned by the Democrat leader in the Senate, Joe Robinson. As he insisted to considerable laughter, he did not, of course, intend to suggest that Robinson "could to the slightest degree be influenced in any vote...by the fact that this association might mean hundreds of thousands and millions of dollars to him in the way of lucrative fees".[407]

Long's Share Our Wealth campaign certainly attracted massive support. As a number of critics have pointed out, however, there is no evidence of him actually implementing it in Louisiana. As Edward Robb Ellis argues, Long "did not raise teachers' salaries, gave no relief to the unemployed, did not provide pensions for the aged, did not end child labour, did not shorten the working day, failed to support unions, weakened the workmen's compensation system, paid state wages far below the prevailing scale".[408] He leaves out of his catalogue Long's revival of the practice of hiring out convict labour to private contractors.[409] And, as Glenn Jeansonne, another powerful critic, points out, Long, the champion of the redistribution of wealth, was quite happy to enrich himself by means of graft and corruption. Long came "to love luxury" and by 1933 owned a mansion in New Orleans "worth between $40,000 and $60,000...a fleet of six Cadillacs costing $5,000 each... and a $3,000 wardrobe of imported suits". When he was assassinated in September 1935 his assets were estimated at anywhere between $2 million and $5 million.[410]

And yet Long was tremendously popular. His appeal in Louisiana was directed towards the rural poor who were the mainstay of his support in the state. Only when he went national did he attempt to extend his appeal to the urban poor and the working class. As for the limited nature of his reforms in Louisiana, Long argued that only so much could be achieved in such a poor state, and that he had achieved more than anyone else ever had.

One last point about Long is that despite his support for segregation and white supremacy, he still attracted considerable black support throughout the South and even in the North. There were black Share Our Wealth clubs in Harlem. The reason for this, according to his biographer, was that Long insisted that those measures he introduced to benefit the rural poor should benefit both black and white, and given the disproportionate number of poor black people, this made him a benefactor of poor black people. Such a stance was, according to T Harry Williams, "almost revolutionary" in the South and the black press "was unanimous in praising him". One black sharecropper, Walter Newton, named his son, the future Black Panther leader, Huey after Long. When Roy Wilkins of the NAACP met Long in 1935, he was surprised to have a white Southern Democrat welcome him with a handshake. Long told him, "I'm for the poor man—all poor men. Black and white, they all gotta have a chance. They gotta have a home, a job and a decent education for their children. 'Every man a king'— that's my slogan. That means every man, niggers along with the rest..." A somewhat nonplussed Wilkins was understandably not convinced. What particularly impressed Southern black people was that Long rarely played the race card. Indeed, on one occasion he famously threatened the Imperial Wizard of the Ku Klux Klan, Hiram Evans, telling journalists that "that Imperial bastard will never set foot in Louisiana, and that when I call him a sonofabitch I am not using profanity, but am referring to the circumstances of his birth".[411] But at the same time, he joined with other Southern Democrats in opposing federal anti-lynching legislation.[412]

Much of the abuse directed at Long is a response to the challenge he made to that great symbol of American liberalism Franklin Roosevelt. The fact was, however, that Long was a progressive who condemned Roosevelt for not going far enough. Roosevelt had no problem with men of the calibre of Frank Hague in New Jersey, Edward Kelly in Chicago, Ed Crump in Memphis or even with the Long machine, once Huey was safely dead, and it had abandoned the Share Our Wealth campaign. Corrupt, authoritarian city and state machines were perfectly acceptable as long as they gave their support to Roosevelt. They were no threat, whereas Long had clearly been intent on standing against Roosevelt in the1936 presidential election. Long dismissed Roosevelt as:

> a phony. I can out-promise him and he knows it. People will believe me and they won't believe him. His mother's watching him and she won't let him go too far... He's living on inherited wealth.[413]

The Roosevelt camp were alarmed enough to commission a report on Long's appeal that concluded that while he could not win the presidency for himself, he could take enough votes away from Roosevelt to deny him a second term. A reactionary Republican administration elected in 1936 would inevitably radicalise the country and this would carry Long into the White House in 1940.[414] Roosevelt determined to head off the challenge. Part of the administration's response was to have the Internal Revenue investigate Long and his supporters with a view to uncovering their graft and corruption. Roosevelt cut off any federal patronage to the Long machine and gave it to his enemies instead. As William Ivy Hair, certainly no great admirer of Long, observes, Roosevelt was "no stranger to devious, underhanded tactics and his fight with Huey Long provides a view of the dark side of his presidency".[415]

According to Raymond Moley, Roosevelt also came to the conclusion that it might be necessary "to woo some of Long's supporters with a counter-offer... FDR actually used the phrase 'steal Long's thunder' in a conversation with me and two other friends of his".[416] The challenge from Long tipped the balance in their favour of those of Roosevelt's advisers who were arguing that he should be more radical. Rexford Tugwell acknowledged that Long "made possible actions that otherwise could not have been undertaken! He helped pass the Social Security Act, the bill for an increase in corporate taxes, and the huge (as it was then regarded) appropriation to combat unemployment". Long denounced all these measures as inadequate, but it was only this challenge from the left that made them possible. Tugwell, who considered Long a "madman", still acknowledged that he was "a major phenomenon".[417] According to Alan Brinkley, the administration's offensive against Long had completely failed to dent his popularity, right up until the time he was assassinated (he was shot on 8 September and died after botched surgery two days later).[418] Long's funeral on 12 September 1935 was attended by some 175,000 people.

Turning left

In 1935 Roosevelt faced an urgent dilemma. He could turn to the right and align himself with the conservatives and big business who felt that the New Deal had already gone too far. A turn in their direction would certainly involve the administration having to support the use of deadly force to crush union militancy. Or he could turn to the left. A decision to turn left would be a political calculation that derived not from any supposed sympathy for the poor and oppressed, but from an assessment of the balance of forces. If Roosevelt turned right, he would be outflanked on the left. He would face a serious challenge from Long, would forfeit the support of the CIO (whose financial contribution was to play a considerable part in his election victory in 1936) and be confronted with escalating levels of class conflict. Moreover, however far he moved to the right, he was unlikely to be able to compete on that terrain with the Republicans. His loss of support to Long would not be compensated by gains from the right and there was always a danger that this would hand the Republicans the presidency.

For Roosevelt these were purely tactical questions. As he was to boast later, "I am a juggler, and I never let my right hand know what my left hand does..."[419] And, of course, there was also the safety of American capitalism to consider. As far as Roosevelt was concerned, a Republican victory would not just be a personal disaster, but would also put US capitalism in serious danger. The Republicans were too reactionary and inflexible to take the measures necessary to head off popular unrest; indeed they would exacerbate it. They would inevitably create the circumstances where growing numbers of people would go beyond the reform of capitalism to its overthrow and replacement. In the circumstances Roosevelt took the decision to turn left. He tried to carry conservative Democrats with him, convincing some that the left turn was necessary, but not others. A lot of effort was put into keeping the press baron William Randolph Hearst on board.

As early as September 1934 Harold Ickes, the secretary of the interior, had dined with the general manager of Hearst's press empire, Tom White:

We talked quite a lot about the recent (Congressional) elections. I pointed out that the country was much more radical than the administration and that it was my judgement that the president would have to move further to the left in order to hold the country. I said, as I have said on a number of occasions, that if Roosevelt can't hold the country within a reasonable safe limit, no one else can possibly hope to do so, and that a breakdown on the part of the administration would result in an extreme radical movement, the extent of which no one could foresee. I pointed out that I thought that a lot of the newspapers that are now so busy attacking the administration, if they had any regard for their own interests would be supporting it because a wild swing to the left would engulf all of us in an extreme situation that might readily get beyond control. I said that I would a whole lot rather give up 50 percent of whatever property I might possess than be forced to give up all of it, and that the latter was a distinct possibility if things got out of hand.[420]

Such was Roosevelt's concern to keep Hearst on board that on 22 January 1935 he personally intervened to block a National Labour Relations Board order reinstating a journalist, Dean Jennings, sacked for his trade union activity from one of Hearst's newspapers.[421] At the end of April he told Ickes that he was "anxious just now not to do anything to stir up William Randolph Hearst".[422]

With Hearst increasingly critical, a meeting was arranged with a Hearst representative, Edmund Coblentz, who "was received like the emissary of a foreign potentate".[423] They dined (Coblentz remembered "Beluga caviar—plenty of it") and discussed outstanding issues for nearly four hours. Roosevelt made clear his opposition to the Wagner or National Labor Relations Act and dismissed Coblentz's complaints regarding Rexford Tugwell's supposed excessive influence within the administration (he "was anathema to businessmen", he told Roosevelt) with the remark that no one should "take too seriously what he says". According to Coblentz, in his report back to Hearst, Roosevelt emphasised that his reforms were intended to combat the growing challenge from the left and that big business had to realise this. Roosevelt argued:

I am fighting Communism, Huey Longism, Coughlinism, Townsendism. I want to save our system, the capitalistic system; to save it is to give some heed to world thought of today. I want to equalise the distribution of wealth. Huey Long says that 92 percent of the wealth of this country is controlled by 8 percent of the population. He would change this situation by giving a five thousand dollar home to each head of family, 25 hundred dollars a year, etc. To combat this and similar crackpot ideas it may be necessary to throw to the wolves the 46 men who are reported to have incomes in excess of one million dollars a year. In other words, limit incomes through taxation to one million dollars a year.

Roosevelt warned of the country going the same way as France where Communism had become a serious danger because of the failure to introduce reforms in time. He complained that there were "certain progressive senators" who hoped to split the Democratic Party and thereby put the Republicans in power so that in 1940 they could "put a radical over as president". If this were to happen, Roosevelt warned, "we will have Communism in this country". His was "the only way to fight Communism". As far as Coblentz was concerned, however, the reforms Roosevelt was proposing amounted to Communism anyway. The problem was that Hearst was one of the 46 men Roosevelt proposed to "throw to the wolves" to save the rest of the capitalist class. The young Hearst might well have embraced the left turn, but that was a long time ago. Instead the old Hearst responded to Roosevelt's overture by condemning the New Deal as "a bastard product of Communism and demagogic democracy, a mongrel creation which might be accurately called demo-communism, evolved by a composite personality which might be labelled Stalin Delano Roosevelt".[424]

The Second New Deal

Roosevelt's turn to the left must not be exaggerated. He was pursuing "a quasi-social democratic strategy".[425] The social reforms that he presided over in the Second New Deal were less radical than those that had been introduced in Britain by the Liberal government before the First World War. His Social Security Act was, according to historian William Leuchtenburg, "an astonishingly inept and conservative piece of legislation...[that] denied coverage to numerous classes of workers, including those who needed security most: most notably farm labourers and domestics".[426] Those excluded were, of course, disproportionately black. While unemployment insurance and old age pensions were introduced, the administration backed away from proposals for health insurance, a retreat of historic significance.[427] And when old age pensions finally began to be paid in 1940, only 20 percent of workers qualified.[428] Roosevelt had established what Michael Katz has described as "a semi-welfare state".[429]

His wealth tax, which was to provoke fury from the right, was, in fact, considerably more bark than bite, intended to rally support rather than redistribute wealth. It actually left the share of national income going to the rich untouched; indeed "the share of the top 1 percent even increased a bit after the passage of the Wealth Tax Act".[430] One estimate claims that the measure only raised the taxes of one man—America's richest man, John D Rockefeller.[431] According to Peter Fearon, in the early years of Roosevelt's presidency taxation had "hit the poor disproportionately hard" and now, when he turned left, "achievement fell a long way short of rhetoric".[432] In his discussion of New Deal taxation policy, Mark Leff argues that claims that Roosevelt's policies "must have eased income inequality...are extravagant at best; high rates on upper income brackets were counterbalanced by less glamorous taxes that obtained more impressive collections from the poor". Under Roosevelt regressive excise taxes as a proportion of total tax revenue rose from 19 percent in 1931 to 40 percent in 1936. What was of "paramount importance", according to Leff, was "the rhetorical wrapping with which Roosevelt packaged his legislative programme". While the Wealth Tax proposals certainly had "rhetorical abrasiveness", they were "without economic bite". This, needless to say, is very different from the conventional view of Roosevelt's reformism in the Second New Deal.

Popular support for the Second New Deal derived less from its limited programme of social reform, however, than from its relief programme. In April 1935 the Works Progress Administration (WPA) was established, providing work for over 3 million people into 1936. This was "the core of the welfare state" as far as the New Deal was concerned.[433] Even though relief was inadequate, nevertheless it was considerably more than the Republicans would have provided. Much more could and should have been done, but Roosevelt set his face against such radicalism. Opinion polls in 1935 clearly showed large majorities for radical reform: "77 percent of respondents wanted the government to find jobs for everyone who wanted to work; 68 percent wanted the government to levy taxes sufficient to pay for public works jobs; 74 percent wanted medical care for the poor".[434]

Of particular importance to the trade unions was the National Labor Relations Act, largely the work of Senator Robert Wagner, one of the few New Dealers with genuine labour sympathies. Indeed, he can make a much better claim to the title of New Deal reformer than can Roosevelt, whose commitment to reform was always opportunistic. The Wagner Act, as the legislation was generally known, was, according to historian David Milton, "the most radical legislation enacted during Roosevelt's tenure, yet he neither initiated nor supported the bill until the last minute". As we have seen, Roosevelt made his opposition to the measure absolutely clear in private, but once it became clear it was going to pass, he leapt on board to claim it for the administration. The act "outlawed company unions, declared traditional anti-union practices by employers illegal, legalised union organising efforts, and established the National Labor Relations Board (NLRB) to administer all the provisions of the act".[435] Attempts to incorporate the outlawing of racial discrimination in the act failed in the face of AFL opposition.[436] Moreover, the legislation was only carried because of congressional fear of the class struggle running out of control. As Representative William Connery told the House, they had seen the strikes in Toledo, Minneapolis, San Francisco and in the South, but he had been reliably informed that this was "mild. You have not seen the gates of hell opened, and that is what is going to happen from now on unless the Congress of the United States passes labour legislation". Similarly, in the Senate, Robert La Follette argued that unless the rights of labour were recognised "a grave national emergency will arise…thousands of persons perchance will lose their lives in bloody open conflict". The Auto-Lite strike in Toledo, he warned, presaged what might come.[437] The passage of the act ensured that the unions, most particularly the UMW, threw their weight behind Roosevelt in 1936. The CIO gave Roosevelt unprecedented financial support, donating $780,000 to his campaign, $469,000 coming from the UMW.

Roosevelt made clear the motives for his turn to moderate reformism on 25 September 1936. He was talking to journalists in the aftermath of the May-June 1936 wave of factory occupations in France and claimed that if it were not for the New Deal, the US might well be facing the same dangers. He told them:

Suppose brother Hoover had remained president until April 1936, carrying on his policies of the previous four years; in other words, hadn't taken any steps towards social security or helping the farmer or cutting out child labour and shortening working hours, and old age pensions. Had that been the case, we would have been a country this past April very similar to the country that Blum found when he came in. The French for 25 or 30 years had never done a thing in the way of social legislation. Blum started in and he jumped right into the middle of a strike the first week he was in office.

Now the French were introducing social reforms, but, he asked, "was it too late?"[438]

The conservative backlash

The capitalist class responded to Roosevelt's reforms with absolute fury. As *Time* magazine reported in April 1936, "With few exceptions members of the so-called Upper Class frankly hate Franklin Roosevelt".[439] This hatred, in turn, outraged Roosevelt, who felt that he had saved these people, his own class, from catastrophe, and this was how they repaid him. According to Raymond Moley, he was amazed that they "did not understand that he was their saviour, the only bulwark between them and revolution".[440] Roosevelt himself would tell the story of "a nice old gentleman" in a top hat who had been saved from drowning by a friend, and then once he had recovered berated "his friend because his silk hat was lost".[441] Marriner Eccles, the head of the Federal Reserve, argued that the rich actually believed that the only way the federal government should help the poor and the unemployed "was by means of the "trickle down method," that is that the government should help "the topmost levels of the economic pyramid" and that these benefits "would then spread downward".[442] Another Washington insider, William O Douglas, complained bitterly of how business and finance, "which were opposed to relief for the poor...quickly learned that the public trough was an attractive place to wallow". In his memoirs Douglas emphasised the importance of the Reconstruction Finance Corporation (RFC), which he described as "the most devastating weapon of the New Deal", loaning vast sums of government money to business in order to safeguard American capitalism. Roosevelt's policies were, he felt, not "in any sense radical". In fact, the New Deal was "a collection of makeshift devices to shore up the capitalistic system". Roosevelt:

> expressed over and over to me as well as publicly, his amazement at the charges that he was its enemy, that he was out to "sovietize" the United States and so on. He truly thought that he was capitalism's best friend, pointing out the way for its survival.[443]

As we have already seen, the key figure at the RFC was Jesse Jones, an absolutely uncompromising supporter of the capitalist system. Jones, a Texan banker, was once described as being able to smell money, "even when the wind was against him".[444] As far as he was concerned, the New Deal was an exercise in "state capitalism at its best and needed no apologies". The capitalist state was intervening to save the capitalist system, "even if it took billions of dollars". Although he had no sympathy for the poor, Jones was even prepared to endorse concessions to the working class if they were necessary to safeguard the system.[445]

The fact was, however, that the majority of the US capitalist class believed not only that no further concessions to the working class were necessary, but that far too many concessions had been made already. In July 1936 Harold Ickes dined with a number of rich people who were all extremely hostile to Roosevelt. He tried to convince them "that people won't indefinitely endure hunger and that if we do not give them an opportunity to earn enough to live on, sooner or later we will run the risk of revolution". He "insisted that Roosevelt really had saved capitalism", but concluded that "there is no use trying to talk to men of that type…they cannot see ahead into the future any further than the ends of their noses".[446]

Among the most determined opponents of the New Deal were the Du Pont family (the three brothers, Pierre, Irénée, Lammot and their partner, John Raskob), who controlled a great swathe of US industry. According to their biographer, they "controlled the world's largest chemical company, the world's largest automobile company and the world's largest rubber company". They also had a stake in the domestic weaponry industry, having a large shareholding in the Atlas Chemical Company that "sold various vomiting and tear gases to corporations and police departments throughout the country". And they bought a controlling interest in a major small arms manufacturer, Remington Arms. The Du Ponts were phenomenally wealthy—Pierre had an income in 1929 estimated at over $31 million.[447]

Initially the Du Ponts had been sympathetic to the New Deal. They strongly supported the repeal of prohibition, which they saw as a way of shifting the burden of taxation onto the working class[448] and the National Recovery Act, which they saw as strengthening the position of big business, especially once it had been made clear that company unions were acceptable under Section 7a. They certainly benefited from the policies of the first New Deal, with profits making a dramatic recovery, but they were outraged by the scale of relief expenditure and the rise of militant trade unionism. According to Pap Ndiaye in his study of the family business, in all of the correspondence between the three Du Pont brothers at this time, "there is not one word about the suffering of large numbers of their compatriots, not one word of compassion, not one remark about the country's social conditions, and nothing but lamentations and unending recriminations against the burden of taxation".[449] They regarded even Roosevelt's moderate reformism as tantamount to communism. The Du Ponts and their kind had come to believe that Roosevelt was a serious danger to the capitalist system and had to be stopped.

In June 1938 the Du Ponts took the lead in establishing the Liberty League to put a stop to the New Deal. The intention was to rally those Democrats opposed to Roosevelt, to ally with the Republicans and, with their almost limitless resources, build a powerful movement against the New Deal. Al Smith, the former governor of New York and the Democratic Party presidential candidate in 1928, but by now the Du Ponts' hired man, became one of the League's figureheads. According to Irénée du Pont, the organisation would hopefully "include all property owners—stocks, bonds, homes or farms...the American Legion and even the Ku Klux Klan". They were trying to establish a broad-based movement of reaction to overthrow the "totalitarian socialistic state" that Roosevelt was setting up in America. At its peak the League would claim 120,000 members, but in reality it functioned more as a propaganda organisation. Between August 1934 and November 1936 the League spent over $1 million producing 135 pamphlets (more than one a week), of which 5 million copies were distributed. All this was to be in vain.[450]

Although it was to throw its support behind the Republicans in 1936, the Liberty League also flirted with the extreme right. The Du Ponts made overtures to the Ku Klux Klan and helped fund a variety of fascist organisations. These included the Sentinels of the Republic, which condemned the New Deal as the "Jew Deal", and the Black Legion, a fascist terrorist organisation based in Michigan. There seems little doubt that the Du Ponts would have covertly financed a Huey Long challenge to Roosevelt in order to split the Democratic vote in 1936 if the senator had not been assassinated. The Democrat governor of Georgia, Eugene Talmadge, an appalling racist and reactionary, attempted to mount his own Southern challenge to Roosevelt through his Southern Committee to Uphold the Constitution, and they supported and helped finance that initiative.[451] Talmadge held a convention of his so-called "Jefferson Democrats" on 29 January 1936. There was a giant Confederate flag behind the podium and a copy of *Woman's World* magazine with a picture of Eleanor Roosevelt talking to a black man on the cover on every seat. The challenge was stillborn.[452] After Long's death any prospect that a challenge from the left would damage the Democrats had quickly faded.

Most shocking was the involvement of the Du Ponts and others later associated with the Liberty League in the contemplation of a coup d'état to seize control of the government, revealed by a retired marine general, Smedley Butler, in November 1934. This conspiracy was investigated by the House Committee on Un-American Activities (a precursor to the post-war House Un-American Activities Committee), but it absolutely refused to even question the likes of the Du Ponts, who had been implicated in Butler's testimony. When the committee finally delivered its report in February 1939, it confirmed that there had indeed been a conspiracy, but refused to indict any of the conspirators. As Roger Baldwin of the American Civil Liberties Union (ACLU) observed at the time:

> Not a single participant will be prosecuted under the perfectly plain language of the federal conspiracy act making this a high crime. Imagine the action if such a plot were discovered among Communists! Which is, of course, only to emphasise the nature of our government as representatives of the controllers of property. Violence, even the seizure of government, is excusable on the part of those whose lofty motive is to preserve the profit system.[453]

The support for various small fascist organisations and the flirtation with a coup show how far the Du Ponts were prepared to go. More important at the time, though, was the advice that the Liberty League's lawyers committee issued to business with regard to the Wagner Act. They declared that the act was unconstitutional and that consequently employers were under no obligation to obey it. This was in the confident expectation that the Supreme Court would strike the legislation down. This advice (that in effect corporate lawyers could decide which laws their clients had to obey) was taken up by employers and employers' associations across the country. There can be little doubt that if Roosevelt had lost the 1936 presidential election and been replaced by a Republican president prepared to set about smashing the unions, the Supreme Court would have lived up to their confident expectations. The class struggle was to produce a different outcome, however.

The last champion of capitalism

As part of the preparation for his 1938 biography of Roosevelt, the popular biographer Emil Ludwig interviewed the president. In the course of the interview Roosevelt made it absolutely clear that the overriding motive behind the New Deal "was my desire to obviate revolution... I wanted to rescue capital." For Ludwig, Roosevelt was engaged in momentous work, "unchained by any theory", trying "to prevent revolution". He was carrying on "a simultaneous struggle against radicalism and reaction", desperately trying "to save his own class, the ruling class, from a revolution, by means of magnanimous concessions". His was "perhaps the last attempt to mediate between rich and poor, without a revolution, for this and nothing else is the theme of his labours". As far as Ludwig was concerned, when Roosevelt died his monument should bear the inscription, "The Last Champion of Capitalism".[454]

In 1935 and 1936, however, Roosevelt was subjected to the most ferocious attacks from members of his own class and he responded in kind. In many ways the Liberty League absolutely played into his hands. With the establishment of the League the rich came out quite openly in defence of their own selfish interests at the expense of everyone else. Instead of packaging their interests as those of the average man for electoral purposes, they had revealed themselves for what they were. Roosevelt ruthlessly exploited their mistake. While the Republicans actually nominated Alfred Landon, a moderate, as their candidate for the presidency, a man who was certainly to the left of where Roosevelt had stood in 1933, the Democrats attacked him as the puppet of reactionaries. When Landon tried to attack Roosevelt's tax policies as regressive, as bearing down most heavily on the working class, his perfectly valid point was drowned out by the noise of what the Democrats had constructed as a Herculean clash between "the people" and "the economic royalists". This was their great campaign theme and Landon was overwhelmed by it. He was later to describe the support he got from the Liberty League as "the kiss of death".[455]

In his acceptance speech at the Democratic Party convention in Philadelphia on 27 June 1936 Roosevelt strongly condemned the "economic royalists" who had "carved new kingdoms...built upon concentration of control over material things...the whole structure of modern life was impressed into this royal service". He was quite ferocious in his attack on these "privileged princes of the new economic dynasties" who had created "a new despotism...this new industrial dictatorship". "The collapse of 1929", he went on, "showed up this despotism for what it was". And in 1932 the people had voted to put an end to this "economic tyranny". He proclaimed that in place "of the palace of privilege we seek to build a temple out of faith and hope and charity". What they were engaged in, he went on, was "a war for the survival of democracy... I am enlisted for the duration of the war." He was giving the Liberty League an object lesson in politics, in effect, making them the issue of the campaign. What he had to say was, of course, just so much rhetoric that he had no intention of ever allowing to determine his policies once re-elected, but it rallied millions to his cause.

Roosevelt regularly revisited this theme throughout the campaign. On 14 October in Chicago, he proclaimed his administration "a people's government", confronting "selfish forces". He made it clear that he "cherished our system of private property and free enterprise" and that he was "determined to preserve it as the foundation of our traditional American system". What threatened the "American system" was that half of the country's "industrial corporate wealth...had come under the control of less than 200 corporations". And these giant corporations did not even compete with each other but "were tied together by interlocking directors, interlocking bankers, interlocking lawyers". This concentration of wealth and power had become a threat "to the economic system which we call American democracy". Once again though, just to make it clear that his radicalism had limits, he proclaimed, "I believe, I have always believed, and I will always believe in private enterprise as the backbone of economic well-being in the United States."

Roosevelt went out of his way to repudiate the Communist Party. At Syracuse on 29 September he made it absolutely clear that he was opposed to Communism: "That is my position. It has always been my position. It will always be my position." Where he differed from the Republicans was over how best to fight Communism. "Communism", he told his audience, "is the manifestation of the social unrest which always comes with widespread economic maladjustment." He had tackled the causes of the problem. It was under his administration "that starvation was averted, that homes and farms were saved, that banks were reopened, that crop prices rose, that industry revived, and that dangerous forces subversive of our form of government were turned aside". The Democratic Party was "against revolution. Therefore, we waged war against those conditions which make revolutions—against the inequalities and resentments which breed them."

He closed his campaign at Madison Square Garden on 31 October. Here he attacked the super-rich who had come to consider "the government of the United States as a mere appendage to their own affairs... Government by organised money is just as dangerous as government by organised mob." He condemned those "powerful influences" that had come together against him: "They are unanimous in their hate for me—and I welcome their hatred." This produced thunderous applause. He went on to say that in his first administration "the forces of selfishness...met their match" and to promise that it would be said of his second administration that they had "met their master".[456]

Roosevelt's use of class war rhetoric was to give the campaign the character of a crusade. As James MacGregor Burns observes:

> even hard-bitten journalists were incredulous over the wild enthusiasm of the crowds. For mile after mile people lined the roads, not only in the cities but in the outskirts as well. Boston Common was overrun by a seething mass of 150,000 people... In New York City the Roosevelt car travelled more than 30 miles without passing a block whose sidewalks were not jammed. As he waved and talked to such crowds Roosevelt seemed to catch their militancy.[457]

This rhetoric was to help produce one of the greatest election victories in US history. The Republicans were swept away by the popular enthusiasm for social reform and for curbing the privileges of the rich.

Roosevelt's inaugural address on 20 January 1937 promised change. He spoke of the "tens of millions...who at this very moment are denied what the lowest standard of today calls the necessities of life", of "millions of families trying to live on incomes so meagre that the pall of disaster hangs over them day by day", of "millions whose daily lives in city and on farm continue under conditions labelled indecent by a so-called polite society half a century ago". Roosevelt pledged himself to lift up the one third of the nation "ill-housed, ill-clad, ill-nourished... The test of our progress is not whether we add more to the abundance of those who have much; it is whether we do enough for those who have too little".[458] The nature of Roosevelt's campaign, his often ferocious attacks on the rich, quite unwittingly provided a powerful impetus to a new wave of working class revolt that was to culminate in the greatest triumph in US working class history. Workers in the General Motors car plants in Flint, Michigan, saw Roosevelt's victory over the "economic royalists" as an invitation to take them on themselves.

Chapter Eight

1937: the year of the sit-down

When they tie the can
To a union man
Sit down! Sit down!

When they smile and say
"No raise in pay"
Sit down! Sit down!

When the boss won't talk
Don't take a walk
Sit down! Sit down![459]

The struggle in auto

The Great Depression had a devastating impact on the US car industry. In 1929 5.3 million vehicles were produced, down to 1.3 million by 1932. At the same time employment fell from 450,000 to 243,000 with many of those still in work on "short time".[460] Short time could mean just a few weeks work over the course of a year: between June 1931 and June 1932 Wyndham Mortimer, a worker at the White Motor Company in Cleveland, earned $53.65. Everyone he knew was either unemployed or on short time.[461]

The first great explosion of working class unrest occurred in January 1933 at Briggs Manufacturing in Detroit, a firm making car bodies for Ford and Chrysler. On 11 January the management imposed a 20 per-cent wage cut, provoking a walkout at their Waterloo plant. The lead was given by Socialist, IWW and Communist workers on the shop floor. In strike after strike in this period success was dependent on the anger on the shop floor being given direction by political activists, men and women, who were committed to organising the class for struggle. The strikers put pickets on the other three Briggs plants in Detroit, closing them down. Within days the company withdrew the pay cuts. The management refused to meet with the men's representatives, however, and on 24 January some 12,000 workers walked out again. This time the company was ready. It was fighting to preserve the open shop on behalf of the whole Detroit car industry. Picket lines were broken by police violence and scabs were brought in. The strike went down to defeat with mass victimisation. Walter Reuther (all three Reuther brothers, Walter, Victor and Roy, were Socialist Party members involved in the strike) wrote at the time that, despite the setback at Briggs, "underneath the surface there was rebellion in the hearts of the workers".[462]

The great rallying of workers to the unions that took place after Congress passed the National Industrial Recovery Act, with its sop to the AFL, Section 7a, did not leave the car industry untouched. Over the summer of 1933 the AFL established 183 Federal Labor Unions in the industry, recruiting some 100,000 workers. As there was not an affiliated AFL union in the industry, workers were recruited into FLUs that were under the jurisdiction of the AFL itself. William Green, the AFL president, put William Collins in charge of organising the industry. He was totally unfit for the task. Collins was a bureaucrat of the worst kind, opposed to militancy whatever the provocation, and, moreover, was under orders not to allow into the FLUs any workers who came under the jurisdiction of the craft unions. He famously assured the employers that he was completely opposed to strikes and had never voted for one.[463] The AFL strategy was to use the machinery established by Roosevelt's National Recovery Administration to secure recognition, relying, in effect, on the government. The failure of this strategy left union members exposed to victimisation at the hands of some of the most ruthless employers in the US.

The AFL strategy did not go unchallenged. On 21 September 1933 skilled workers, tool and die makers, members of the Mechanics Educational Society of America (MESA), struck at General Motors in Flint, Michigan. The strike quickly spread throughout the city and to Detroit, affecting every major company except Ford (MESA had not made any headway in that industrial police state), and many small engineering firms. Some 14,000 men walked out. MESA had been established in February 1933, a militant craft union that posed as a self-improvement society to avoid victimisation. It organised the skilled toolmakers who made the cutting, stamping and grinding machinery used in the car industry. These workers had seen their wages and conditions savagely attacked. Leading them was Matt Smith, a British immigrant and strong socialist who had been one of the leaders of the shop stewards' movement in Manchester during the First World War. Smith had been imprisoned during the war for his opposition to conscription. In the aftermath of the British General Strike of 1926 he was blacklisted—he was sacked from 11 jobs in six weeks—and emigrated.[464] Smith was one of a number of British skilled workers, veterans of the class struggle back home, who helped organise the US car industry. Indeed, in the 1930s there were some car plants that would not employ anyone with an English or Scottish accent for fear of union trouble.[465] Smith's militancy was unfortunately to be compromised by his narrow craft outlook, but in September and October 1933 MESA members took on the car companies for six weeks.

The strike was only partly successful in closing down production as the big plants turned to small workshops for retooling. To counter this, on 30 October hundreds of strikers mounted a "riotcade", with carloads of pickets carrying out surprise raids on scab workshops, invading the premises, destroying blueprints, sabotaging machinery, breaking windows and overturning cars. One participant, Joe Brown, described how over 4,000 workers set out:

> We were out to do a job on the job shops. The route was laid out in advance. When we reached the first shop on the route we piled out of the cars, smashed all the windows, broke the doors in, burned the blueprints, tore up expensive tool diagrams and smashed fixtures. Then we ran back to the cars and headed for the next shop. Man, was that ever an exciting experience! We called it "educating the bosses"... We started around nine in the morning and did not finish till past four in the afternoon.[466]

This direct action broke the deadlock and company after company came to terms. Although only small material gains were made (5 cents an hour rise), nevertheless, as one historian observes, "MESA had breached the historic open shop in the automobile industry".[467] By the end of 1934 MESA had 34,000 members.

Production workers in the FLUs now demanded militant action. Workers in the Buick and the Fisher Body plants in Flint and in the Hudson plant in Detroit voted for strike action on 4 March 1934. They demanded union recognition, the reinstatement of victimised workers and a 20 percent pay rise. The intention was to use strike action in these plants as a springboard to close down the whole industry. Militant action would rally the workers to the union. All that stood in the way was the AFL leadership. Collins was determined to avoid a strike and contacted the government, warning of the threat that his members posed to the industry and urging intervention. Roosevelt responded with a promise of mediation by the National Labor Board. Playing the Roosevelt card, Collins secured a suspension of the strike. Discussions got nowhere and on 21 March the workers voted to strike. Once again Roosevelt, at Collins's instigation, intervened. With the employers refusing to even meet with the unions, Roosevelt met the two sides separately.

On 25 March he announced a settlement that established a toothless Automobile Labor Board, which left union members helpless in the face of a wave of victimisation and, most damaging of all, for the first time gave government recognition to company unions. The settlement effectively undermined Section 7a. It was enthusiastically welcomed by the car companies as bolstering their stand against the unions. It was, in Irving Bernstein's words, "a total victory" for management.[468] The AFL accepted the settlement with disastrous consequences. Union membership in the car industry collapsed, particularly in the key centres of Flint and Detroit. Men tore up their union cards, both in disgust at the AFL's betrayal and in order to avoid victimisation. Those who didn't were sacked and blacklisted.

The battle was not over, however. In Toledo, Local 18384, as we have already seen, defied the AFL leadership and struck at the Auto-Lite components plant on 12 April 1934. The strikers turned to the American Workers Party (AWP) for support. The result was a hard fought struggle that saw strikers and their supporters battling police and troops before the company surrendered. It was the first of the great victories won by the US working class in 1934 that began to turn the tide.

Under pressure from the surviving FLUs the AFL established a National Council for the car industry in June 1934. The left from strongholds in Toledo and Cleveland pushed for the chartering of an independent car workers' union. Meanwhile the AFL replaced Collins with another identikit bureaucrat, Francis Dillon. In April 1935 he was confronted with another strike in Toledo called by Local 18384, once again in defiance of the AFL leadership. This time the union closed down GM's Chevrolet plant in the city that supplied all the transmissions for the Chevrolet division. The strike leaders, James Roland, Bob Travis, George Addes and others, once again all Socialists, Communists or Musteites, were determined to spread the strike. Urged on by Abraham Muste, they hoped to kick-start a company-wide strike. All their efforts to bring out other GM plants were blocked by Dillon. As Sidney Lens later wrote:

> The strike was spreading with 30,000 workers in other plants...out in sympathy. The men were on the verge of victory, since it was obvious that a few more days of the tie-up would spread the strike throughout the GM system. But ever fearful of the rank and file, the Federation declared the strike unauthorised and ordered the men back to work.[469]

Once Dillon had successfully isolated the Toledo workers, he was able to bully them back to work, although only with considerable difficulty and great abuse. Even though unsuccessful, the strike accomplished "the final discrediting of the AFL in auto".[470] The aftermath of the strike demonstrated the need to organise company wide—GM fired hundreds of men at the well-organised Toledo plant, shifting some 50 percent of transmission production to unorganised plants in Saginaw, Michigan, and Muncie, Indiana.

By the time the AFL finally called a convention to establish a new union for the car industry, the United Auto Workers, in August 1935, its leadership was completely discredited and regarded with contempt. Collins's and Dillon's misleadership had seen opportunity after opportunity squandered with membership collapsing from 100,000 to only 22,000, with thousands victimised and blacklisted. The situation was most dire in Flint and Detroit, where membership fell to 757 and 2,197 respectively. And yet when William Green gave the new union its charter, he insisted on appointing Dillon as union president with a handpicked team that excluded anyone on the left or with the taint of militancy, that is, anyone who had actually been trying to build the union. Wyndham Mortimer led a delegation to protest about this to the AFL Executive Council. They thought they had stumbled into a meeting of business executives by mistake. The full-time officials were "discussing stocks, bonds, personal investments and the like". Bill Hutcheson of the Carpenters was arguing with Ed Wharton of the Machinists about whether Hutcheson's $50,000 investment in Consolidated Edison was a good move. Wharton preferred to invest in AT&T. And this was at a time when "there were still millions of unemployed...who wondered where their next meal was coming from".[471]

At the newly-formed UAW's convention in April 1936 delegates took the first opportunity to remove Dillon, replacing him with Homer Martin, a former preacher turned car worker. He was a powerful orator who could rouse an audience, but a poor organiser, a worse strategist and increasingly anti-Communist. Wyndham Mortimer was elected first vice-president. He was a Communist Party member, although this was never admitted even in his memoirs—he was actually a member of the party's Central Committee but his membership was registered under a pseudonym. One of the leaders of the union in Toledo, George Addes, was elected secretary-treasurer. The union was reinforced by the affiliation of three of the largest MESA locals and of two independent unions that had previously rejected any AFL connection. Strengthened and under their new leadership, the UAW looked not to the AFL but to the CIO. Organising the car industry was going to involve a fight and they knew they could count on the CIO for help.

"The dark clouds of fear"

General Motors was the largest corporation in the world. It operated 110 plants in 19 countries, and owned both Vauxhall in Britain and Opel in Germany. GM had its core business in the US, operating 69 plants in 35 cities in 14 states with total assets of $1.5 billion. In 1928 its profits after tax were $296 million, but by 1932 this had fallen to only $8 million. By 1936, however, the company had made a remarkable recovery with profits after tax back up to $239 million. Executive pay reflected this success. In 1936 Alfred Sloan, GM's president, was paid $561,311. The turnaround in the company's fortunes had, of course, been achieved at the expense of its workers. GM was absolutely committed to the open shop, and, to this end, dramatically increased its expenditure on labour spies, company police and weapons. From 1932 until 1936 GM spent $1 million on spies and was the Pinkerton Agency's biggest client.[472] The company had successfully generated "widespread terror...by mass firings and victimisations... Reprisals were commonplace at all the major plants...the company went to extraordinary lengths to repress union activities".[473]

When Wyndham Mortimer arrived in Flint to launch an organising campaign in June 1936 he found that "a cloud of fear hung over the city, and it was next to impossible to find anyone who would even discuss the question of unionisation". The UAW had, on paper, five locals in the city with a combined membership of only 122. Most of the union officers were either spies or members of the fascist Black Legion or both. The militants had by and large been victimised and "were now walking the streets". Within minutes of registering at a hotel— Mortimer had not even taken his coat off—he received a phone call warning him to leave town now "if you don't want to be carried out in a wooden box". This was the Black Legion serving him notice, a threat that had to be taken seriously because a number of union organisers had been shot in recent years. Indeed, the Black Legion was a powerful force within the Michigan Republican Party, and had a strong presence in local government and many police departments throughout Michigan and Ohio. According to B J Widick, both a participant in and chronicler of these events, between 1933 and 1936 there were "over 50 murders in Michigan that could be attributed to the Black Legion". In such a climate Mortimer had to begin organising on a clandestine basis, bypassing the existing union officers and patiently building up a secret network of militants.[474]

GM was completely confident that it would be able to keep the UAW out. When William Knudsen, a top company executive, visited France in September 1936 he told a Renault executive, still reeling from the May-June factory occupations, it could never happen in the US.[475]

What drove workers to fight back was the speed-up. While there was a multitude of grievances, "speed-up was the focal point...in the 1930s". The car companies had taken full advantage of mass unemployment to relentlessly increase work rates while at the same time cutting wages, confident, as one worker was told, that if he didn't like it there were 400 men outside after his job. Speed-up was a permanent feature of mass production, but in the car factories:

the drive system became even more bluntly coercive. As a foreman who worked at the Flint Chevrolet plant throughout the 1930s later recalled, "It was predicated on getting every bit of work out of a person...that he could stand"... Physical abuse was even used by foremen to supplement other forms of coercion.

Workers were regularly sacked to intimidate the others. When the line was speeded up, foremen would watch for those who could not keep up and they were fired. Men were worked until they dropped. Such was the punishing nature of the job that a production line worker was regarded as finished by the age of 40. And, at the same time, rates of pay were arbitrarily set, with workers often not knowing what they were being paid until they got their wage packet.[476]

As GM moved back into massive profit, however, the balance of power on the shop floor began to shift. Any interruption of production cost money, and to keep the line moving the management began to make concessions. Small victories built the confidence necessary for great battles. Wyndham Mortimer recalled one such victory at the Fisher Body No 1 plant in Flint in October 1936. The two Perkins brothers were fired for union activity and their fellow workers stopped work, demanding their reinstatement. The company conceded but the workers:

> refused to resume work until the fired men were back on the job. General Motors ordered the Police Department to find and bring these two men back to the job. The Flint radio station broadcast spot announcements urging them to return. No work was done, however, until the Perkins boys walked into the plant and resumed their jobs. One of them had gone to a show with his girlfriend so that by the time they were found and brought back to the plant it was 10pm.

GM had surrendered to direct action and, on the shop floor at least, had been forced to negotiate with union men, with a committee headed by Bud Simons, a CP member. This victory, Mortimer continues, "had a terrific impact on the rest of the workers... The dark clouds of fear that had hung over Flint were rapidly disappearing." The workers were beginning to "feel their strength and power. Fear of the boss evaporated to the point where workers were openly talking union".[477] The UAW began to increase in membership and to grow in confidence.

Bob Travis was brought in from Toledo to take over from Mortimer and a bi-weekly union newspaper, the *Flint Auto Worker*, edited by Henry Kraus, was launched. By December the paper had a sale of over 50,000 "that unemployed auto workers led by Communist Party member Charles Killenger delivered door to door all over the city".[478]

In the run-up to Christmas 1936 there were a growing number of disputes in the industry. On 27 November 1,200 workers at Midland Steel in Detroit, a former MESA stronghold but now UAW, "sat down and occupied their workplace". John Anderson, another British trade union veteran and Communist Party member, led the fight. This was "the first wave of a flood tide of worker unrest". The company surrendered on 4 December, "the first time in the city's history a major car company had been forced to come to terms with a union representing all its workers".[479]

At the Kelsey-Hayes Wheel plant in Detroit militants carefully planned a confrontation with management. Department 49 was the union stronghold, but what was needed "was some dramatic incident to spark the action and draw in other departments as well". A little while earlier a strong union member, a Polish woman, working in the department had collapsed because "the constant increase in tempo was more than she could handle". It is worth quoting Victor Reuther's account at length:

> Since the speed-up was the major source of resentment, we spoke to the Polish girl in my sector, and she agreed to faint again. This time it would be a signal for a strike in 49... To take advantage of our membership in both shifts, we set the fainting incident for the hour when the shifts were about to change and both sets of workers would be present. D-Day would be Tuesday 10 December... We organised picket squads, and since we were planning a sit-in, a committee was formed to take care of feeding the strikers inside the plant and their families outside. May Reuther took a sick leave from her teaching job... On the day of the strike, I reported to work earlier than usual to size up the situation before the deadline came... At precisely 20 minutes before that shift was to end, our faithful friend went into a dead faint, and I ran and pulled the main switch and shouted "Strike! We've had enough of this speed-up!" The call for strike action spread through our whole department and into neighbouring sectors.

Kelsey-Hayes surrendered on 23 December, conceding union recognition and a substantial pay rise (the wages of many workers were doubled). The sit-down strikers "marched out into the glare of flash bulbs and the cheers of thousands who had gathered to congratulate them." And, as Reuther emphasises, a union local that had begun the strike with only 78 members ended it with 3,000 and by the end of 1937 had 35,000 members throughout the district.[480]

GM, meanwhile, had its own problems. On 17 December there was a sit-down at the Bendix Products plant (part owned by GM) in South Bend, Indiana, that ended in a union victory. On 23 December strikes broke out at plants in Atlanta[481] and Kansas City, and on 28 December workers in the Fisher Body plant in Cleveland began a sit-down strike. The decisive battleground was to be in Flint, however. On 30 December workers in Fisher Body No 1 and 2 plants occupied.[482]

Sit down! Sit down!

According to Len De Caux, the sit-down strike:

> was the stratagem of the man on the job... To the man on the conveyor line, the thing to do in a showdown was to pull the switch. All on that power line would have to stop working. If united on the beef, they'd stay stopped until it was settled. Meanwhile, in the nature of line production, a stoppage in one department would soon stop others—and the boss would be tearing his hair out... In the 1920 sit-downs I saw in Italy, the workers ran up the red flags, claimed the plants for the people, and tried to keep them running. The American sit-downers claimed the jobs were theirs, not the plant's. Significantly, perhaps, they often acted as if the plants were also theirs.

As De Caux insisted, in the class struggle "the initial impetus came from the men on the job", although the action was generally sparked by union activists, "often radicals".[483] In 1937 the sit-down strike was to transform the balance of class forces in the United States.

In some ways the sit-down strikes in the US were a testimony to the immense power of big business, to the success corporations like GM had in resisting unionisation. What hundreds of thousands of workers were to decide in the course of the year was that occupying their workplace was a way of giving themselves the strategic advantage at a time when the employer still seemed to hold all the cards. In the car industry the experience of the workers was that any attempt to build a union resulted in victimisation before it was securely established. The workforce was infiltrated by company spies, who would often pose as good union men, identifying those to be sacked. If you worked for Ford, dismissal was often accompanied by a beating (union activists were routinely sacked for "fighting", which conveniently explained their injuries). If victimisation provoked a strike, the picket lines would be broken by police and company guards, with strikers beaten, arrested and sometimes killed. Scabs would be brought in to take the strikers' jobs and the least determined would begin to return to work, leaving the most determined, the militants, out in the cold. The sit-down strike changed all this.

The sit-down strike enabled a strategically placed minority of workers to close down production and demonstrate to their workmates that the boss could be taken on and beaten. This was crucial because at the end of 1936 the UAW had only some 4,500 members in Flint out of a workforce of 45,000. By occupying, the sit-down strikers avoided defeat on the picket line (storming a defended factory was a completely different proposition from dispersing a picket line), being replaced by scabs, and, in the car industry, if they were in the production process, they could bring even a giant like GM to its knees. The sit-down strike in the US in 1937 was an organising weapon. It was the way both to win over the majority of the workers and to batter the employer into submission.

The UAW was committed to strike action against GM in 1937. Roosevelt's re-election and rout of the "economic royalists" seemed to provide a mandate for taking the company on—after all, the workers were only demanding that the management obey the National Labor Relations Act. The way the struggle developed, however, was in the hands of the rank and file. As we have seen, strikes had already broken out in the GM plants in Atlanta and Kansas City, and on 28 December workers in the Fisher Body plant in Cleveland had occupied. Decisive, however, were developments in Flint.

On 30 December workers in Fisher Body No 2 plant occupied in protest against the sacking of three inspectors for union membership. The union was still weak in this plant, and if they were to have any chance of winning it was absolutely essential to close Fisher Body No 1 plant where the union was strong. At this stage it was felt that any

FIGHTING BACK

defeat would seriously damage union credibility. In Fisher Body No 1 Bud Simons and his committee, with the support of Bob Travis, the union organiser, decided to take action over a key set of dies the management were planning to remove from the plant so they could start up production elsewhere. They occupied the plant that same day. The part played by Communist Party and Socialist Party militants was crucial. They were able to present their workmates with a strategy for winning and with a blueprint for running an occupation. As one worker later remembered, "guys in the back of the room took a couple of pieces of paper out of their pockets—'What to do in case of a sit-down'".[484]

And while the Flint Fisher Body plants were occupied, outside the UAW launched a solidarity and recruitment campaign. In the days of the AFL officials would have made every effort to undermine the struggle in order to demonstrate their usefulness to management, but the UAW and the CIO recognised that the only way to break management resistance was to spread and intensify the struggle. When John L Lewis was first told of the sit-downs, he asked his brother Denny, a UMW official, how he should respond. Denny told him to "tell them to invite their friends".[485] There was no going back. On 31 December GM plants in Norwood, Ohio, walked out and the Guide Lamp plant in Anderson, Indiana, was occupied. On 4 January 1937 workers occupied the Chevrolet plant in Toledo and on the following day plants in Janesville, Wisconsin, were occupied. The strike spread until by early February there were over 40,000 GM workers either in occupation or on the picket line.

Fisher Body No 1 provided a model for the sit-down strike. In his *The Many and the Few*, Henry Kraus provides a useful, if flawed, account. An elected strike committee chaired by Bud Simons ran the occupation, although its decisions "were subject to the daily check-up of the membership meetings". Sub-committees were established with responsibility for supervising all the various activities involved in maintaining the occupation. As Kraus wrote:

> Everyone had to work, naturally, putting in six hours strike duty a day, three hours on and nine hours off. This would be picket duty at the gates, outside patrols, health and sanitation inspection, kitchen, police, etc. The kitchen was open day and night, serving coffee and sandwiches at all times...

The strikers were organised into squads of 15 under a captain, living and working together in the plant. Education classes were organised. Security was taken very seriously with a "special patrol" going round the plant every hour. This functioned as "the eyes and ears of the sit-down, chasing down all rumours and suspicious circumstances". It changed its route round the plant every day. The workers entertained themselves, forming their own orchestra with mandolins, guitar, banjo and mouth organ. There was ping pong, boxing and football. The owner of the Rialto cinema, Maxie Gaeler, was a union sympathiser, and sent in variety acts to entertain the strikers. He put on film shows in the plant, including a screening of Charlie Chaplin's *Modern Times*. And the sit-down strikers and their supporters sang; they sang union songs for their own entertainment, to maintain morale and as a propaganda weapon.[486]

Preparations were made to defend the plants against police and vigilante attack. Metal sheets were fixed over the windows with holes cut in them so that fire hoses could be deployed against any attackers. Missiles, particularly the heavy door hinges, were stockpiled, ready for use. Firearms were banned. The strikers held regular drills, preparing themselves for a showdown. As a last resort, drums of oil were placed at the windows with hand pumps ready to spray the approaches. According to John L Lewis, they "had wads of waste ready to light and throw down until they could have ringed the factory with a wall of fire...it would have been Greek fire".[487]

The organisation of solidarity outside the occupied plants was of crucial importance. Keeping the strikers fed three hot meals a day was a massive undertaking, along with organising support for the men's families. What won the strike, according to William Weinstone, the Communist Party leader in Michigan, was the "combination of an inside strike with an outside mass mobilisation". It was this that "rendered the use of the sit-down most effective". Daily meetings were held outside the plant together with "large-scale demonstrations...to meet any critical situation".[488] And thousands of workers from Toledo, Detroit and elsewhere poured into Flint to support the sit-down.

Another crucial feature of the strike was the involvement of women. A very effective Women's Auxiliary was established by Dorothy Kraus which, as Sidney Fine writes:

set up its own speakers' bureau and publicity department, engaged in picketing on a regular basis, staffed a first-aid department…maintained a nursery where wives could leave their youngsters while they themselves engaged in strike duty, collected food and money for the strike, and contacted sit-down "widows" who complained about the absence of their husbands to explain the strike and enlist their support.[489]

There was also a Women's Emergency Brigade, set up by Genora Johnson, a Socialist Party member, to reinforce the picket lines. The brigade, which eventually numbered over 350 women, mobilised "every time there was a threatened battle". "We carried heavy wooden clubs," Johnson recalled. Volunteers were warned that they would "face tear gas and bullets" and the possibility of being "killed by the police". In the first group of 50 volunteers was 72 year old Rebecca Goddard, and Johnson tried to persuade her to withdraw because of her age. She was assured that Rebecca's six children, 20 grandchildren and ten great-grandchildren were all union and she intended to play her part. Many of the women involved were themselves GM workers. The Women's Emergency Brigade in their red berets were to play a crucial role in winning the battle.[490]

GM responded to the occupation of the two Flint plants almost immediately. On 2 January the company obtained an injunction from Judge Edward Black, which not only ordered the evacuation of the plants, but also effectively prohibited any activity to further the strike, including picketing. What could have been a premature testing of the union's strength and resolve was successfully turned into a propaganda triumph. The union discovered that Judge Black owned over $200,000 worth of GM shares, and under Michigan law such a personal interest barred him from hearing the case.

Having failed to recover the plants by legal means, on 11 January the company tried to retake them by force. The Flint police, essentially an extension of the company, attempted to storm Fisher Body No 2, firing tear gas into the plant, and attacking the strikers and their sympathisers. The so-called Battle of the Running Bulls saw the police drenched by the strikers' hoses (in sub-zero conditions) and pelted with anything that came to hand—Victor Reuther was to remark later that victory hinged on the ready availability of door hinges! The police responded with gunfire, wounding 13 pickets, one of them critically, and accidentally wounding one of their own number. Among the wounded were two striking bus drivers, taking time off from their own dispute to support the GM occupation. The pickets captured a number of police cars, turning one of them over with its occupants still inside. A critical role in rallying the strikers and their supporters was played by the union sound car, with Victor Reuther exhorting the pickets to stand firm and directing the erection of barricades. At one point Reuther saw a window opening across from the plant with a shotgun aimed down at the sound car. He called out to the union men on the factory roof and "immediately a bunch of hinges flew all the way across the avenue and smashed the window". The shotgun disappeared. At one point in the battle Genora Johnson took the microphone and urged women bystanders to join the picket and stand with the men. Both men and women came forward as reinforcements. The number of women on the picket line deterred the police from further gunfire and they retreated. The union had driven them off.[491]

Governor Frank Murphy, a New Deal Democrat, responded by sending in the National Guard, eventually over 3,000 men, to prevent any further violence. He placed them under the command of a professional soldier who could be relied on to obey Murphy's orders rather than those of the car companies. Meanwhile, Murphy tried to persuade the union to evacuate the plants and GM to open negotiations. Under intense pressure the UAW president, Homer Martin, agreed to a "truce" whereby the strikers would evacuate the plants which would remain closed while negotiations began. The strikers were to march out on 17 January. This would have been a recipe for defeat, but fortunately GM's bad faith led to the union repudiating the agreement and the occupation continued. This episode decided the CIO leadership that Martin could not be left to handle the negotiations. As far as Lewis was concerned the strike had to be won no matter what because the fate of the CIO itself was at stake in Flint.

In Washington the administration was divided over how to respond to the crisis. Vice-President John Nance Garner led those advocating the use of force to end the sit-down, while the secretary of labour, Frances Perkins, desperately tried to persuade GM to negotiate. Roosevelt certainly had no intention of authorising the use of federal troops, but if Governor Murphy had decided to send in the National Guard to drive the workers out at bayonet point, there is every reason to believe that the president would have gone along with his decision. He never publicly objected to the use of lethal force against striking workers in other strikes. As for Murphy himself, he seems to have been determined to avoid the use of force if at all possible, but nevertheless did his best to force the union to back down by threatening its use. Unknown to the union, on 18 January Murphy quietly sold GM shares worth over $100,000, and ill-advisedly bought Chrysler shares instead.[492]

Meanwhile GM was mobilising against the UAW. Vigilante attacks increased and a number of union activists and organisers were badly beaten. Evidence later came to light that Flint city officials conspired to have Bob Travis, Victor and Walter Reuther and Kraus himself killed. And on 25 January vigilante action organised by GM officials drove the union out of Anderson and Saginaw. In Anderson vigilantes beat union members and wrecked the union hall with the police only intervening to arrest the union men once the mob had finished with them.[493] The GM management believed that the tide was beginning to turn in their favour. Increasingly confident of victory, GM resisted all the pressure both from the governor and from Washington to open negotiations. On 29 January this led to an angry telephone exchange between Frances Perkins and Alfred Sloan in which she called him "a skunk" and "a scoundrel" and told him he would go to hell when he died. Sloan replied that she could not talk to him like that because he was worth $70 million. He obviously thought this an important point because, according to Perkins, he repeated it some 20 times. Sloan's income in 1936 was $2,876,310.[494]

With their position weakening, the strikers decided to reclaim the initiative. GM was not hurting enough and the union was being worn down by a process of attrition. At this point Kermit Johnson (Genora Johnson's husband) proposed the seizure of Chevrolet No 4 plant. This would restore morale and deal the company a crippling blow—No 4 produced all the engines for the Chevrolet (a million engines in 1936).[495] The plan was opposed by Walter Reuther, but supported by Bob Travis. They decided that a diversion of some sort was necessary and came up with a feint, a fake attempt to seize Chevrolet No 9 that company spies would leak to the management. Only four people knew that the real plan was to take the No 4 plant once all the company guards had been drawn to No 9.

On 1 February the plan was put into effect with a fierce fight taking place at No 9 plant. The workers here were heavily outnumbered by company guards and a number were badly beaten—two, Russell Hardy and Morley Crafts, were carried away unconscious. Nevertheless, the stratagem worked and the way was left clear for the occupation of No 4. According to Edward Levinson, with all the guards over at Chevrolet No 9, the plant was occupied "with no more difficulty than a few harsh words to amazed foremen".[496] A crucial role was played by the Women's Emergency Brigade that blocked one of the entrances to No 4 and stopped police getting into the plant and evicting the strikers. This turned the tide. The union had dramatically seized the initiative. The strikers were jubilant. They had inflicted a crippling blow on GM. Confidence was restored.

For GM the situation was now desperate. Instead of the strike heading towards defeat, it had been revitalised and promised to continue through February into March. GM had produced 50,000 cars in December 1936; in the first week of February production was down to 125. Ford and Chrysler could not resist taking advantage, even though GM was battling their common enemy. Ford increased production from 16,000 cars a week to over 28,000 and Chrysler increased production from 20,000 to over 25,000. They were eating into GM's market share in a big way. Earlier, on 15 January, GM had convened a secret meeting of the industry heads to propose a general lockout to smash the UAW. Henry Ford, completely confident he could defeat the union on his own, refused to cooperate, and the proposal for a united stand collapsed.[497]

Sloan still hoped to be able to force Governor Murphy to send the National Guard in to clear the occupied plants. To this end, on 2 February the company secured an injunction from Judge Paul Gadola ordering the evacuation of the plants the next day and once again prohibiting picketing. The National Guard made it clear to Murphy that any attempt to retake the plants by force would require a declaration of martial law in Flint, the arrest of union leaders and left wing activists, an effective ban on all union activity, and even then, he was told, there was no guarantee that the troops would actually be able to retake the plants in the face of determined resistance. A telegram from the strikers in Fisher Body No 1, drafted for them by Bob Travis and Lee Pressman, warned Murphy that the use of troops would "mean a bloodbath of unarmed strikers...a bloody massacre of the workers". All that they were fighting for was for General Motors to "obey the law and engage in collective bargaining":

> We have decided to stay in the plant. We have no illusions about the sacrifices which the decision will entail. We fully expect that if a violent effort is made to oust us many of us will be killed, and we take this means of making it known...that if this result follows from the attempt to eject us, you are the one who must be held responsible for our deaths.[498]

Political oblivion was staring him in the face. And Lewis raised the stakes when he made it clear to Murphy that if troops were sent in, he would join the men in the plants so that "the militia will have the pleasure of shooting me out of the plants".[499] This, needless to say, was not the stance of the average union leader. It is impossible to imagine Green taking such a stand. Lewis, in Len de Caux's words, "knew this strike was crucial. He gave it all he had." It was a "make or break showdown for the UAW, maybe for all the CIO". To ensure victory, he took on "the Wall Street powers behind GM. He took on Washington and the president".[500]

On 3 February thousands of union reinforcements from Akron, Detroit, Toledo, Norwood, Lansing, Pontiac and elsewhere poured into the city, many of them armed with clubs, iron bars, hammers and other weapons, ready for a fight. Murphy spoke to Roosevelt on the phone, telling him that he did not see any alternative in view of the injunction to the use of force. Roosevelt told him to "go right ahead with it".[501] The decision was Murphy's, with Roosevelt positioning himself to minimise any blame and to maximise any credit that might derive from the situation.

The idea that Roosevelt actually supported the workers in their struggle is positively ludicrous. According to Frances Perkins, his attitude was that the sit-down strike "was wrong and hazardous...they ought not to do it in a country like this". He acknowledged that the workers had rights, but if they would only be patient, "the government will get around to seeing that those rights are recognised". With regard to the use of force to evict the strikers, he "made no official or unofficial recommendation".[502] In the event, Murphy backed down. He had decided that he was not "going down in history as 'Bloody Murphy'".[503]

Later he argued that not to have backed down would have "precipitated labour conflict of the greatest magnitude for the entire nation".[504] Was this a realistic fear? It seems certain that a massacre in Flint in February 1937 would have provoked an unprecedented response from workers throughout the country and would have decisively changed the character of the class struggle. By retreating Murphy successfully contained the conflict.[505]

The union faced down the injunction by celebrating Women's Day with a demonstration of hundreds of women and children through the city. Mary Heaton Vorse, the veteran labour journalist, described how the Women's Emergency Brigade marched through the city before joining the picket line at Fisher No 1:

> Here they take part in one of the most amazing demonstrations this country has ever seen. Veterans in the labour movement insisted they had never seen anything like it. Six deep the pickets marched around and around the factory. The picket line enfolded the great plant. Thousands of people on the picket line. Thousands of strike sympathisers looking on. Thousands of singing men and women guarding the sit-down strikers from the threat of violent eviction... Not a policeman was in sight.

And as she pointed out, many guardsmen sympathised with the strikers.[506] With force not available, GM had no option but to negotiate. As Bob Travis whispered to Lewis during the negotiations, words that will warm the heart of every militant, "We've got 'em by the balls; squeeze a little".[507] One way that Lewis put the GM management on the defensive was by demanding to know which one of them had authorised the stationing of a Pinkerton detective outside his home. A last-minute attempt by the AFL to derail the proceedings was brushed aside by Lewis with contempt: Haile Selassie, the Emperor of Abyssinia, had more members in GM than the AFL.[508] On 11 February a six-month agreement was reached that recognised the UAW in the plants where it had struck, but, more important, gave the union the green light to organise throughout the company. The sit-down strikers left the plants in triumph, and when the National Guard was withdrawn from Flint, some of them left singing "Solidarity Forever".[509] The GM management were not reconciled to defeat; indeed the company lawyer promised Lewis that next time they would "give you the kind of whipping that you and your people will never forget".[510] And there followed months of guerrilla warfare on the shop floor across GM as the union contested management power—in the four months after the settlement there were 170 strikes, many of them short sit-downs.[511]

By February 1937 UAW membership in the industry had already increased to 88,000. By March it had risen to 166,000, by April to over 250,000 and by the middle of October to over 400,000. The CIO had won a decisive victory. By that same October CIO membership was some 4 million.

Chapter Nine

On the attack

The victory over GM inspired a working class revolt that was spearheaded by the sit-down strike. During 1937 there were 477 sit-down strikes lasting at least one day involving over 400,000 workers. In January there were 25 sit-downs, in February 47, in March 170 (the peak month) and in April 58. Over 100 of the sit-downs involved AFL members. And, of course, there were a great many more sit-downs that lasted less than a day before the employer gave in.[512] As Len De Caux recalled:

> Workers everywhere—AFL, CIO and unorganised—began sitting down. Early in 1937, sit-downs were pulled by hosiery, shoe, hotel, restaurant, steel, transport, tobacco workers; by seamen, shipbuilders, clerks, printers, pressmen, janitors, electricians; by Woolworth store girls, rag weavers, watchmakers, garbage collectors; by Postal and Western Union messengers, farmhands, bed makers, food packers, movie operators, gravediggers...[513]

In Chicago there was "a frenzy of union organising" with sit-down strikes of varying length in some 60 firms in the first two weeks of March.[514] There was even a sit-down strike at Joliet prison. Seamen on 11 ships of the Great Lakes Transit Company sat down in support of a wage demand. The police were reported as having "tried to come aboard one boat in south Chicago but the captain and his crew manned the fire hose and kept the slimy strikebreakers on the dock until they finally went away".[515] Women sat down in a Chicago meatpacking plant following an accident in which one of them lost her fingers. According to CPer Stella Nowicki, "We just stopped working right inside the building, protesting the speed and the unsafe conditions".[516]

In Gillespie, Illinois, 450 coal miners staged a stay-down strike, 360 feet below ground.[517] Sit-down strikes were widespread in maritime shipping with, according to one account, "probably hundreds of individual shipboard strikes against shipping companies opposed to independent union action". The *Los Angeles Times* proclaimed "Guerrilla War at Sea".[518] The city of Milwaukee, Wisconsin, had more than 20 sit-down strikes. Over 1,000 hotel workers sat down in or walked out of 19 hotels in a dispute that lasted seven hours before management gave in. At the Rhea Manufacturing plant some 900 clothing workers, overwhelmingly women, occupied:

> Four floors were occupied and connected with two-way radios. A dance contest took place and women on the fourth floor lowered ropes to the ground where friends and relatives attached boxes of food and blankets for the sit-downers. Children came to say goodnight to their mothers. A reporter from the *Milwaukee Leader* wrote "it is hard to know if the Rhea sit-down was a strike or a workers' holiday".

The company surrendered after 17 hours. A few days later workers in the same building employed by another clothing firm, the Belin Garment Company, occupied; they took over at 9am and the firm had capitulated by 4.30pm. The longest sit-down in Milwaukee began on 26 June when 130 members of the United Electrical Workers (UE) occupied the Solar Battery Company, demanding a closed shop and a pay rise.[519] The sit-down lasted 23 days before the company gave in. In Albert Lea, Minnesota, Woolworth workers occupied the store on 18 March and the next day workers at the American Gas Machine company's two plants in the city also sat down. What was distinctive about this struggle was that they were all members of the syndicalist Independent Union of All Workers (IUAW), which had been established at the Hormel meat-packing plant in nearby Austin in 1933. The workers decided to bow to a court injunction and evacuate the store and the two factories on 2 April. They set up picket lines to continue the fight, but once they had evacuated the police cracked down. They attacked the picket lines, destroyed the IUAW headquarters and arrested 62 union members. Once news of this assault reached the Hormel plant in Austin:

> at least 400 men put aside their tools and walked out. They stopped at their homes to pick up assorted weapons and then drove in a caravan

to Albert Lea. There they marched down the main street to the jail and demanded that all the prisoners be released.

They were in the process of breaking into the jail when Governor Elmer Benson intervened and ordered the release of the prisoners. From the jail they marched on the nearest American Gas plant and evicted and disarmed the special deputies guarding it. Once again Benson intervened and the company backed down, although the settlement included a condition that the IUAW should join the CIO. Even the CIO was preferable to a syndicalist union![520]

The longest sit-down anywhere in the country involved UE members working at Emerson Electric in St Louis. Inspired by the victory at GM, they occupied on 8 March, led by CPer William Sentner. The strike galvanised the whole St Louis working class, with the Emerson workers actively trying to spread the strike to other plants. Following the firing of union activists at the Century plant, Emerson workers were prominent in the 1,500-strong picket that shut the place down. The Emerson occupation lasted 53 days.[521]

Not every sit-down ended in success. The occupation of the Hershey chocolate factory in Hershey, Pennsylvania, on 2 April was broken after five days when vigilantes stormed the plant. The workers were kicked and beaten when they left the plant.[522] Some 300 workers who occupied the Fansteel Metallurgical plant in Chicago on 17 February barricaded themselves on the second and third floors. The police used a battering ram in an attempt to break into the plant, but were forced to retreat when acid was poured over them. They finally succeeded in driving the workers out when they mounted a siege tower on a truck so they could fire vomiting gas through the second floor windows. The police attacked early in the morning and "hurled hundreds of gas shells through the windows". The strikers "fought back with nuts, bolts and pieces of scrap iron", but after two hours "they began to stagger out, sick and retching". Twenty three of the strikers were given prison sentences, with the CIO organisers, Oakley Mills and Marty Adelman, receiving 180 days and 240 days respectively.[523]

One other episode is worth noting here: the occupation of the Maytag washing machine factory in Newton, Iowa, on 23 June 1938. The workers, members of the UE, had been locked out over a 20 percent wage cut and the company attempted to break their resistance with a Back to Work march. To the delight of the management the tactic seemed to have worked with large numbers of workers, including some of the union leaders, coming in through the gates. They proceeded to occupy the plant with the letters CIO being painted on the water tower.[524]

The Detroit crucible

Though the sit-down offensive was nationwide, it was centred on Detroit. As Steve Babson points out, in Detroit the victory over GM "had an electrifying effect":

> [It] excited debate among workers in a wide range of industries. "Little by little we were getting information", recalled Estelle Gornie, a machine operator in one of Detroit's largest cigar factories. "And we sat down; we can also do it... So we decided on a certain day, a certain hour. And we sat down... We got rid of the manager and took the factory over." Estelle and her militant co-workers at General Cigar were not alone as they fortified their plant against possible counter-attack. By February 20, 1937, little more than a week after the end of the GM sit-down, 2,000 women cigar makers had occupied Detroit's five largest cigar plants. They were soon joined by thousands of others in every major Detroit industry.

In February and March in Detroit some 35,000 workers sat down in "nearly 130 factories, offices and stores...constituting a virtual 'rolling' general strike".[525]

The revolt of the women cigar workers, overwhelmingly Polish-American, was prompted by longstanding grievances that were compounded by victimisation. In mid-February women workers who had occupied the Webster Eisenlohr plant approached the UAW for help. They were advised to go to the AFL cigar makers' union, which had already turned them away, so they sat down in the UAW offices and refused to leave. Stanley Nowak was sent to help them organise. Within six hours "the necessary committees were elected to conduct strike affairs and formulate demands, to provide sleeping accommodations, to see to the care of strikers' children, to establish a kitchen, and set up strike headquarters in the Polish Club". When the news of the sit-down spread, workers occupied the other Detroit cigar making plants and demanded UAW assistance.[526] The union was deluged with requests for assistance. Henry Kraus recalled meeting a group of workers from a sausage-pickling factory who demanded UAW help. He told them to go to the Amalgamated Meat Packers Union, but they refused to have anything to do with an AFL union. Their spokesman asked him, "Couldn't you send somebody down at least to show us how to get started? There are 500 of us sitting down..."[527] On another occasion Nowak was sent to an American Aluminum Company plant where the workers had occupied. He asked them if they had elected a strike committee and the reply was, "Is that what we're supposed to do?" How had they occupied without any organisation? One of the workers told him that "we've all been talking about it...we figured if others can do that, we can too".[528]

On 17 February George Edwards, a former student activist, one of the leaders of the Kelsey-Hayes sit-down and now a UAW organiser, wrote enthusiastically to his sympathetic parents:

> We are riding the crest of the greatest labour upsurge I have ever dreamed about in this country. Today in Detroit there are no less than a dozen sit-down strikes in three auto plants, three in cigar factories, two in bakeries, two in meat-packing houses—and all of them want to join the UAW. That, of course, they can't, but we are free to help organise them. It is work—but it is certainly thrilling work for we are winning every hand.[529]

The UAW organised "flying squadrons" to reinforce picket lines throughout the city, providing assistance for workers in every trade, determined to make the once open-shop city of Detroit a "union town". The appearance of the UAW flying squadron meant that "the police would have more than they could handle if they used force" and that "the union was going to win".[530]

On 27 February staff at Woolworth's downtown store in Detroit, overwhelmingly young women, many of them teenagers, staged a sit-down strike, evicting the management and barricading themselves in. The company refused to negotiate until staff at another Detroit Woolworth's occupied. They won a 5 cents an hour pay rise, union recognition and half pay for the duration of the occupations when management surrendered on 6 March. Two days later the victorious strikers celebrated with a dance at the Barlum Hotel, where the staff promptly occupied, winning a substantial pay rise. The Detroit Woolworth's occupations inspired shop workers in New York where on 14 March 12 stores were occupied. Woolworth refused to negotiate and police evicted the women. After they were released on bail they reoccupied the stores, were once again evicted and once again, after being released on bail, promptly reoccupied. With public opinion behind the strikers, the company finally gave in and the women won union recognition and a 10 percent pay rise.[531]

The most important struggle in this working class offensive, however, was the occupation of the giant Chrysler Corporation's car plants that began on 8 March. At 1.30pm in a carefully planned and well-organised operation workers seized all nine Chrysler plants. On 11 March, when the company announced that all the strikers had "terminated their employment", the workers responded by occupying the corporation's Detroit headquarters, evicting company executives in the process. Chrysler secured a court injunction, ordering the evacuation of the plants on 15 March, but the UAW once again mobilised for battle and the authorities backed down. The workers set up a committee to go through the company's espionage files. They found that the management had "systematically recorded the activities of every key union activist, citing what time he went to the toilet, how long he stayed, what he said, how many times he was absent or came late to work, whether he passed out union literature and if so what kind, and so on".[532] Later revelations of Chrysler's spying operations were to reveal that the best friend of Richard Frankensteen, one of the union leaders in the Dodge plant, was a spy. They regularly socialised together, went on family holidays together and their children played together. But John Andrews was a Corporations Auxiliary spy and had been providing daily reports on Frankensteen since they had first met for $40 a month.[533] The union issued a warning that spies would not be tolerated and that Pat Quinn, the union head of security in the Dodge plant, was a former Irish Republican Army officer, a veteran of the Irish War of Independence, and "knows just how to deal with traitors".[534]

Elsewhere in the city, however, the police did act. On 20 March over 300 police stormed the Bernard Schwartz cigar factory. They fought it out with "30 women armed with heavy wooden cigar molds... the vastly outnumbered women retreated floor by floor to the roof" where they surrendered. Outside the factory hundreds of supporters, including many car workers, fought with the police. At the same time police threw strikers out of Newton Packing and a number of shoe shops that had been occupied. This police action, countenanced by Murphy, provoked outrage and was widely seen as preparing the way for a police assault on the Chrysler sit-down strikers.

There was a determination to mobilise the entire Detroit labour movement to resist this repression and a protest demonstration was called for 23 March. By now the CIO leadership was trying to rein in the militancy. The sit-down strikes had been necessary to force the employers to deal with the unions, but now the concern was to show that the unions were "responsible" partners and could actually control their members and curb militancy. Adolph Germer of the CIO warned strongly against the 23 March demonstration, telling Wyndham Mortimer that it would result in another Haymarket massacre. The demonstration went ahead with over 100,000 people filling Cadillac Square to hear calls for a general strike if the police action continued.[535] Soon afterwards Governor Murphy sold his Chrysler shares.

The CIO leadership got their way at Chrysler, however. In the face of considerable opposition, they persuaded the workers to evacuate the plants on 25 March with the promise that they would not reopen while negotiations took place. At the giant Dodge plant the recommendation to evacuate had to be put to the vote five times before the leadership got their way. While he was determined to rein in militancy, Lewis was still prepared to be brutal during negotiations. He called the president of the Chrysler Corporation "a son of a bitch" to his face at one point and threatened "to come round this table and wipe that silly smile right off your face".[536] Lewis finally concluded "a GM-style agreement" with Chrysler on 6 April.[537]

Looking back at these months, Sidney Lens, at the time a member of the small Trotskyist sect the Revolutionary Workers League, remembered that "the militancy of the workers in those days was quite an experience". He remembered a sit-down at a sheet metal works where the police prepared to evict the strikers by force. The strikers threatened to tip the sheet metal on them if they invaded the factory and when "they actually began to move the big overhead crane, the police withdrew". Lens chronicles the gap that was opening up between the CIO leadership and the militants. After the GM victory Lewis's strategy was to tell employers, "Give me recognition and I'll stop irresponsibility." Decisive for Lens was the Yale and Towne Lock Company sit-down in Detroit that began on 9 March. Here the strikers refused to evacuate the plant despite an offer to keep it closed while negotiations took place. On 15 April the police moved in:

> During the ejection...the police beat up quite a few young girls who were sitting in. Tear gas was all over the place. Spontaneously workers from Kelsey-Hayes Wheel Company, Babcock and Bartell and many other plants came to protect the women and free Walter Reuther from the paddy wagon... The UAW sound truck, singing an entirely different tune from that played during the victory in Flint, now told the men to go back to their jobs or to the union headquarters; the whole matter would be settled "peacefully". When more than half the men had gone the police surrounded the sound truck and destroyed it. Another attack against the decimated crowd led to the complete abandonment of the plan to put the girls back into the plant.[538]

George Edwards, who was inside the plant at the time, remembered how the police "fired dozens of rounds of tear gas shells into it and arrested all the people who were there, including me". He got 30 days in jail.[539]

By now Lewis was assuring employers that "a CIO contract is adequate protection for any employer against sit-downs, lie-downs, or any other kind of strikes".[540] Militancy might be necessary if employers refused to recognise the unions, but if they were reasonable then the CIO would collaborate as a responsible partner and they could avoid trouble. As far as he was concerned this strategy was triumphantly vindicated when, only a week after the GM victory, US Steel, long a bastion of the open-shop, recognised the Steel Workers Organizing Committee (SWOC) without a fight. This success was achieved, as we shall see in the next chapter, by a campaign that very deliberately excluded any rank and file initiative. As far as US Steel was concerned, resisting the union might well provoke its workers into full-scale rebellion, whereas Lewis promised that SWOC would be a defence against militancy. Certainly for an important section of the capitalist class, the trade union leadership, both AFL and CIO, was coming to be seen as a necessary defence against shop-floor radicalism. This was without any doubt one of the reasons why, against all expectations, the Supreme

Court upheld the Wagner Act on 12 April 1937; the alternative was escalating class war.[541]

One last episode is worth recounting as a demonstration of the tremendous potential of working class action. In the Michigan state capital, Lansing, the UAW had successfully established a stronghold at the Reo car plant, an independent producer employing some 2,500 men. Here a month long sit-down strike in March had forced the company to recognise the union and from this base UAW Local 182 had proceeded to organise the other car plants in the city, Oldsmobile, Fisher Body and others. By May the local had a membership of over 15,000 workers. They also adopted a policy of positive solidarity, providing support for any workers in struggle. One dispute took place at the small Capital City Wrecking Company where some 20 workers walked out following the sacking of union activists. The UAW provided support on the picket line and ignored a court injunction prohibiting picketing. Rather than confront the union on the picket line, the police raided a number of union activists' homes at 2am on 7 June, arresting eight people. Among the homes raided was that of Local 182's leader, Lester Washburn. He was on his way back from union business in Detroit at the time, so they arrested his wife. He arrived back home at 2.30am to find his three small children on their own. By 3.30am he had contacted the union leadership in every plant and they had agreed to call a one day general strike, to declare a "labour holiday". At the shift changeover that morning union officers and activists were on the gate at every plant calling the workers out in protest against the raids. They were, a union statement said, holding a "labour holiday" to celebrate the bravery of Sheriff Allan MacDonald "in dragging a harmless and innocent woman out of bed in the middle of the night and leaving alone in the house her three small children".

In the course of the morning thousands of UAW members and sympathisers took to the streets. In the words of the historians of the "labour holiday", they:

> seized virtual control of downtown Lansing. They forced the closing of stores, factories, and theatres; halted all traffic and even picketed police headquarters, the city hall, and the state capitol. The police force was completely immobilised while the workers paraded the streets, their numbers growing each minute as more workers emerged from the

closed stores and factories. Some sang "Solidarity Forever", while others carried clubs, sticks and two-by-fours. By early afternoon, just about everything that could be closed was closed.

In the face of threats to storm the jail, Governor Murphy ordered the release of the prisoners and the Capital City Wrecking Company agreed to recognise the union and reinstate the victimised militants.[542]

Ford next!

After the victories over General Motors and Chrysler the UAW slogan was "Ford next!" But Henry Ford's private police state was to prove an altogether tougher proposition.

On 26 May 1937 the UAW organised a mass distribution of leaflets at the River Rouge plant in Dearborn. The union got a permit for the leafleting, invited a large contingent of observers to deter violence, and saw to it that the great majority of the volunteers handing the leaflets out were from the union's Women's Auxiliary. Walter Reuther, Richard Frankensteen and other union officers were there, watching from the overpass. Here they were attacked by some 50 men from Ford's Service Department, punched to the ground, kicked, stamped on and thrown down the steps. Reuther was knocked to the ground and then picked up bodily and bounced off the concrete "about eight different times". He later recalled how his attackers "kicked me in the face, head and other parts of my body". While this attack was under way, the men and women handing out the leaflets were also attacked. Women were punched and kicked. One observer, the Reverend Raymond Sanford, saw a young woman kicked in the stomach by one of the Ford men while a policeman watched.[543] William Merriweather, one of the union men handing out leaflets, was beaten so badly that it was thought his attackers had killed him; his back had been broken and he suffered serious internal injuries. Another activist, Tony Marinovitch, had his skull fractured by the Ford men, and Ralph Dunham was so severely beaten he was hospitalised for two weeks. Another union man, Alvin Stickles, was actually captured by the Ford men, dragged into the plant and beaten up in a Service Department office before being released. When Bill McKie, a veteran British communist now in the American CP, protested that they had a permit to leaflet, he was told, "That don't mean a damn here".[544] The violence was, as Robert Lacey, the biographer of the Ford Company, puts it, "unashamed, exuberant almost".[545]

The UAW leadership had believed that the presence of observers would deter violence, but the Ford strategy, masterminded by Harry Bennett, was to intimidate its workers by the very public display of the company's capacity for violence and the impunity with which they could carry it out. The "Battle of the Overpass", as it became known in union lore, was intended to show Ford workers that the company was a law unto itself, that police and courts actually acquiesced in its brutality. While GM and Chrysler might have been overwhelmed by the working class revolt, Henry Ford was determined to fight it out, and he had put his Service Department chief, Harry Bennett, in charge of seeing off the challenge.

Ford had earlier established a reputation as a paternalistic employer. Before the First World War he had famously introduced the "Five Dollar Day" in his plants, earning considerable praise from social reformers. This reputation had always been fraudulent, however. The Five Dollar Day had been introduced to reduce a ruinous monthly labour turnover rate of between 40 percent and 60 percent produced by appalling working conditions, and to see off a challenge from the IWW that was trying to establish itself in Detroit. Even this paternalist veneer was to be abandoned in the 1920s. The company's industrial relations were to become increasingly repressive, developing into a fully-fledged industrial police state in the 1930s. While this embrace of repression was getting under way, Henry Ford also discovered anti-Semitism.

In the early 1920s Ford was to become an enthusiastic champion of the Protocols of Zion and an international publicist of the threat that international Jewry posed to white civilisation. In the summer of 1923 he told a journalist, "You probably think the labour unions were organised by labour. But they weren't. They were organised by Jewish financiers." He earned the admiration and praise of fellow anti-Semite Adolf Hitler who told the *Chicago Tribune* in March 1923 that he regarded "Heinrich Ford" as "the leader of the growing fascist movement in America". He particularly admired Ford's "anti-Jewish policy... We have just had his anti-Jewish articles translated and published." Hitler praised Ford in *Mein Kampf* and had a picture of the great man on the wall of his private office.[546]

The vehicle for Ford's anti-Semitism was the *Dearborn Independent*, a weekly newspaper that he had bought in 1919 and that was to achieve a national circulation in the 1920s of over half a million. In May 1920 the paper carried the first of many anti-Semitic articles, "The International Jew: The World's Problem". Over succeeding weeks and months the paper exposed the Jewish financiers who were responsible for the assassination of Abraham Lincoln, condemned jazz as a Jewish attack on morality in America, warned of a Jewish plot to inoculate white families with syphilis and much more. Many of the paper's anti-Semitic diatribes were published in book form later that year and this was followed in 1921 and 1922 by three more volumes collecting later articles. The first of these volumes, *The International Jew*, was to become one of the most important and pernicious anti-Semitic tracts of the 20th century. In the 1920s it was translated into 16 languages and by the end of 1922 had gone through six editions in Germany, where it was a staple of the Nazi movement.

Although Ford was to retreat from his public advocacy of anti-Semitism in 1927 and even apologise for it, he remained an anti-Semite. He continued to covertly support the activities of American anti-Semites, employing Fritz Kuhn, the leader of the German-American Bund, a pro-Nazi organisation, as a chemist and financing Gerald Smith's anti-Semitic propaganda campaigns. On his 75th birthday, 30 July 1938, he received personal congratulations from Adolf Hitler, who awarded him the Grand Service Cross of the Supreme Order of the German Eagle (other recipients were to include Mussolini, Admiral Horthy, General Franco, Monsignor Josef Tiso, Charles Lindbergh and a GM executive, James Mooney). Copies of *The International Jew*, imported from Nazi Germany, were widely circulated on the far right in the late 1930s, and Ford ignored repeated requests to repudiate the book. When the Second World War broke out, Ford blamed it on "international Jewish bankers".[547] On 26 June 1940 there was a private party at the Waldorf Astoria hotel in New York to celebrate the Nazi victory over France. Among the guests were James Mooney of GM and Henry Ford's son, Edsel.[548]

While Ford's plant in Germany[549] could rely on the Nazis to deal with the trade unions, in the US the company had to confront the UAW on its own. Under Harry Bennett the Service Department had grown into a sizeable private army that imposed a reign of terror both inside and outside of Ford plants. According to the historian Stephen Norwood, Ford had "the world's largest and most formidable private army".[550] At its height the Service Department had some 3,000 full-time members, ready to keep the workforce in line and see off outsiders. Bennett was a member of the State Prison Commission and had prisoners parolled to the Service Department. He combined this public service with close connections with organised crime in Detroit and New York. And, of course, he had very good relations with the FBI with whom he shared intelligence about the left.

As well as its army of heavies, the company operated an extensive spy network with perhaps one in ten of the 90,000 workers at River Rouge, whether willingly or coerced, informing on the rest. The labour journalist Benjamin Stolberg wrote that:

the fear in the plant is something indescribable. During the lunch hour men shout at the top of their voices about the baseball scores lest they be suspected of talking unionism. Workers seen talking together are taken off the assembly line by Servicemen and fired. Every man suspected of union sympathies is immediately discharged, usually upon the framed-up charge of "starting a fight", in which he often gets beaten up.

Stolberg quotes a National Labor Relations Board decision of 2 December 1937 that described the River Rouge plant as having "taken on many aspects of a community in which martial law has been declared".[551]

According to Ralph Rimar, a former senior member of the Service Department who had worked for what he described as Ford's "Gestapo" for ten years, in the Ford empire "there was no liberty, no free speech, no human dignity... To those who have never lived under a dictatorship, it is difficult to convey the sense of fear which is part of the Ford system." He described how:

Our spy network covered Dearborn and the city of Detroit, reaching into the home of every worker and into the private offices of the highest state and city officials. Years of espionage had provided the company with accumulated files of all the activities of every Ford worker... My own agents reported back to me conversations in grocery stores, meat markets, restaurants, gambling joints, beer gardens, social groups, boys' clubs, and even churches. Women waiting in markets to buy something might discuss their husbands' jobs and activities; if they did, I soon knew what they had said... Nick Torres, one of our Servicemen, was boxing instructor at a boys' club in Dearborn. His information helped me secure the dismissal of many men...

Rimar estimated that over the years he had been responsible for the firing of over 1,500 men for suspected union sympathies.[552] Between 1937 and 1941 the company was to sack over 4,000 men for suspected union sympathies.

Even after the Battle of the Overpass the UAW continued to attempt to leaflet the River Rouge plant with a catalogue of beatings and arrests. On 8 December there were 60 arrests, on 16 December 208 arrests, and on 21 January 1938 there were 352. Bennett responded with an attempt to have Walter Reuther killed. On 8 April 1938 two gunmen tried to kidnap him from his home, but they interrupted a birthday party and were driven off by the guests.[553] The organising effort continued, however, with the UAW actually setting up its own radio department which recorded sketches and plays that were broadcast on community and commercial radio stations. Upton Sinclair's novel about Henry Ford, *The Flivver King*, was broadcast in both English and Polish.[554] But the UAW was unable to break the River Rouge.

Elsewhere the violence unleashed by the Ford Company was even more excessive than in Detroit. In Dallas, Texas, a mass meeting of the Ford plant workforce was called at which a company executive warned them of the consequences of siding with John L Lewis: "If it takes bloodshed, we'll shed blood right down to the last drop." The Dallas plant set up an "outside squad" which, with the help of the police, dealt with union organisers and sympathisers across the city. On 10 July 1937, in broad daylight, a lawyer representing the UAW, W J Houston, was brutally beaten and knocked to the ground, with his attackers jumping on his prone body. After a week in hospital he left the city. The Ford men behaved with complete impunity. In his account of the activities of the Dallas outside squad, historian George Green details a series of horrific assaults over the summer and autumn of 1937:

> the whipping and kicking of an auto worker from Kansas City, who was not a member of any union, the slugging into unconsciousness (and whipping with a cat-o'-nine-tails) of a former auto worker from Kansas City who applied for a job at Dallas Ford, and the beating of

three tourists from California at the fair ground parking lot because of a CIO sticker on their car... On 9 August the outside squad was tipped off by the Dallas police that an American Federation of Labor organiser was attempting to unionise the local millinery industry. Veteran organiser George Baer was assaulted in daylight and his face was repeatedly smashed with blackjacks until most of his teeth were missing and an eye was knocked out of its socket. Dumped into a field, he later crawled to a highway and a passing motorist took him to hospital. He lost the teeth and the sight of one eye.[555]

Baer was lucky to be alive. His attackers were convinced they had killed him and had left him for dead. The injuries he suffered "made an old man out of a vigorous young man".[556] As Keith Sward observes, the methods of the Dallas outside squad "approached a degree of savagery that was extreme even for Ford Service".[557]

The UAW sent Norman Smith as its organiser to Memphis, Tennessee. In early September 1937 he was brutally beaten by men armed with battery cables and coke bottles. Smith refused to be intimidated, but Ford workers understandably kept well away from him. But this was not enough for Ford. On 5 October he was once again attacked. He was beaten with pistol butts and a hammer and was left half dead with a fractured skull. The UAW withdrew him from the city before he was killed and closed its Memphis office.[558] The support that the authorities gave to Ford in keeping the UAW out was clearly demonstrated in Kansas City. Here a union man was jailed for being in possession of a slingshot while the district attorney decided not to prosecute the 25-strong outside squad who had been stopped by the police in possession of 14 revolvers, 12 shotguns and 60 other assorted weapons.[559] For the time being Ford's methods worked and the UAW was kept out.

Despite this catalogue of violence, on 27 April 1938, to the horror of trade unionists throughout the country, Roosevelt had a two-hour luncheon meeting with Henry Ford. The purpose seems to have been some sort of gesture of goodwill to US big business. According to Harry Bennett, Ford absolutely "hated Roosevelt" and Ford's private secretary, Ernest Liebold, has recorded Ford's delight when he believed he had discovered Roosevelt's Jewish ancestry. For his part, Roosevelt told Ford that his mother was particularly pleased they were meeting and that she regarded him as "a great man...a good man". Ford told the president that he believed there were Wall Street financiers behind "much of the labour strife so prevalent in the country", although he restrained himself from mentioning the Jews. He praised Vice-President Garner. The administration was not going to put any pressure on Ford on behalf of the CIO.[560]

Communists and the unions

When Roosevelt had been elected president in 1932, the CP had still been faithfully following the Comintern's Third Period line. This involved a ferocious hostility to the rest of the left. As for the AFL, in March 1930 a cable from the Comintern patiently explained to its American disciples that the unions were "PLAINLY FASCIST" and there-after the AFL was routinely referred to as "the fascist American Federation of Labor". John L Lewis was inevitably a "fascist", while Sidney Hillman was a "fascist gangster".[561] The election of Roosevelt was seen as a step along the road to fascism. The *Daily Worker* denounced him as a "Wall Street lackey" and Earl Browder, the CP general secretary, condemned the New Deal as "the same as Hitler's programme... hunger, fascization and imperialist war".[562] The Wagner Act was condemned as "the most dangerous strikebreaking instrument yet devised by the Roosevelt regime" and as a "tentative move toward Hitler's goal of illegalising all strikes". It was part of "the process of fascization in the United States".[563]

This all changed with the Comintern's "Popular Front" turn in the mid-1930s. The threat of fascism in Europe and Stalin's desire to position himself as an ally to Britain and France against Germany meant an abrupt shift from the utter sectarianism of the Third Period to its polar opposite. Communists were to work with any and all "progressive forces". The Roosevelt administration changed overnight from preparing the way for fascism into a bastion against fascism. Indeed, in March 1936 Earl Browder was summoned to Moscow to be told that the Comintern wanted the party to support Roosevelt in that year's presidential election. In an interesting demonstration of Stalinist dialectics, Browder convinced the Comintern that if the CP supported Roosevelt it would cost him millions of votes. The best way the CP could assist his re-election was to stand a candidate but only to campaign against the Republicans. The party's nominating convention at Madison Square Garden had bands playing "Yankee Doodle" and the slogan "Communism is Twentieth Century Americanism" displayed everywhere.[564] The party's manifesto was "clearly reformist", and, in effect, the CP campaigned for the New Deal and against the Republicans. Browder's strategy was, as his biographer points out, "to make the Communists a small but vociferous part of the New Deal coalition". He "endorsed the New Deal as the Popular Front's specifically American form".[565] It is important to note, however, that this turn was not a response to changing circumstances in the US, but to the changing priorities of Russian foreign policy. So when, in August 1939, the Soviet Union allied with Nazi Germany, the turn was abandoned overnight. The politics of the Popular Front will be examined further in the next chapter.

The Communist Party's Popular Front turn had inevitable consequences for its industrial work. The party gave up the Third Period policy of setting up revolutionary trade unions in favour of building rank and file organisations inside the AFL unions. This commitment to rank and file organisation was short-lived, however. While many party members remained among the best rank and file militants, the CP leadership increasingly looked to an alliance with the leadership of the CIO. As we have already seen, as early as November 1936 Browder had a secret meeting with John Brophy, the CIO director, where an agreement was reached for the party to provide organisers, particularly for the campaign to organise steel. According to William Z Foster, "Lewis, Hillman, the Communists, and other progressives" formed a "left-centre bloc…a working alliance". As part of its contribution, out of the 200 full-time organisers in steel, "some 60 were party members". Steel, Foster writes, became the party's "first order of business" with Bill Gebert designated as "the party's liaison with the SWOC". There was an expectation of a great historic struggle in steel that would radicalise SWOC, but that was not to materialise. Instead the CP was to find itself actively collaborating in the top-down organisation of steel on the trade union bureaucracy's terms, and this was to involve acquiescing in the determined exclusion of any rank and file initiative.[566]

As the Popular Front turn developed, the CP increasingly began to direct its efforts to securing positions in the trade union bureaucracy.

This aspect of the Popular Front turn has been neglected in the literature on the history of the CP. It was very much an international phenomenon, with the British Communist Party, for example, taking a similar direction in its trade union work. The building of a bureaucratic left in the unions became the party's objective and to achieve this party members, when and where necessary, hid their political affiliations. This was a strategic change of direction of tremendous significance. In 1938-39 the party disbanded its union fractions and closed down its shop papers, in part as a gesture of good faith to the CIO leadership. Equally important, however, is that the fractions were becoming an embarrassment for the party's own union officials as the defence of the interests of the shop floor inevitably came into conflict with the imperatives of bureaucratic politics. One consequence of disbanding union fractions was that it removed Communist union officials from the influence of rank and file party members on the shop floor. The struggle on the shop floor was increasingly subordinated to the bureaucratic politics of "the left-centre bloc". The dangers this involved were nowhere better demonstrated than in the UAW.

As early as the Chrysler sit-down strike, when local party members opposed the UAW leadership's decision to evacuate the plants while negotiations continued, Browder intervened to set them straight. "We are", he told them, "a fully responsible party, and our subdivisions and fractions do not independently take actions which threaten to change our whole national relationship with a great and growing mass movement".[567] What he meant, of course, was that the militancy of the party members in the car factories could not be allowed to compromise the party's relations with the CIO leadership. Another dramatic demonstration of this tension between rank and file and bureaucratic concerns was to be provided in November 1937 when the night-shift at the Fisher Body plant in Pontiac staged a sit-down strike in protest against management failure to honour agreements. GM responded by sacking four leading militants, whereupon the workers "again occupied the Fisher Body plant, welded shut the gates and moved in blankets and food". Other GM plants in Pontiac came out in sympathy. Both Communist Party and Socialist Party members were involved in leading the strike, which had the support of Walter Reuther, Wyndham Mortimer and William Weinstone, the Michigan CP leader.

To begin with the *Daily Worker* supported the strikers. The CIO leadership, however, demanded that the strike be brought to an end. Rather than fall out with their allies in the bureaucracy, the CP leadership insisted that party members in Pontiac come out and condemn the strike they were helping to lead. On 2 December the *Daily Worker* carried a statement by Weinstone declaring "unequivocally and emphatically that the Communists and the Communist Party had never in the past and do not now in any shape, manner or form advocate or support unauthorised and wildcat action and regard such strikes as gravely injurious to the union's welfare".[568] The result was disaster. The strikers returned to work defeated, the four men remained sacked, the UAW suspended the leadership of the Pontiac local, and union membership in the Pontiac plants collapsed. Browder subsequently removed Weinstone from the leadership of the Michigan CP for compromising the party's relations with the CIO leadership.[569] Communist policy towards the CIO leadership at this time has been summed up by one historian as a policy of appeasement.[570]

Even more telling in a way were developments at the UAW convention in March 1939. Here the left candidate, George Addes, was assured of victory in the election for union president, with Mortimer as first vice-president. But it was not to be. Party members at the convention were confronted with a deal that had been struck by Browder and Sidney Hillman of the CIO whereby the CP would support R J Thomas, the CIO leadership's moderate candidate for the presidency, and, moreover, support the abolition of the post of vice-president, even though this was explicitly aimed at removing Mortimer from the union leadership. This was never so much as discussed with party members working in the car industry. Browder actually attended the convention to make sure they toed the line. As one veteran party member, Al Richmond, later put it:

> There was no prior consultation with Communist auto workers, who were most intimately acquainted with conditions in the union and the industry. They did not participate in making the decision although the burden of implementing it would be theirs, they would have to live with its direct consequences and would be held accountable for them by their fellow workers. The growing consideration was the Left-Centre Bloc at the top, or more specifically the relationship with Hillman and Murray.

FIGHTING BACK

As far as Richmond was concerned, the party line in industry increasingly involved "a rape of principle by tactic".[571] Such concerns were, however, soon to be overtaken by the problems that the Hitler-Stalin Pact and later the Second World War posed for the Communist Party.

Chapter Ten

The battle for steel

For John L Lewis the central strategic objective of the CIO was organising the steel industry. Breaking the resistance of the historic bastion of the open shop would not only safeguard union organisation in the mines, but would also dramatically shift the balance of class forces in the US. He had long recognised that the Amalgamated Association of Iron, Steel and Tin Workers was not up to the job. Its leadership was incapable of leading a fight; indeed it regarded union militants as a more dangerous enemy than the employers. When thousands of workers had rallied to the union in 1934, eager to take on the steel companies, it had responded by expelling them. Now, through the agency of the CIO, Lewis proceeded to launch a new organising drive, intended to bring the steel companies to terms.

In June 1936 he had established the Steel Workers Organizing Committee (SWOC), which incorporated the Amalgamated Association but, in fact, was under the complete control of the UMW. Resources were poured into the organisation, a headquarters was established and 35 offices were opened throughout the steel districts. SWOC took on over 400 full-time and part-time staff, including some 60 Communist Party members and another 40 assorted radicals and socialists. Lewis appointed one of his most trusted lieutenants, Philip Murray, to head up the organisation. The limitations in the thinking of the SWOC leadership were made clear by the secretary-treasurer, David McDonald, a former UMW official, who emphasised the CIO's commitment to "the classical American economic system", to the "preservation of American business organisations" and its "continuing opposition to economic philosophies which seek to destroy the present economic system".[572] SWOC was no threat to the capitalist system.

The significance of UMW control was that they were determined to create a union in steel that was run along the lines of the UMW, an autocracy, a union dominated by the official leadership. They wanted a union with the bureaucracy in command rather than a rank and file driven union such as was created in the struggles in the car industry. As Len De Caux put it, "SWOC was as totalitarian as any big business".[573] Nevertheless, both Lewis and Murray recognised that the organisation of the steel industry required dedicated, courageous organisers, men and women who were ready to risk their lives if necessary, and who could speak to the concerns of the rank and file. For this they turned to the left, in particular to the Communist Party. Earl Browder enthusiastically embraced the opportunity. A veteran CPer, Bill Gebert became the liaison between SWOC and the party. The Communist Party had a large immigrant membership (1936 was the first year in which US born members became a majority of the party membership) and a stable of foreign language newspapers. This allowed its members to play a crucial role in organising among the thousands of immigrant workers—Lithuanians, Poles, Croats, Serbs, Slovenians, Ukrainians and Russians—who worked in the steel mills. The party was also to play a crucial part in winning black workers over.

The steel industry had a long history of successful strikebreaking going back to the Homestead lockout of 1892.[574] Indeed, less than 20 years earlier the steel companies had inflicted a crushing defeat on the AFL in the Great Strike of 1919, a bloody defeat in which 26 strikers had been killed. In the 1930s these same companies still maintained their private armies and operated extensive spy systems to keep their workers in subjection. According to Horace Davis, writing in 1933, "the spy system coupled with the blacklist" was the steel bosses' "most important weapon for retaining control". Although they might sometimes hire the services of private detective agencies, generally the steel companies relied on their own spy networks. US Steel, for example, according to Davis, "hires and pays its own spies and receives their reports". The US Steel spy apparatus was operated out of the company headquarters in the Carnegie Building in Pittsburgh, with a company executive, Charles Tuttle, in charge. Tuttle "maintained one of the best current libraries on labour and radical activities in the country... These publications are scanned for names which are carefully filed and indexed". US Steel, according to Davis, "makes special efforts to have officials of unions and political leaders on its payroll". As he presciently observed, however, "the effectiveness of the spy is not great enough to check a really widespread organisation move".[575]

The drive to organise steel promised to be a decisive struggle that would determine the future of the American working class. This had certainly been the case in 1919. As part of the Communist Party's contribution, William Z Foster, himself one of the leaders of the 1919 strike, published a number of pamphlets on organising in steel. These are classic guides to organising that still repay reading. In October 1936 he published *Organizing Methods in the Steel Industry*, a clearly written 24-page pamphlet that set out the strategy and tactics necessary to take on the steel giants. Foster insisted that in order to be successful:

> the organisation campaign must be based upon the principles of trade union democracy...every effort must be made to draw the widest possible ranks of the workers into the activities of the leading decisive committees, and also into the work of the organisers and the union generally. Only with such democracy, or systematic mass participation, can the great task of building the union be successfully accomplished.

Democracy was crucial. The steel workers "can only rely on themselves and the support they get from other workers", and while they should make use of politicians, "it would be the worst folly to rely on Roosevelt". Indeed, the coming struggle should be used to lay the foundation "for an eventual Farmer-Labor Party". More specifically, he went on to warn of the need to guard against company spies and advised that "in local situations of acute struggle" organisers and headquarters would need "organised protection". Mass meetings and demonstrations were "fundamental to the carrying on of a successful organisation campaign" and every effort "should be made to bring the maximum number of women and children to the steel mass meetings".

He detailed how different groups of workers should be approached. "Special efforts" had to be made to counter "anti-foreigner, anti-Negro and anti-Red tendencies" among "American whites". This meant being prepared to do active work in organisations like the American Legion. It was imperative to employ "special Negro organisers'". Black workers had to be involved in the union as officers and as organisers, and the union should also immediately launch "an active campaign against the prevalent Jim Crow practices in the steel towns and steel industry". The recruitment of foreign-born workers required "organisers speaking the principal foreign languages in the mills" and union literature had to be available in these languages. There had to be "systematic recruitment work in the many fraternal and other organisations that exist among this group of workers". Special attention should also be paid to young workers, with youth organisers appointed and youth committees set up. A Women's Auxiliary was essential and there "should be a corps of women organisers in the field". He advocated "flexible tactics" towards the company unions that the steel companies had established, with every effort being made to win them over, and incorporate them into the union. Attention should be paid to the churches with the union offering speakers to put the union case and sympathetic priests and preachers being invited to speak at mass meetings. Indeed, the union should even send "speakers into all organisations of professional and business people in order to break down as far as possible the opposition of these elements to the organisation of steel workers". This recognised that in many steel towns sections of the middle class, professionals and small businessmen, resented the domination of the steel companies. He urged that the union should make use of the radio, buying time to reach the workers in their homes. All this was in expectation of "a great strike...this perspective must be constantly borne in mind".[576]

Early in 1937 Foster followed this pamphlet up with another, *What Means A Strike In Steel*. This was clearly informed by the struggle that was going on at General Motors. As far as he was concerned the US was in a period of great mass struggles and a steel strike might well be the decisive conflict. Foster warned that they were "shaping up for the greatest labour struggle in American history, one that will involve unparalleled masses of striking workers, and probably several industries in the very heart of the industrial system". He still warned against trusting Roosevelt ("The government is allied with many great capitalist interests") and urged that united action by steel workers and coal miners was the way forward. This, he wrote, "appears to be the aim of the CIO and, if so, it is a sound strategy". Such a "joint strike...would constitute by far the greatest strike in American history". Wherever necessary workers should be prepared to launch local general strikes and he pointed to the examples set by San Francisco, Minneapolis and Terre Haute. "It may well be", he argued, "that the method of the stay-in strike will be applied to many steel plants in the event of a general strike call". Much depended on whether the GM sit-down was successful. As far as he was concerned, however, "the most important of all forms of mass strike activities is mass picketing. Good picketing is a decisive factor in every big strike." Absolutely crucial once again was "the development of a democratic strike leadership through national and local broad strike committees". AFL strikes were usually "managed by small and remote committees of bureaucratic officials", whereas "the best strike experience the world over" showed that broad strike committees that maximised rank and file involvement were the way to win. And "the democratisation of the strike leadership should start at the top".[577]

In her study of the Chicago labour movement, Elizabeth Cohen argues that Foster's *Organizing Methods in the Steel Industry* "became a blueprint for CIO policy".[578] This was only partly true, because the crucial importance he attached to union democracy and rank and file initiative was to be deliberately ignored. This was possible because Foster's perspective of a decisive class battle taking place in 1937 was not to be. Instead of the rank and file taking to the field, the union leaders were able to remain in control.

The American ruling class was divided over how to respond to the great working class revolt that was getting under way. While there were important sections of the capitalist class that favoured bloody repression, there were others who felt that confrontation was both too costly and too dangerous. Instead they looked to Lewis and the leadership of the CIO to control the workers and prevent the conflict getting out of hand. Walter Lippman, an influential establishment newspaper columnist, warned employers that the more:

> they treat Mr Lewis and the CIO leaders as public enemies to be resisted at all costs, the more impossible they make it for Mr Lewis to develop discipline and a sense of responsibility in the ranks of his young and inexperienced followers. The more they compel Mr Lewis to lead strikes to obtain recognition for organised labour, the more they compel him to depend on his most militant followers... I think it impressive and significant that in the automobile industry Mr Lewis and Mr Martin have tried as earnestly as they have tried to suppress unauthorised strikes.

Employers, he suggested, "will perhaps find it pleasanter to work with Mr Lewis than to fight him".[579] This would certainly involve unwelcome concessions, but many employers now recognised that with the emergence of the CIO the balance of class forces had begun to change. While these employers did not have a problem with union-busting and strikebreaking, they were beginning to conclude that the outcome of such struggles was increasingly uncertain. Once conflict was unleashed, neither the employers nor the union leadership could determine the forces that might become involved. Working class militancy and solidarity could trump the efforts of even the most powerful industrial giants. One management that was seriously considering recognising the union to avoid confrontation was that open-shop bastion US Steel.

The SWOC campaign was having considerable success. The union had intervened in the 1936 presidential election campaign, urging steel workers to vote for Roosevelt and defeat the steel bosses' candidate, Landon. When Roosevelt won, SWOC distributed 500,000 leaflets headed "STEEL WORKERS WIN", arguing that to complete the victory steel workers now had to "win in the mills, on the job".[580] By the end of December 1936 SWOC claimed to have 125,000 members organised in 150 lodges. While Roosevelt's victory was important, with many workers believing that the unions had a friend in the White House, many steel workers still held back. There was too much history of defeat and victimisation. What was to decisively turn the tide was the UAW victory at General Motors. One SWOC organiser actually reported men telling him, "Wait till you win the auto strike. Then we'll join." The CIO victory at GM had an equally powerful impact on US Steel's management.

The US Steel deal was concluded between John L Lewis and company chairman Myron Taylor on 1 March 1937. For the company the deal made sound business sense: after a dreadful recession it was now "earning substantial profits".[581] The company's output had fallen from 24.5 million tons in 1929 to only 5.5 million tons in 1932, but in 1936 it was back up to 18.9 million tons and in 1937 was to reach 20.7 million tons. A bitter, protracted strike would put all this at risk. The defeat of GM certainly demonstrated that the CIO was a force to be reckoned with. There was a real fear that the company would go down to defeat in a confrontation with SWOC. Lewis had shown that he was fully prepared to unleash rank and file militancy if he had to. Instead of risking confrontation, the company decided to accept Lewis's assurances that recognition, collective bargaining and a union contract would be a guarantee against militancy. This was to have momentous consequences. Certainly it involved a tremendous boost for both SWOC and the CIO, shifting the balance of class forces in the US. This had not been accomplished by rank and file struggle, however, but by a deal between management and union bureaucrats, a deal that was handed down from on high. The first US Steel workers knew of the negotiations was when the deal was announced. As Jack Metzgar puts it, for many steel workers, the union "was something that 'came in' from the outside, not something that rose indigenously from themselves".[582] The US Steel deal served to consolidate Murray's bureaucratic control over SWOC, whereas unleashing rank and file militancy might have threatened it. Foster's expectations of "the greatest labour struggle in American history" and its accompanying radicalisation, an absolutely realistic prospect if US Steel had resisted, never took place.

Aliquippa

The surrender of US Steel was followed by a rush of other smaller companies to conclude deals with SWOC. Within two months another 88 companies had signed up with the union. And steel workers rallied to the cause in growing numbers. In the week following the US Steel deal 35,000 workers joined the union. By May 1937 SWOC membership had risen to some 280,000.

While company after company surrendered without a fight, the union also won its first big strike victory over one of the most determinedly anti-union companies, Jones and Laughlin. The company had run the city of Aliquippa in Pennsylvania as a police state where all efforts at organising had been defeated by victimisation and beatings, with men run out of town. It operated an extensive spy system. The town's reputation was so bad that it was known in trade union circles as "Little Siberia". The architect of this tyranny was Tom Girdler, who described himself during his time at Jones and Laughlin, as "an unofficial caliph", "a sort of political boss" and boasted of running "a benevolent dictatorship". According to Girdler, the company policed the town "in our own way and we policed it well". Their intelligence was so good that they "knew who got off the train".[583] In Aliquippa workers were sacked for joining the Democratic Party, let alone the Communist Party. Union organisers were routinely run out of town and when one particularly obstinate individual, George Issoski, failed

FIGHTING BACK

to respond to arrest, beatings and death threats, the company had him "disappeared". Clint Golden had to go under cover in the town to discover that he had been secretly committed to a state mental hospital on the company's recommendation without even his family being informed. The union had to call on the help of the governor to secure his release.[584]

The man put in charge of organising Aliquippa in the aftermath of the US Steel deal was Joe Timko, an experienced UMW official, a veteran of the miners' struggle in Harlan County, Kentucky. Golden warned him that Aliquippa was "a dark town...a 100 percent company town... Fear hung over the place".[585] When Timko held his first meeting 18 steel workers turned up and within a fortnight 14 of them had been fired (they had between them worked for the company for 181 years). Timko took them on as organisers, and as more men were victimised he took them on as well, until he had a team of over 50 men working for the union. Just a year earlier the company's methods would have driven the union out, but now more and more workers were prepared to make a stand. With anger boiling to the surface, the union called a strike on 12 May. At 11pm, as the shift came off work, they were greeted by the cheers of thousands of men, women and children assembled outside. As Meyer Bernstein, a former student now working for Timko, recorded:

> Aliquippa rose up against a tyranny that had held it for years. For all practical purposes, the workers took over the reins of government. They were in complete control... The strike was a rank and file affair. SWOC may have called it, but it is now in the hands of anyone who can lead.

Confronted with the scale of the revolt, Jones and Laughlin capitulated—"the toughest corporation in America brought to its knees in exactly 40 hours". Even once the deal was signed, a huge crowd, perhaps 20,000 strong, many "armed...with clubs, ball bats, chair legs, lead pipe and plain beaverboard", continued to besiege the mill, waiting for the scabs and the management to leave. Union recognition was not enough—they wanted payback. Timko had to hire a band to lead them away from the mill on a victory march through the town. This was more than winning union recognition: Aliquippa had been liberated from corporate tyranny. One worker remarked that it was worth the union dues just "to be able to walk down the main street of Aliquippa, talk to anyone you want about anything you like, and feel that you are a citizen".[586] It was, as Robert Brooks observes, "a perfect example of a successful organising strike". Once the workers had returned to work, there was still a series of short stoppages, including a three-hour sit-down strike by 400 workers in one section, before the management finally recognised that the union was here to stay. The Aliquippa victory led to another rush of smaller firms eager "to get on the SWOC bandwagon".[587]

The Little Steel strike

There were other employers determined to both stop and roll back the advance of the CIO. Among them was Remington Rand, an office equipment manufacturer. In May 1934 over 6,000 workers had walked out on strike demanding union recognition. The company had been forced to concede, but the management was determined to break the union. Company president James Rand planned out a strategy for union-busting that went into effect in May 1936. On 25 May the company deliberately provoked a strike by sacking union leaders at a number of plants and once the workers were out put its strategy into effect. The company launched a propaganda campaign against the union, brought in over 500 professional strikebreakers, mobilised local police forces, organised Back to Work movements and, after a bitter battle, reopened its plants. The company proclaimed itself victorious in June and James Rand began publicising his strikebreaking methods as a recipe for turning the tide in the class struggle.

Rand put forward the so-called "Mohawk Valley Formula" as a scientific method of strikebreaking derived from his experience in union-busting at his company's Ilion plant in the Mohawk Valley. The "formula" would begin with a propaganda assault on the union, labelling it as under the control of Communist outsiders. This campaign should preferably be led by a "citizens' committee" ostensibly independent of the company. The union had to be portrayed as a threat to "law and order" (Remington Rand had set about deliberately provoking violent incidents during the 1936 strike). This would enable "public opinion" to be mobilised against the union, and the citizens' committee could then begin organising anti-union vigilantes. The union had to be confronted with overwhelming force consisting of police, professional strikebreakers, vigilantes and, if possible, the National Guard. Once this force had been deployed, the company should sponsor a "Back to Work movement", preferably involving workers actually employed at the strike-bound plant, but if they were not available outside scabs could be brought in. A march back to work under heavy police protection would break the strikers' morale and result in the speedy collapse of the union. During the Remington Rand dispute, the company had wildly exaggerated the numbers returning to work. The establishment of a loyal company union was crucial in consolidating victory.[588]

In reality, the formula offered no scientific guarantee of success. General Motors had used these methods in its battle with the UAW, but without success. The Mohawk Valley Formula would only bring victory in the right circumstances. Working class militancy and solidarity could and did defeat employers trying to implement it. Indeed, after a protracted war of attrition Remington Rand itself was forced to come to terms with the union. In July 1947 the company attempted to break a strike at its Ilion plant with a Back to Work march. It collapsed in the face of a 1,500-strong mass picket determined "that no strikebreakers should pass that picket line".[589] What the wide circulation and enthusiastic reception of the formula indicated, however, was that there were still many employers determined to make a stand for the open shop.

Among these employers were the independent steel companies Republic, Bethlehem, Sheet and Tube, National, Inland and ARMCO, known collectively as Little Steel. These firms were only "little" in comparison with US Steel. Bethlehem employed almost 80,000 workers, Republic 46,000, Sheet and Tube 23,000, National 14,000, Inland 11,000, and ARMCO 12,000. Over the months SWOC had successfully established itself in the Bethlehem plants and was making headway in Sheet and Tube, Republic and Inland. The employers, led by Republic's Tom Girdler, formerly president of Jones and Laughlin of Aliquippa, were determined to confront the union before it became too strong. As Girdler made clear, there would be no deal struck with "an irresponsible, racketeering and violent body like the CIO".[590] To this end, the Little Steel companies armed themselves to the teeth, and made ready for open unashamed class war that they intended to win, if necessary by massacre. They assembled huge arsenals so as to be able to shoot down their employees. Sheet and Tube had 369 rifles, 453 revolvers and 190 shotguns with 76,000 rounds of ammunition and over 100 gas guns, as well as four machine guns. Republic had 64 rifles, 552 revolvers and 245 shotguns with 77,000 rounds of ammunition and over 200 gas guns. The Little Steel companies were better armed than most police departments.[591] Republic Steel had only recently shown its capacity for violence when it broke a strike in Canton, Ohio, in May 1935. Company police had rampaged through the town, firing tear gas and live rounds indiscriminately. A pregnant woman was shot and wounded two miles from the plant and an elderly man was killed when a tear gas shell hit him on the head. Terror had been the order of the day.[592] Now, as far Girdler was concerned, they were confronting a "hydra-headed monster". The CIO was "tyranny disguised as a labour movement" and its organisers were "unpleasant, fierce-mannered, psychotic, thriftless strangers with clubs". Whereas Michael Tighe, the president of the old Amalgamated had been "a fine old gentleman" who could be safely ignored, John L Lewis was "out to make tribute-paying captives of our workmen" and would have to be fought. Union power, Girdler wrote in his memoirs, "horrifies me as a physician is horrified when he finds a cancer has developed in the person of someone he loves".[593]

The Little Steel companies' militant determination to crush the union by any means necessary contrasts with the increasing moderation of the SWOC leadership. Murray was not a man best-equipped to lead a struggle against such opposition and on top of that the surrender of US Steel had worked to undermine any official commitment to militancy. Certainly the use of the sit-down strike, the most potent weapon in labour's arsenal, was ruled out. Indeed, the previous year black workers had occupied the American Casting Company plant in Birmingham, Alabama, on Christmas Eve. The company surrendered after a few days, conceding a 20 percent pay rise. The SWOC leadership subsequently fired the two organisers, Joe Howard and C Dave Smith, both CPers, who had led "Alabama's first sit-down strike in history", for acting without authorisation.[594] And while SWOC's leadership was becoming more moderate, the Communist Party had resolved not to offer any challenge to its control over either the union or the forthcoming strike.

Republic Steel began firing workers for union membership at the start of May 1937. On 20 May it locked out workers in its Canton and Massillon plants with the intention of forcing the union into battle before it was fully prepared. The stratagem worked. Rank and file pressure to take action proved irresistible, and anyway, after the Aliquippa victory, the leadership was confident that Little Steel would soon come to terms. Even in those plants where union membership was still low, there was confidence that workers would rally to a strike call. On 26 May workers at Republic, Sheet and Tube and Inland were called out on strike. Bethlehem Steel was not to be called out until 11 June. At its height there were to be over 80,000 workers on strike, affecting some 30 steel mills across eight states. Another 20,000 workers, mostly coal miners, were to strike in sympathy. The strike would be decided by the struggle in northern Ohio. Initially, however, attention focused on Chicago. In Ahmed White's words, the strike "was soon awash with violence".[595]

Massacre

On 26 May at the Republic Steel plant on Burley Avenue, Chicago, hundreds of workers staged a sit-down strike. Instead of throwing the union behind this initiative, John Riffe, a SWOC organiser, assured the police that the union was "going to conduct this according to the law". The police allowed him into the plant to order the men out. As historian Michael Dennis puts it, Riffe "made it clear that SWOC would not support the most effective weapon available to organised labour... An opportunity to tip the balance in favour of the striking workers had been lost".[596] Once the plant was evacuated, the police proceeded to prevent any attempt at effective picketing, dispersing the strikers through arrests and beatings. Pickets were kept six blocks from the plant. On Sunday 30 May, Memorial Day, the union held a rally at Sam's Place, a former dancehall, now the strikers' headquarters. After speeches the protesters, men, women and children about 1,500 strong, many in their Sunday best, decided to march on the Republic Steel plant in a symbolic assertion of their right to picket. They were confronted by the police, who replied to jeers and a few stones with tear gas, then opened fire with their revolvers, before charging with clubs. One of the demonstrators, George Patterson, remembered "the cops there shooting away... At first I thought they were blanks...then I began to see people fall." Jesse Reese, a black steel worker, remembered his astonishment at seeing the police beat white women: "I'd seen them beat black women, but this was the first time in my life I'd seen them beat white women with sticks".[597] Meyer Levin, a novelist working for the union as a volunteer, only realised the police were firing live rounds when a boy near him was shot in the foot. He helped his father carry him to safety.[598] A clergyman later testified that he saw two policemen beating a young man. They "were standing over him, taking turns at slugging him with their clubs as hard as they could... I was close enough to hear the terrible impact of each blow as it landed on his head".[599]

This attack left ten workers, Earl Handley, Alfred Causey, Sam Popovich, Joe Rothmund, Anthony Tagliori, Hilding Anderson, Otis Jones, Leo Francisco, Lee Tisdale and Kenneth Reed, dead. Handley was shot in the leg and left to bleed to death in a police van despite the protests of other prisoners. Kenneth Reed had been shot three times; Alfred Causey had been shot four times and was badly beaten as he lay dying; 17 year old Leo Francisco was shot and died two weeks later from blood poisoning. Fifty year old Sam Popovich was so badly beaten about the head that initially it was assumed he had been beaten to death, but the autopsy revealed that these injuries were post-mortem and that he had been killed by a shot to the head. His widow was so distraught at his death that she drowned herself. Three of those killed had been shot in the side while turning away from the police and the other seven in the back while trying to get away. Of the other 40 demonstrators with gunshot wounds, 27 had been shot in the back and nine in the side. Among these victims were two women and an 11 year old boy. Another 38 people were hospitalised by the beatings they received at the hands of the police, a number of them permanently disabled. Of course, many of the injured avoided hospital for fear of arrest. Clancy Sigal, then a young boy, later recalled how some of the wounded made their way to his family's laundry shop where they were provided with sandwiches and coffee. Sigals' was known as "safe harbour". He was stationed on the roof, keeping a look out for the police.[600]

According to the later report of the La Follette Committee, the police treated the wounded and injured with "the most callous indifference to human life and suffering. Wounded prisoners of war might have expected and received greater solicitude".[601] The police arrested 150 people. They later justified their attack to the La Follette Committee on the grounds that they had intelligence that the plant was to be stormed and occupied. When Captain James Mooney was asked the source of this intelligence, he replied that it came "from some newspapermen. They didn't give me their names".[602]

The massacre was reported in the press as a heroic stand by brave embattled police under attack from a red mob intent on storming the Republic plant and revolution. The *Chicago Tribune* headline read "Riots Blamed On Red Chiefs" and the *New York Times* had "Steel Mob Halted". Even the national media, *Time, Life* and *Newsweek*, carried the same story. There had been no brutal massacre of unarmed demonstrators, but rather a pitched battle with a revolutionary mob in which the police had thankfully prevailed. This was what the American people were told by the "free press". There was one minor problem because a Paramount newsreel photographer had actually filmed the massacre. This was solved by the simple expedient of suppressing the film on the grounds that it might provoke public disorder.[603] This was a very real fear. Roosevelt had won the 1936 presidential election by mobilising millions of working class voters with a promise to break the power of the "economic royalists". Now the lackeys of those same "economic royalists" were murdering working people for daring to unionise. The situation was on a knife edge.[604] As we have seen, William Z Foster's strategy for organising steel had recognised the likelihood, indeed the inevitability, of a violent response by the steel companies. He quite correctly urged a militant response to such action on their part. The call should go out for solidarity from other workers. The steel workers and their supporters should fight for a general strike in Chicago on the San Francisco model. If there was no effective response to company violence the dispute would be lost.

How did SWOC respond to the massacre of its members? SWOC's Mid-West director, the former UMW official, Van Bittner, promised the Chicago police that there "will be no more trouble", and that if there were any more attempts at provoking violence, the police "should notify me and I will put a stop to it". The union went into a rapid retreat. Instead of confronting the challenge, the union threw itself on the tender mercies of the Chicago authorities and began scapegoating the Communists. There was to be no attempt at mobilising the widespread outrage at the massacre; in fact every effort was put into preventing any such mobilisation. The Communists made no attempt to challenge this retreat. Foster's strategy was abandoned with the Communist priority now being to keep in with the CIO leadership.

There was widespread support for the steel workers among the rank and file of the Chicago AFL unions, but the Chicago Federation of Labor (CFL), dominated by full-time officials, incredibly refused to condemn the conduct of the police. John Fitzpatrick, the CFL president and one of the leaders of the 1919 steel strike, had over the years become just another AFL reactionary. He dismissed the shootings as "a CIO matter". He had the police clear demonstrators demanding solidarity from the CFL hall.[605] For his part, William Green blamed the massacre on "the evil influence of the CIO leadership".[606] The AFL leadership made clear to the steel companies that if it would help they were prepared to charter scab unions. The potential for solidarity was still there if only the CIO had campaigned for it. Meyer Levin got round the suppression of the newsreel of the massacre by taking photographs from the newspaper coverage. When they were arranged in their time sequence, "they made a complete pictorial record of the event from the start of the march to the dead in the hospitals. I had slides made from these clippings." The slide show was put on at a packed protest meeting at the Opera House where it had an electrifying impact: "The vast auditorium was a cauldron of rage" and there was "a naked revolutionary urge".[607]

Defeat

While the Chicago massacre was a stunning demonstration of the willingness of the Little Steel companies and the police to use lethal force, in fact the fate of the strike was decided in the steel districts of Northern Ohio. In town after town the strikers were attacked, the National Guard was sent in and the strikers were starved into surrender with troops escorting scabs back to work. In Youngstown on Saturday 19 June the union had a Women's Day on the picket line. There were over 2,000 women and children on the demonstration. The police, in what was clearly a deliberate provocation, tear-gassed women pickets. John Steuben, a SWOC organiser and CPer, later wrote of how:

> news of the gas attack on the women spread like wildfire, and hundreds of strikers rushed to the Republic plant. For six hours in pitch darkness,

the workers defended themselves and their wives against a brutal attack deliberately precipitated by police, deputy sheriffs and vigilante gunmen.

Eventually the police withdrew but by this time one worker, John Bogovich, had been shot dead and another, James Eperjesi, had been mortally wounded. The labour journalist Mary Heaton Vorse was on the picket line and could testify that:

> [Eperjesi] was not shot in self-defence. He was fired on point-blank by deputies standing in a truck. I know because I was there.

She was injured herself in the attack. According to Steuben, the scene "looked like civil war".[608]

David McDonald, the secretary-treasurer of SWOC and a future president of the United Steelworkers, described the situation as reminiscent of "the coal wars of the 1920s all over again". He described how he had to restrain the workers in Youngstown from further conflict. "Youngstown was a pyre of combustibles" and, as far as he was concerned, Steuben "was about to set a match". Steuben, McDonald complained, had convinced the workers that "only by a massive show of force—backed with arms if necessary—would the workingmen prevail. And they were hungry enough and angry enough to believe him." McDonald persuaded them to put their faith in the president. As he acknowledged, however, the federal government, on this occasion, "told us to go to hell".[609]

On 11 July in Massillon another attack took place. Here, without any warning, the police machine-gunned the union headquarters:

> When the shooting was over and the dead and wounded were cleared away, a night of terror followed. The boarding houses of strikers on Cleveland Avenue were stormed. Doors were broken down, men, women and children were dragged from their beds, searched and arrested—all without warrants... They arrested 165 union members and hauled them off to jail. The search failed to disclose a single weapon on the persons or in the homes of the strikers except one pocket knife in the possession of Harry Jones.

Two strikers, Fulgencio Calzada and Nick Valdoz, were killed that night.[610] Altogether 18 strikers were to be killed before the Little Steel dispute was over. As Steuben pointed out, while men were being gunned down, beaten, gassed and arrested, "the press and radio and halls of Congress resounded with the hypocritical cry of 'CIO violence'".[611] There was a good demonstration of the fear the Little Steel companies inspired at this time when workers from Republic Steel travelled to Washington DC to give evidence to the National Labor Relations Board. They were kept in safe houses by board officials because of fears that Pinkerton agents had been sent "to locate these men and gun them down".[612] By the time the strike was over, more than 2,000 pickets had been arrested. The breaking of the Little Steel strike was, as Sidney Lens, without any exaggeration, puts it, "one of the most shameful reigns of terror of our times".[613]

In the end the steel workers were beaten and starved back to work. McDonald remembered having to tell the strikers in Canton that the funds to feed the strikers and their families had run out. The workers in the food line "had a beaten, hopeless look in their eyes". When he made the announcement they "never changed expression. They just looked at me". Despite this, his account of the Little Steel strike ends not with an indictment of Roosevelt's betrayal, but with congratulations for the way the union leadership beat off the Communist challenge![614]

Was the defeat inevitable? Certainly the employers had provoked the strike before the work of organisation was complete, but even so a very strong case can be made that what ensured defeat was the leadership's determination to remain responsible and moderate and the employers' willingness to use whatever violence was necessary, backed up by the local state. If the UMW had actively mobilised behind the Little Steel strikers, the outcome might have been different, but this was not to be. In fact, UMW officials did their best to minimise solidarity from the miners. Moderation on the part of the union leadership and murderous violence on the part of the employers combined to defeat the attempt to unionise Little Steel.

What was Roosevelt's part in this bloody defeat? In an interview on 29 June he famously pronounced "a plague on both your houses". According to Melvyn Dubofsky and Warren Van Tine, he "acted as he did for good political reasons".[615] It is quite difficult to see what political reasons can possibly be good enough for a liberal president to effectively declare himself neutral in a battle for union recognition where unarmed trade unionists were being gunned down in cold blood. What we see here is a particularly glaring example of a common phenomenon whereby liberal historians bend over backwards to find some justification for Roosevelt's most outrageous actions. In his biography of the president Frank Freidel argues that Roosevelt negotiated his way through "the no-man's land between the opposing forces" with "considerable skill", although he does concede that the Chicago massacre was so blatant that "some expression of sympathy" was in order. He is quite clear about why none was forthcoming: Mayor Kelly "was an important ally...keeping an Illinois senator in line on votes critical to the president".[616]

John L Lewis's response to Roosevelt's betrayal was much more robust. On Labor Day John L Lewis broadcast a defence of the CIO, an indictment of its enemies and a condemnation of its false friends. The CIO, he told a radio audience estimated at 25 million, was born:

> out of the agony and travail of economic America... To millions of Americans, exploited without stint by corporate industry and socially debased beyond the understanding of the fortunate, its coming was as welcome as the dawn to the nightwatcher... [The CIO] exemplifies the resentment of the many toward the selfishness, greed and neglect of the few. The workers of the nation were tired of waiting for corporate industry to right their economic wrongs, to alleviate their social agony and to grant them their political rights. Despairing of fair treatment, they resolved to do something for themselves.

Considerable progress has been made, he told his listeners, "although much of this progress was made in the face of violent and deadly opposition which reached its climax in the slaughter of workers paralleling the massacres of Ludlow and Homestead". He chronicled "the fury of the police" in Chicago and the betrayal of "the infamous Governor Davey of Ohio", a New Deal Democrat, who to secure election had "reiterated promises of fair treatment for labour". And then he went on to indict, in the most ferocious terms, American politicians more generally, including Roosevelt himself, although he never mentioned him by name:

> The steel workers have now buried their dead, while the widows weep and watch their orphaned children become objects of public charity. *The murder of these unarmed men has never been publicly rebuked by any authoritative officer of the state or federal government* [my emphasis].

Some of them in extenuation, plead lack of jurisdiction, but murder as a crime against the moral code can always be rebuked without regard to the niceties of legalistic jurisdiction by those who profess to be the keepers of the public conscience.

And, of course, this last point was surely even more valid when the murderers were policemen and, to all intents and purposes, above the law. He ended with a bitter personal condemnation of Roosevelt's stand:

Labour, like Israel, has many sorrows. Its women weep for their fallen and they lament for the future of the race. It ill behooves one who has supped at labour's table and who has been sheltered in labour's house to curse with equal fervour and fine impartiality both labour and its adversaries when they become locked in deadly embrace.[617]

While Lewis was to never forgive Roosevelt for his failure to support the CIO in its battle with Little Steel, nevertheless his own response to the defeat was to rein back militancy. With US Steel signed up, defeat at the hands of Little Steel would not be a fatal blow to the CIO. The union bureaucracy could ride out the setback. Murray began a purge of CP organisers within SWOC, maintained a rigid authoritarian control over the organisation, and insisted that the union enforce contracts, even when its members rebelled. As Bert Cochran points out, "Communists were simply removed from the payroll, district by district." There was no internal union democracy; there were no conventions. SWOC was "a top-heavy, centralised Lewis-Murray, then a Murray, dictatorship".[618] It was not to be formally constituted as a union until 1944. It is remarkable that the Communists let this happen with very little protest. Foster was to complain later that the CP had been "in a strong enough position locally at the time to have insisted that representative steel workers be brought into the top leadership", but "they failed to do so" with the result that in many cases "mere chair-warmers and time-worn bureaucrats retained full control of all decisive positions".[619] While he was to blame Earl Browder for this, in fact it followed from the CP's alliance with the CIO leadership which would not have survived any attempt at a rank and file challenge.

The change in official attitudes inside SWOC is nicely captured by an episode recounted by Clint Golden and Harold Ruttenberg in their book *The Dynamics of Industrial Democracy*. Both men had been involved in the campaign to unionise steel and Golden was a veteran trade unionist with a left reputation. In the book they discuss the problem that a militant like Stanley Orlosky posed for the union. People like him had been essential when the union was fighting for recognition, but now he had had to be expelled from the union and fired from his job. Orlosky had been a coal miner and UMW member since 1911. He had been blacklisted in the 1920s and went to work in the steel industry where he had become a SWOC activist. Golden and Ruttenberg quote him:

> Being a good union man is agitating—that's what I always knew as a good union man—and I got fired for agitating... The company has had it in for me since 1933. I'm a thorn in the flesh to it. Now the union sides with the company and I'm out.

The problem with Orlosky, they argue, was that his idea of "grievance settlement was to get everything or strike". He had played a leading role in the early days; indeed, his "leadership was essential to the establishment of the union against bitter opposition". Once the union was recognised and had entered into agreements with the company, however, "such leadership was a handicap to the development of cooperative union-management relations". Golden and Ruttenberg's only lament is that there are still too many other workers with Orlosky's unhelpful attitude.[620] Others adapted to the new reality. Joe Timko, who had organised Jones and Laughlin in Aliquippa, is a good case in point. A Jones and Laughlin executive confessed that while Timko had been "one of the toughest organisers and hardest-fighting strike leaders we had ever come up against", he had not hesitated to put a stop to unofficial strikes even on safety issues.[621]

Although Lewis had fallen out with Roosevelt, Murray remained close to the Democrats. Even in Chicago, SWOC was to kiss the hand that beat it. In the 1939 mayoral election SWOC wholeheartedly backed Mayor Kelly, whose police had only recently murdered its members and supporters. Indeed, the union actually ensured that on the platform with Kelly at every meeting and rally was one of the survivors of the Memorial Day massacre, Harry Harper, who had lost an eye as a result of the beating he received at the hands of Kelly's police. The architect of this obscenity was Joseph Germano, a full-time official, who controlled the local union by old-fashioned strongarm methods.

According to Robert Slayton's authoritative account, he had prevailed upon the reluctant Harper "possibly by threatening violence". Germano was very much part of the corrupt Chicago Democratic machine and was to go on to become a key supporter of Richard Daley.[622]

An echo of the class war

One of the most remarkable relief projects that the New Deal administration introduced as part of the Works Progress Administration (WPA) was the Federal Theatre Project. This was established to provide work for unemployed actors, designers, musicians, stage hands and directors. It was intended to make live theatre available to people who might otherwise never get to see a live production. And it was hoped by many of those involved that out of this relief project might come a permanent, subsidised American national theatre. At its height the Federal Theatre Project was to provide work for 13,000 people. The parallel Music Project employed some 12,000, the Writers' Project over 6,000 and the Arts Project 5,000. As Ray Allen Billington observes, "A tidal wave of culture inundated the United States".[623] Without any doubt, Federal Theatre made theatre history, staging challenging productions that reached audiences untouched by commercial theatre. The objective was "free, adult, uncensored theatre". The project director, Hallie Flanagan, outlined the thinking behind the initiative:

> In an age of terrific implications as to wealth and poverty, as to the function of government, as to peace and war, as to the relation of the artist to all these forces, the theatre must grow up. The theatre must become conscious of the implications of the changing social order, or the changing social order will ignore, and rightly, the implications of the theatre.[624]

In this spirit, the Federal Theatre put on dramas and entertainments of all kinds across much of the country, many of them making radical statements about the state of America.

The Living Newspaper productions dramatised current events and issues. There were productions dealing with the crisis in agriculture, the need for public ownership of the utilities, socialised medicine, the history of syphilis and slum housing. One production, *Injunction Granted*, was directed by Joseph Losey, a CPer at the time. It was, in the words of

Jane DeHart Matthews, "a militantly pro-labour account of the working man's fight for liberation through unionisation", with Communist Party literature being sold in the foyer. In spite of many objections, not least from Flanagan herself, the production went ahead.[625] Less fortunate was the production of *Ethiopia*, an anti-fascist dramatisation of the recent Italian invasion of Ethiopia. The production had been in rehearsal for six weeks, involving 300 people, when the White House took steps to stop it. The Federal Theatre was barred from making "any representation of a foreign state" without State Department approval.[626] The director, Elmer Rice, resigned in protest against this censorship. The success of the Living Newspaper inspired Ernst Toller, the German revolutionary playwright, to offer a play, *Europe, Last Edition*. However, the project made "powerful enemies" and, in the end, these were "instrumental in the final closing of the project".[627]

One of the most successful productions was a stage version of Upton Sinclair's bestselling anti-fascist novel *It Can't Happen Here*. MGM had bought the film rights and had spent $200,000 developing the project before fear of the commercial consequences in Germany and Italy led to it being dropped. The Federal Theatre took it up with gusto and in October 1936 the play opened simultaneously in 21 theatres in three languages—English, Yiddish and Spanish. It opened in Los Angeles, Boston, San Francisco, Tampa, Birmingham, Bridgeport, Chicago, Cleveland, Denver, Detroit, Yonkers, Indianapolis, Omaha, Miami, Newark, Seattle and Tacoma. It opened in three theatres in New York. Each production was unique. Across the country *It Can't Happen Here* was seen by over 300,000 people.[628]

The most famous production, however, was one that never went on, at least not as a Federal Theatre production: Marc Blitzstein's *The Cradle Will Rock*, produced by John Houseman and directed by Orson Welles. This was an opera about the campaign to organise the steel industry. As part of his research for the production Blitzstein had read various pamphlets by William Z Foster, including his *Organizing Methods in the Steel Industry*.[629] He dedicated the opera to Bertolt Brecht. Blitzstein:

> transformed a steel strike into a bitterly sarcastic, wittily derisive opera.
> Complete with bloated capitalists, sadistic cops, heroic union organis-
> ers, and the proverbial prostitute with a heart of gold, it fairly burst

with moral fervour and contemporaneity. *The Cradle Will Rock*, however, was no mere *New Masses* cartoon set to music. It was the first serious musical drama written in America which provided a new vernacular for the man in the street—an achievement, according to Aaron Copeland, that made truly indigenous opera possible. Artistically superb and politically explosive, it was, above all, superb theatre.[630]

According to Welles, Blitzstein almost believed that his opera "had only to be performed to start the revolution".[631]

The Federal Theatre was not exempt from the struggles of the time. Budget cuts led to sackings. On 27 May 1937 in New York 7,000 WPA workers in the various arts divisions went on strike in protest, including *The Cradle Will Rock* actors and crew. Flanagan gave the strikers her support, making the point that "if they are dropped from the rolls they must go back to destitution" and asking critics of the strike what they would suggest as "a better method" of protest.[632] *The Cradle Will Rock* was due to open at the Maxine Elliott Theatre on 16 June, in the middle of the Little Steel strike with strikers being beaten and gunned down. Despite the fact that 18,000 advance tickets had been sold, the opening night was cancelled and the production never opened. The ostensible reason was budget cuts, but the real reason was to save the Roosevelt administration from the embarrassment of the Federal Theatre staging an openly pro-CIO drama when the Little Steel bosses were busy trying to smash the union. It was, according to Flanagan, "obviously censorship under a different guise".[633] This act of censorship provoked what Susan Quinn has described as "the *Cradle* insurgency".[634]

Houseman found another theatre, the Venice Theatre, where the opera could be staged, only for the musicians' and actors' unions to prohibit their members from performing. Nevertheless, they were determined to make a public demonstration against censorship. On 16 June they collected the audience that assembled outside the Maxine Elliott, over 600 people, and marched them the 20 blocks to the Venice. Lincoln Diamant, one of the audience, later remembered how an

> impromptu parade was organised...at the head was a truck. In the truck was a piano with posters for *Cradle Will Rock*...sitting on a piano stool was Marc Blitzstein, and he was playing from the show. The audience was marching about five abreast up Seventh Avenue... Oh, it was fantastic![635]

When they arrived at the Venice they found a fascist flag hanging inside, left over from an Italian variety show. It was torn down to applause.

The opera was staged with Blitzstein alone on the stage playing the piano, and with the cast circumventing the ban by singing their parts from the stalls. Of the musicians, a lone accordionist accompanied Blitzstein. Houseman later remembered the moment when Olive Stanton stood up to sing the first part. It was almost impossible to convey, he recalled, "the throat-catching, sickeningly exciting quality of that moment or to describe the emotions of gratitude and love with which we saw and heard that slim green figure". If she had lost her nerve, then none of the others would have dared. When the performance ended there was "pandemonium... New York had never seen such a night of sheer theatrical defiance".[636] This ad hoc performance was to be put on at the Venice for the next two weeks.

That same night of 16 June there were other protests against the cuts elsewhere in New York. At the Lafayette Theatre in Harlem the audience and the cast staged a sit-down protest at the end of a performance of *The Case of Philip Lawrence* while at the Federal Music Theatre the musicians and audience staged a sit-down after a performance of Brahms chamber music. In New York the Federal Theatre was to lose 30 percent of its staff with 1,700 jobs going. Flanagan chronicled other protests against the regime of cuts and layoffs:

> a sit-down hunger strike of dancers, which lasted from June 21 to June 25; in the art project there was an overnight sit-down strike, with women threatening to jump from the windows. Harold Stein, manager of the other arts, was held an overnight prisoner in his office by 600 demonstrators...[637]

The Federal Theatre Project was finally shut down altogether by Congress in the summer of 1939. By the time it was closed down the Federal Theatre's 158 companies had entertained a total audience of some 25 million people.

Chapter Eleven

On the defensive

The defeat at the hands of Little Steel and the onset of the Roosevelt Depression were serious blows to the CIO, bringing its apparently irresistible onward march to a halt. Employers, politicians, both Democrats and Republicans, and the AFL rallied against it with every intention of rolling back its advance, perhaps even of destroying it. The defeat at Little Steel was to be followed by the even more serious setback in textiles and the failure to break through in the South.

Under the leadership of Sidney Hillman of the ACW the CIO had undertaken to organise the textile industry, which employed some 1.25 million workers. They were employed by thousands of firms, employing anywhere from 100 to 10,000 workers, across 29 states. To this end a Textile Workers Organizing Committee (TWOC) was established, incorporating the United Textile Workers that had never really recovered from the crushing defeat it had suffered in 1934 and had a mere 38,000 members. Preparations were made for an industry-wide organising drive. Over 500 organisers were taken on and a large war chest was put together (between 1937 and 1939 TWOC was to spend $2 million). According to one historian, this "was undoubtedly the best-planned organising campaign ever undertaken".[638]

The TWOC leadership took the decision to concentrate its efforts in the areas where there was already a union presence. What this meant was that of the more than 500 organisers put into the field, only 150 were assigned to the South. This was a serious strategic mistake. It was in the South that the 1934 defeat had been hardest felt, with the most brutal repression and widespread victimisation. Wages were 25 percent lower than in the North. The employers exercised an absolutely tyrannical rule over their workforce and could rely on the support of the

Democrats in opposing the CIO. Police, vigilantes—most notably the Ku Klux Klan—and the National Guard were readily available if required. It was always going to be difficult and dangerous to crack the South, but it was strategically vital. The North was already losing jobs to the South and this situation would undoubtedly worsen if the North unionised while the South remained an open-shop stronghold. Between 1925 and 1940 one of the great Northern textile centres, Fall River, Massachusetts, moved 73 mills with a capital value of $60 million—three quarters of its production capacity—to the South. If TWOC was to be successful, it had to organise the 500,000 textile workers in the South.[639] More generally, the South was the bastion of reaction in the US and establishing a strong trade union movement there would enable a frontal assault on the Southern Democrats.

Hillman was determined to avoid industrial conflict in the hope that moderation and respectability would win the employers over. Unionisation, he argued, would help modernise the industry, increase efficiency, improve productivity and raise profits. TWOC campaigned on the basis that union recognition and collective bargaining were a positive benefit for employers. Hillman actually published an article in the business magazine *Barron's* on "why textile unionism means profit".[640] And there were some firms in the North that were prepared to embrace this approach, especially in the hope that TWOC would organise the South and thereby reduce its competitive advantage. In the South, Hillman looked to political support as a way of overcoming employer resistance but, despite his close relationship with the White House, this was not forthcoming. Employers in the South were not convinced unionisation would be to their advantage.

TWOC offered employers a collaborative relationship, but if they refused these advances and the rank and file were militant, determined and confident enough, it fought. A four-week strike of silk workers across New Jersey and Pennsylvania in the summer of 1937 ended in victory. In the Amsterdam district of New York, the carpet and rug manufacturing district, in the spring of 1938 TWOC took on the Bigelow Sanford Carpet Company in a militant seven-week strike. The union:

> kept a double picket line of 8,000 people encircling the three-mile area occupied by this firm's mills; enlisted the boycott aid of the League of

Women Shoppers, sponsored radio broadcasts which denounced the company's "nothing to arbitrate" stand as an anachronism; got Teamsters and truck drivers to refuse to move its goods from its warehouses or pick them up at the railroad loading points in 25 cities from Boston to Seattle, from Atlanta to San Francisco, and otherwise unleashed a social power of vast effect.[641]

Even in the North, however, the Roosevelt Depression effectively crippled TWOC's organising efforts, as jobs went and mills closed.

The South was another world altogether. Here the US was "exceptional". Between 1936 and 1939 19 union organisers were killed in the South. Union meetings were accompanied by burning crosses and revivalist preachers were bought in to condemn the union. The press was full of attacks on the Jew, Sidney Hillman. On 26 March 1938 the CIO News carried a report on organising in the South:

> Often an organiser dare not enter a town in daylight; he relies upon a union-minded merchant or a handful of key men to keep in touch with those workers who are sympathetic to the union. Mass meetings are seldom held, except in large cities, and unionists in the same village may not even know their fellow union members. In many areas, mill workers provide union organisers with day and night bodyguards for there have been beatings and shootings by mill police, thugs and vigilantes.[642]

Despite heroic efforts TWOC failed to make a breakthrough. By May 1939, when it became the Textile Workers Union, it had only 10,000 members in the South. Ferocious repression coupled with the Roosevelt Depression had resulted in complete failure. Nationally, the picture was more mixed. In his 1938 study of the CIO, Benjamin Stolberg argued that:

> Hillman's method was to half-organise the workers as quickly as possible, without any real union agitation... TWOC has hastily signed any agreement it could get, and it couldn't get much. Having no militancy or cohesion, which alone can gain favourable [results]...the TWOC could gain nothing but Pyrrhic victories. For the TWOC is a rope of sand.

He still thought the drive had been worthwhile though because "it has given the workers in this industry as a whole the idea of unionism.

Not much more. But the idea is there".[643] Steven Fraser, in his 1991 biography of Hillman, is, with the benefit of hindsight, more damning. According to him, TWOC "simply crumbled like sandcastles in the rain". It was "neither a mass movement nor a credible trade union". Instead it was "a bureaucratic mirage, requiring stronger and stronger doses of ritual invocation to sustain the illusion of its existence".[644]

Black workers and the CIO

The organisation of the mass production industries necessitated overcoming the divisions between black and white workers which had been put in place by years of white racism. For most black workers the AFL had not been a friend, but an enemy, determined to exclude them from the workplace. In the South the Great Depression had seen some white workers join in "nigger removal" campaigns. On the railways white workers had resorted to murder in an attempt to drive black workers out of the industry. Between 1931 and 1934 at least ten black railwaymen had been killed and many more maimed and injured by white vigilantes in Mississippi, Tennessee and Louisiana.[645] This "unofficial" terrorism had its official counterpart. In 1939 the AFL-affiliated International Brotherhood of Boilermakers won a closed shop in the Tampa shipyards. The union's whites-only policy meant that 600 black workers were forced out of the yards.[646]

There were unions that did welcome black members, recognising that without the support of black workers effective organisation was impossible. The UMW had a long tradition of organising black miners, and the two clothing workers' unions, the ILGWU and the ACW, had a similar policy. This is not to say that these unions did not include racists among their members, but even they recognised that their own self-interest required unity in the workplace. This self-interest allowed the arguments of anti-racists to get a hearing, helped de-legitimise overt racism, and created the conditions whereby anti-racists could begin to win their workmates over. There were still often immense difficulties. Henry Kraus remembered writing in the UAW newspaper in early December 1936 about the triumphant sit-down strike at Midland Steel in Detroit. Black and white workers had united to defeat the employer and he had celebrated the "strong unity shown between white and coloured Midland workers". A dance was held to celebrate the victory. At the event a black worker asked Dorothy Kraus to dance and when she agreed she was called a "nigger lover" and a fight between black and white workers was only narrowly avoided. As Henry Kraus observed, "union success was no assurance of social enlightenment".[647] Union success with black and white workers fighting alongside each other did, however, create the best circumstances in which it could be fought for.

While recognising the CIO's limitations, Robert Zeiger concludes:

> There is no question that the CIO represented something new in American labour history. To be sure, both the Knights of Labor and the Industrial Workers of the World had built interracial unions, and the UMWA had organised blacks and whites together under often dire circumstances. But the CIO represented the first large-scale effort to bring workers of all ethnic and racial identities into a sustained, well-resourced, and politically realistic common movement. CIO organisers might occasionally betray their regrettable racial views, and black workers might be sceptical, but by the late 1930s, large numbers of African American workers had joined the new CIO unions in steel, meatpacking, food processing, and other industries. "A new type of union is in the field", declared a veteran black labour activist in 1939. For half a century, I H Bratton recalled, "I've fought for full equality for the Negro worker. Today, I've found those things in the CIO".[648]

While the CIO was certainly a massive step forward for black workers, even CIO unions were often reluctant to challenge employers' policies that benefited white workers with regard to promotion and seniority. The extent to which such policies were challenged was often directly dependent on the strength of the left. More generally there was still the problem posed by the racism that pervaded American society both North and South. These two factors came together during the Second World War, when the promotion of black workers in factories and shipyards across the country led to "hate strikes". These vicious outbreaks, sometimes involving thousands of white workers, were, it has to be said, dwarfed by the number of strikes during the war years where black and white workers fought together. Most serious was the three-day Detroit pogrom that took place in June 1943, leaving 25 black people and nine white people dead. While white mobs were allowed to

FIGHTING BACK

roam without interference, the police launched an all-out assault on the black community in order "to put them in their place". Nineteen of the black dead were killed by the police and hundreds more, men and women, were brutally beaten, clubbed and pistol-whipped. Brigadier General William Guthner, who commanded the federal troops sent to the city, described the police as "very handy with their guns and clubs... very harsh and brutal... They have treated the Negroes terrible up here and I think they have gone altogether too far".[649] White racism was a serious weakness for the US labour movement.

The AFL

The AFL played an important part in the assault on the CIO. As far as William Green was concerned (he was a lay preacher after all!) Lewis's revolt against the AFL was positively Satanic. "The first dual union movement", he told one audience:

> occurred in heaven itself. Michael the Archangel rebelled against God and His authority. The executive council in heaven did not hesitate to act. After examining the facts, it expelled his Satanic Majesty and his dual movement from heaven.[650]

Other AFL leaders relied more on old-fashioned red-baiting mixed in with general abuse. The president of the Machinists, Arthur Wharton, in a speech welcoming the fact that "employers have expressed a preference to deal with AF of L organisations", went on to condemn "Lewis, Hillman, Dubinsky, Howard and their gang of sluggers, communists, radicals and soap box artists, professional bums, expelled members of labour unions, outright scabs, and the Jewish organisations with all their red affiliates".[651] At the AFL's Denver convention in October 1938 Green promised delegates that the AFL was going to build "the greatest fighting machine that was ever created within the ranks of organised labour". This "fighting organisation" was not to be built to organise the unorganised or, heaven forbid, take on the employers. Instead, it was going to be dedicated to driving the CIO "out of existence".[652]

One of the most damaging blows the AFL inflicted on the CIO was through its cooperation with the House Un-American Activities Committee (HUAC), chaired by Democrat Congressman Martin

Dies, a protégé of Vice-President Garner. John Frey, a senior AFL official, appeared before the committee on 13 August 1938. The *New York Times* summed up his testimony:

COMMUNISTS RULE THE CIO,
FREY OF AFL TESTIFIES;
HE NAMES 284 ORGANIZERS

Frey testified for three days, effectively launching the red scare and establishing the "naming of names" at its heart. Many of those he named as Communists had no connection with the Communist Party, but that was neither here nor there. The object was to smear regardless. He accused the CIO of succouring the Communist Party, warned that the Communists were infiltrating the Democratic Party and that they were being aided and abetted by the La Follette Committee.[653] The AFL hoped to have his testimony published in book form, but nothing came of this.

The AFL assault on the CIO was not just verbal. The AFL was prepared to ally itself with even the most reactionary employers, to grant charters to company and scab unions, to strikebreak, indeed to use just about any methods to damage its rival. In Chicago in December 1938 some 600 journalists and clerical staff, members of the CIO-affiliated American National Guild (ANG), struck at the Hearst press in protest against victimisations. This "titanic contest" against one of the most powerful and reactionary men in the US was to last for 508 days. Throughout the dispute the AFL backed Hearst, with the AFL print unions crossing the picket lines and the AFL giving the company union—the management-created Editorial Association—a charter. The Editorial Association signed a no-strike agreement with the company. The Chicago Federation of Labor president, John Fitzpatrick, condemned the ANG as an "outlaw" organisation, denied that the strike was legitimate and condemned it as a Communist plot. The CFL actually paid to have sandwich-board men stand on the picket line with posters proclaiming that there was no strike and allowed the Hearst papers to carry a "union approved" label. Despite the incredible ingenuity and tenacity of the strikers in the face of violence and slander, the odds were too great and they went down to defeat. When William Green spoke at the Editorial Association's first national convention in October 1940 he went out of his way to make it clear that the AFL was not there to fight the employers but "those revolutionary forces that are seeking to destroy America".[654]

The AFL threw itself behind employer attempts to drive the Mine, Mill and Smelter Workers Union (MMSWU) out of the Oklahoma, Kansas and Missouri zinc and lead districts. This bitter struggle had been going on since before the formation of the CIO. A bitter strike in 1935 had seen the employers organise a scab union to help beat off the challenge. Whereas in 1935 the AFL had backed the affiliated MMSWU in its battle with the scab Blue Card Union, now that MMSWU had defected to the CIO, quite incredibly, the AFL proceeded to give the scab union an AFL charter. On 11 April 1937 armed vigilantes from the company union, under the watchful eye of the police, launched an all-out, coordinated attack on the MMSWU in a number of towns, beating its members and wrecking its halls. MMSWU was successfully driven out. At the AFL's Denver convention, the triumphant Blue Card Union delegates were a mine owner, a company lawyer and a foreman! No objection was raised.[655]

One other struggle is worth examining here—the conflict between Hutcheson's Carpenters union and the CIO breakaway, the Industrial Woodworkers of America (IWA). The Carpenters had jurisdiction over the lumbermen and had been fighting a company union, the Industrial Employees Union (IEU), that had been established by the US army during the First World War to drive the IWW out of the woods. With the breakaway of the overwhelming majority of its discontented lumber members to establish the IWA, the Carpenters threw their weight behind the company union.

The most bitter episode in this conflict took place at Westwood, a company town in northern California. The IWA was carrying on an organising drive in the area, when, on 8 July 1938, the Red River Lumber Company announced a substantial pay cut. The IWA called a strike. When the IEU ordered its members to cross the picket line many of them promptly changed unions. The company responded to this development at 5am on 13 July. Armed vigilantes sealed the town off from the outside world and proceeded to round up IWA members and expel them and their families from the town. Single men were driven out immediately and married men were given two hours to leave. By the next day there were no IWA members left in the town. Some 600 people were expelled and armed vigilantes in neighbouring towns refused them entry. The AFL response to this attack on elementary civil liberties was to give the company union a charter with workers being advised by management that if they wanted to work they had better join. The American Civil Liberties Union appealed to Roosevelt "to denounce the denial of civil liberties in the Westwood outrage"; he did not reply. One suspects that if armed union men had run the management out of Westwood, Roosevelt would have shown considerably more concern. The Republican Governor of California, Frank Merriam, actually congratulated the citizens of Westwood for driving out "the communistically-led CIO".[656] The AFL tried to crush the new CIO union by boycotts and violence. One episode saw a Teamsters official jailed for 12 years for burning down a box factory in Salem that had gone CIO.[657]

The AFL grew in the years between 1935 and 1941 from some 3.5 million members to 5.2 million. Many of these were signed up as a result of "backdoor deals" whereby companies brought in the AFL in order to keep out the CIO. According to Sidney Lens, "in hundreds of instances employers sought out AFL leaders to sign contracts for employees who had not yet been hired or who were not yet organised... Unquestionably hundreds of thousands of workers are under such contracts. Not a few AFL officials considered this strategy a major weapon in their arsenal".[658] The reasons for the employers' preference for the AFL were put quite succinctly by J Warren Madden, the chairman of the National Labor Relations Board. Employers objected to CIO unions, he observed, "because of their radicalism and also because their leaders are scrupulously honest... They weren't people that you could do business with...like the heads of some of the old craft unions where what the employers did was to pay off the head of the union, instead of paying the working people".[659]

While the AFL certainly grew because it very deliberately offered employers a moderate collaborationist alternative to CIO radicalism and militancy, this was not the whole story. There were many AFL members who were inspired by the CIO's successes and sought to emulate them. AFL members carried out something like 100 sit-down strikes themselves, despite their leaders' repudiation of the tactic. Unions such as the Teamsters certainly grew through corrupt sweetheart deals, but they grew even more through militant organising, much of it inspired by the Minneapolis Trotskyists. Between 1933 and

1939 the membership of the Teamsters grew from 75,000 to 440,000. Although their growth was particularly impressive, the Teamsters were not alone in this expansion. From this point of view, the split in the trade union movement can be seen as tragic, but the fact remains that if AFL unions had not been threatened by the rise of the CIO, they would never have launched the organising drives that contributed to AFL growth. The CIO was a necessary catalyst and without it the AFL would undoubtedly have remained moribund.[660]

Chapter Twelve

Roosevelt and the left

Roosevelt won the 1936 presidential election with the promise that he would master the "economic royalists" and lift up the millions "who at this very moment are denied what the lowest standard of today calls the necessities of life". He announced his own test of how much progress the administration made—not "whether we add more to the abundance of those who have much; it is whether we provide enough for those who have too little".[661] By his own test, he failed miserably.

The only conclusion that one can really draw from the economic policies that he implemented once his re-election was secured was that his campaign speeches were just empty rhetoric. His speeches were intended to mobilise working class support, while his actions were, as always, intended to protect the capitalist system and the interests of the ruling class of which he was a member. His failure to condemn the murderous conduct of the Chicago police and his "neutrality" while the Little Steel strike was broken by armed force speaks for itself.

Roosevelt also intended to make savage cuts in government spending with a view to balancing the budget in 1938. He believed that the recovery was now strong enough to be sustained without government spending and in these circumstances his fiscal conservatism reasserted itself. Henry Morgenthau, the Secretary of the Treasury, had been urging such a course for some time, and now, with the election out of the way, Roosevelt decided this was the way forward. The policy was opposed by important figures within the administration but Roosevelt ignored them. Marriner Eccles, the chairman of the Federal Reserve Board, a man who had drawn the same conclusions from the Depression as John Maynard Keynes, was particularly strongly opposed. He insisted that the recovery was still fragile, that what progress had been made was down to government expenditure and that to cut back now would be a disaster. His warnings were ignored. The cuts in expenditure coincided with the first deductions from workers' wages of their contributions to social security and pensions. This has been described as "a $2 billion Socal Security tax" with Roosevelt determined that it should have no progressive redistributive effect.[662] According to James Olson, in 1936 government expenditure contributed over $4 billion to national income. Roosevelt's cuts reduced that contribution to only $800 million in 1937. The consequences, he observes, "were immediate".[663]

The economic contraction was greater and more rapid than in 1929. As the Trotskyist Maurice Spector observed at the time, Roosevelt had accomplished an economic contraction "in the brief span of a single year" that it had taken "the Hoover Administration... three years to chalk up".[664] Nearly all the gains registered on the New York Times Business Index since 1933 vanished.[665] Industrial production dropped by over a third between October 1937 and May 1938. National income fell by 12 percent. Unemployment rose dramatically to 20 percent, accompanied once again by short-time working and wage cuts. At its peak there were 10 million unemployed, victims of Roosevelt's Depression. In steel, by December 1937, 153,000 workers had been laid off and another 309,000 were on short time. By April 1938 employment in the Detroit car plants had fallen from 250,000 to just over 70,000. Ford alone had laid off 75,000 workers. An embittered Marriner Eccles later confessed that he had been left wondering "whether the New Deal was merely a political slogan or if Roosevelt really knew what the New Deal was".[666] It is astonishing how little effect this self-inflicted catastrophe has had on Roosevelt's reputation among liberal historians.

The economic disaster forced Roosevelt and Congress to reinstate government spending programmes and this successfully prevented the economy spinning out of control. In June 1938 Congress passed a $3.75 billion relief bill which rescued the WPA, and the Reconstruction Finance Corporation was brought in "to pump loans to faltering banks and railroads".[667] By November 1938 the WPA was providing work for some 3.3 million people. All this was nowhere near enough. In 1939 unemployment remained at over 17 percent (9.48 million) and even in 1940 was still at 14.6 percent or 8.12 million. There was still widespread short-time working. The economy was not to recover to its 1937 levels of output until the US was actually embroiled in the Second World War in 1942, when government spending was allowed to grow without restraint.

Roosevelt paid a severe political price for this self-inflicted catastrophe. The suffering that his administration unleashed on the poor inevitably eroded his support and strengthened his enemies. The congressional elections of November 1938 saw the Democrats lose 72 seats in the House of Representatives, although they still had an overwhelming majority. They had a majority in the Senate, but here between 20 and 30 conservative Democrats, mainly Southerners, were emboldened by Roosevelt's declining fortunes to form a conservative bloc with the Republicans. The vice-president, John Nance Garner, allied himself with this group. Roosevelt's economic policies had effectively broken the movement that had secured his re-election, resulting in what amounted to a conservative majority in Congress. The New Deal was over.

The Roosevelt Depression brought an end to the advance of the CIO. Union membership suffered severely in the downturn, with unemployment rising and a return to short-time working. In November 1938 the CIO claimed over 4 million members, but the number paying dues was perhaps a third of that. The UAW was particularly hard hit. This fall in membership was reflected in the low level of shop floor struggle. The number of strike days taken in 1940 was the lowest in the US since 1931. The great working class revolt that had shaken America had, in Sidney Lens's words, been "checked":

> By 1938, after two sensational years, the radicalisation process was fully under control... The spontaneous and "unauthorised" action of the rank and file, which had made the CIO, was now corralled. In its place was an increasing emphasis on respectability and responsibility.[668]

The politics of reputation

The Roosevelt Depression raises interesting questions of political reputation. Why did such a disaster not inflict more damage on Roosevelt's reputation? If there had been no outbreak of war in Europe it is extremely likely that Roosevelt would have been a two-term president, who would have left office having completely failed to pull the US out of the Depression. He would be seen as a fiscal conservative who had reluctantly presided over limited measures of liberal social reform, enough to take the edge off social unrest, but his economic failure would be writ large. His fiscal conservatism would be seen as being central to his ideological make-up and as having produced the economic disaster that wrecked his presidency.

The Second World War saved him from this judgement. But even so, it is still surprising how much of Roosevelt's reputation as a liberal reformer has remained intact. Consider, for example, if the hurricane that devastated the Florida Keys in September 1935, killing 250 veterans, had taken place during Hoover's presidency. Without any doubt, it would figure as part of the indictment of the man, as an example of his callous disregard for the common people. It has never figured in assessments of Roosevelt. Similarly, his consistent refusal to support anti-lynching legislation would have been considered a damaging criticism of any other president, but allowances are made for Roosevelt. The public torture and murder of black men and women were not worth the expenditure of political capital as far as Roosevelt was concerned. Indeed, in all his time in office, Roosevelt did not support any civil rights legislation, something that suggests it was not on his agenda at all. This astonishing failure is actually seen as shrewd politics by many of his admirers, rather than the terrible betrayal it really was— similarly the repression of the unions' organising campaigns, whether it was the textile workers in 1934 (15 dead) or the steel workers in 1937 (18 dead).

Let us briefly consider two other questions—the Spanish Civil War and the question of anti-Semitism.

The Spanish Civil War arguably did more damage to his reputation among liberals and the left at the time than any other. The Roosevelt administration was an active participant in the international decision to strangle the Spanish Republic by means of a policy of non-intervention. The US government went along with the British in refusing to offer any assistance to the Republic; refusing to sell it arms even while the fascist powers were pouring men and munitions into Spain. The Republic was under sustained, large-scale fascist attack by land, sea and air, and was deliberately deprived of the means to defend itself. This malevolent neutrality ensured its destruction. The Italians sent over

70,000 troops and 750 aircraft to fight in Spain. Italian submarines sank ships bound for Republican ports. The Germans sent some 19,000 soldiers and airmen to Spain.

While the US government embargoed the Republic, sections of big business gave whatever assistance they could to Franco. Henry Ford refused to sell trucks for cash to the Republic, but sold them on credit to the military rebels. GM and Chrysler also sold the rebels vehicles. Texaco kept the rebels supplied with oil on credit, running up a debt of $6 million before the war was over. Roosevelt later acknowledged that the non-intervention policy had been a mistake but this was, one suspects, intended to appease his critics rather than indicating any genuine lament for the Spanish Republic. Effectively the administration knowingly collaborated in the destruction of the Republic, refusing it assistance while the fascist powers accomplished its defeat. And once the intended objective was achieved, Roosevelt pacified the Republic's supporters in the US by letting it be known that he regretted its destruction. Whatever his later claims, the Roosevelt administration played an important role in the Republic's overthrow.[669]

An attempt was made, with the active support of Roosevelt's wife, Eleanor, to bring 500 Basque refugee children to the US. This was strenuously opposed by the Catholic Church and Roosevelt bowed to this pressure. He allowed the scheme to founder so that "an unknown number of refugee children whom the effort might have saved died instead of exposure, disease and starvation. Eleanor was dismayed and disgusted".[670]

What of Roosevelt's stand against anti-Semitism? A useful demonstration of the Teflon nature of his reputation is provided by the letter of greeting he sent to "a well-publicised Nazi rally in New York's Madison Square Garden" on 6 October 1934. The event was organised by the Friends of the New Germany and was picketed by hundreds of members of the Young People's Socialist League. As Blanche Wiesen Cook observes, the silence of his biographers on this well-reported episode is extremely interesting.[671] In November 1938, in response to the Kristallnacht pogrom in Germany in which 91 Jews were murdered and some 30,000 arrested and despatched to concentration camps, Roosevelt withdrew the US ambassador from Berlin for consultations. The State Department was looking for a gesture that would not "provoke retaliation that would hurt us". Roosevelt refused to support the relaxation of immigration quotas in order to allow Jewish refugees from Germany into the US. Although he "could scarcely believe that such a thing could occur in a 20th century civilisation", he limited his response to extending visitors' visas by six months or longer if necessary.[672] As Wiesen Cook puts it, considering that he is believed by many to be the best friend American Jews ever had, his behaviour at this time is "unexplainable".[673]

Early in 1939 Robert Wagner attempted to pass a bill that would have allowed 20,000 Jewish children under the age of 14 into the country over a two-year period, on top of the existing quota. The so-called Wagner-Rogers bill died in committee with the president refusing to support it and no cabinet member speaking up in its support. As one of Roosevelt's cousins, Laura Delano, put it, "20,000 charming children would all too soon grow up into 20,000 ugly adults".[674] Roosevelt was not prepared to pay the political price. And while Roosevelt expressed sympathy for German Jewish refugees, this was accompanied by his privately condoning the strenuous efforts of his assistant secretary of state, Breckenridge Long, to keep them out of the US. The German passenger ship the *St Louis* arrived at Havana, Cuba, in May 1939, carrying 930 refugees, the last the Nazis allowed to leave the country. Almost all of them had bought entry permits that the Cuban government invalidated and only 24 were allowed to disembark. The rest found themselves facing the prospect of a return to Germany. Over 700 of them had already applied to the American quota scheme and had been allocated numbers for future entry. Roosevelt was urged to advance the quota date and let them in. He refused. Other countries agreed to take in the refugees so they did not have to return to Germany (Britain took in 288, France 224, Belgium 214 and Holland 181). Of those who were returned to mainland Europe, over 250 did not survive the war.[675]

It is worth noting here the role that Roosevelt's wife, Eleanor, has played in helping sustain his reputation as a liberal. She had been an active supporter of the labour movement since the early 1920s. She had joined the Women's Trade Union League in 1923 and in the winter of 1926 had actually joined a picket line outside a New York box factory. In the 1930s she had become a union member herself, when she joined the Newspaper Guild. Most famously, in 1939 she refused to cross a picket line of striking waitresses outside the George Mason Hotel in

Washington to attend a ball in her husband's honour.[676] She was also a strong supporter of an anti-lynching law and a very public opponent of segregation. Roosevelt's refusal to support these causes appalled her. She was also outraged by his refusal to support the Republican cause in the Spanish Civil War. As far as she was concerned, Spain was "the moral equator".[677] She urged that Jewish refugees be allowed into the country. And as for Breckenridge Long, she considered him a fascist, although Roosevelt forbade her to call him that.[678] Both at the time and since there has been an assumption that Roosevelt must have secretly sympathised with his wife's liberal opinions. There is no real evidence for this. In fact, tolerating her opinions and behaviour helped keep some of the people he was betraying in the Democrat camp.

The Popular Front

How did the Communist Party respond to the Roosevelt Depression? During the tumultuous years 1935 to 1939 the party had established itself as the dominant force on the left; indeed, as far as many were concerned, it was the left. This had been made possible by the dramatic change from the sectarian ultra-leftism of the Third Period to the embrace of the Popular Front. There has been a debate regarding the provenance of this change in strategy: was it the work of members of the American party responding to the New Deal and the rise of the CIO or was it a decision imposed by the Comintern?[679] Certainly there were many party members seriously unhappy with aspects of the Third Period. It had after all been quite brutally imposed on the American party in the first place, with the Lovestone leadership being expelled for opposing the turn.

During the 1934 dockers' strike in San Francisco, Third Period trade union policy had been completely disregarded by the local party leadership. Sam Darcy had abandoned the futile attempt to build revolutionary trade unions, dropped the condemnation of AFL unions as fascist, and instead concentrated efforts on building a rank and file movement within the ILA and involving other AFL unions in the struggle. This, as we have seen, had been triumphantly successful. Darcy had wanted to carry this approach over into the political field by supporting Upton Sinclair's EPIC campaign for the governorship of California. This was not really a presaging of the Popular Front with its abandonment of revolutionary politics, but was a return to pre Third Period revolutionary politics. In 1934 Darcy would have completely rejected as inconceivable the embrace of the New Deal that the Popular Front was to involve. As it was, the party leadership in New York rejected any idea of support for Sinclair and instead ordered Darcy to stand against him. He was ordered to conduct a classic Third Period campaign, complete with denunciations of Sinclair's fascist intentions. Darcy, without any enthusiasm whatsoever, faithfully obeyed.[680]

This shows that whatever reservations and disagreements with the Third Period party members might have had, in the end they accepted as a condition of party membership that the Comintern dictated party strategy. The Communist Party only adopted the Popular Front turn when the Comintern gave the order. If the Comintern had continued the Third Period strategy, the party might well have lost members rather than grown, but it would never have revolted against Moscow. Such a prospect was absolutely inconceivable. The extent to which Moscow dictated party strategy is, of course, best shown by the way that the Popular Front strategy, despite the enthusiastic support of the overwhelming majority of party members, was nevertheless abandoned overnight on the orders of the Comintern at the time of the Hitler-Stalin Pact.

The Popular Front was the Comintern's response to the changing needs of Soviet foreign policy. Stalin's failure to reach some sort of understanding with the Nazis in 1933 led to the decision to seek an alliance with Britain, France and the US.[681] This foreign policy decision led to the abandonment of the revolutionary struggle to achieve a Soviet America in favour of a commitment to strengthening those forces perceived to be sympathetic to an alliance under the banner of anti-fascism. Indeed, anti-fascism became the cornerstone of Communist policy, so much so that anyone who continued to argue the case for revolutionary politics was accused of aiding fascism. It is worth noting that if Stalin had reached an understanding with the Nazis in 1933-34, similar to that achieved in 1939-41, there would have been no Popular Front.

The Popular Front turn was certainly successful in terms of the growth of the party. In 1936 membership stood at 41,000, by 1937 it was up to 62,000, by 1938 up to 82,000, and in 1939 the party claimed to have briefly reached a membership of 100,000. This did not, as

Browder later acknowledged, involve any strengthening of the revolutionary forces in American society. Looking back some 30 years later he proudly argued that the CP in this period became "the most single-minded practical reformist party that America ever produced". The Popular Front, he said, had not advanced the cause of revolutionary socialism in the US by even "one inch". On the contrary it had "buttressed the Roosevelt New Deal and postponed revolutionary prospects indefinitely".[682] This is hard to argue with.

The wholehearted embrace of Roosevelt and the New Deal was not an immediate response to the Comintern's decisions. It was accomplished over time, and really only came to fruition after Roosevelt's "Quarantine" speech of 5 October 1937. On this occasion he very specifically identified Germany and Japan as threats to international stability and called for their isolation.[683] It was only after this speech that the Communist Party really began arguing that Roosevelt was the leader of the American Popular Front whether he liked it or not. Browder himself charted the development of party policy as proceeding from "stubborn opposition to Roosevelt" in 1933-34 to "a little support for Roosevelt", although "our main fire was directed against his enemies" in 1935-36, until in 1937 "Roosevelt's programmatic utterances...when combined with the legislative programme of the CIO" actually came to constitute "a People's Front programme of an advanced type". The Communist Party pledged its support to the president: "We Communists welcome his speeches, agree with their central thoughts and quietly and calmly tell the president he has nothing to fear from us, on the contrary, he will receive our help." In 1938 the party was distributing leaflets proclaiming that "We Do Not Propose to Let the President Down".[684] Unfortunately, this decision to rally behind the president came just as his fiscal conservatism was plunging the country into renewed Depression and the New Deal was coming to an end. Roosevelt's own concerns were increasingly with the threat that Germany and Japan posed to the interests of American capitalism. But, of course, party strategy had more to do with Soviet foreign policy concerns than with what was happening to the American working class. In many respects all that distinguished the CPers from New Deal liberals at this time was their devotion to the Soviet Union.

What did this mean for party members? George Charney remembered how on one occasion during the Third Period he had been censored for leaving the slogan "For a Soviet America" off a factory leaflet. All this changed with the embrace of the Popular Front:

> Overnight we adjusted our evaluation of Roosevelt and the New Deal. Where we had been prone to damn all things American, we were now reassured that patriotism was not necessarily reactionary or the "last refuge of scoundrels", that there was a difference between bourgeois democracy and fascism, that we had to cherish democratic traditions and, above all, that transcending the class struggle, a basis existed for common action between the Soviet Union and the bourgeois democratic nations of the West. It is difficult to describe the profoundly transforming impact of these ideas on the party.

While the industrial struggle still had priority in theory, in practice "the centre of gravity shifted to the community and election cycles... In the twinkling of an eye the orientation changed, [and] everyone became an expert on election strategy." "Anti-fascist unity" became the overriding concern, whereas socialism belonged to "the future, inevitable, of course, but quite nebulous". What mattered was the People's Front so that the party, "which had hitherto been oriented to the naked forms of the class struggle such as picket lines and relief struggles, now acquired an astonishing flair for electoral politics". This change inevitably had an effect on party leaders and officials: "The proletarian garb favoured by functionaries was replaced by the business suit; our professional revolutionaries could hardly be distinguished from office executives; bus travel was replaced by Pullman".[685] The party was working within the New Deal coalition, helping to elect liberal and left Democrats to office, courting a new found respectability. Peggy Dennis accompanied her husband, Gene, one of the leaders of the party and its future general secretary, to Washington DC, where they lobbied sympathetic Congressman on behalf of the organisation. She writes, rather optimistically, that through these men "many of Gene's and Browder's memos were relayed to the president's attention".[686] The party was in the political mainstream.

Whereas the Communist Party had once proudly situated itself in an international revolutionary tradition, now it increasingly celebrated itself as part of a home-grown American revolutionary tradition, a tradition that included the likes of Thomas Jefferson and Abraham Lincoln. Indeed, the party was the modern day bearer of their political heritage.

In 1938 the party published a book, *I Like America*, by its leading literary critic, Granville Hicks. This was the party's most important popular rehearsal of the politics of the Popular Front, written for a liberal audience. Here Hicks presented a resolutely reformist account of the way forward. He condemned the inequality and injustice prevalent in American society, protested against the brutality with which the police and vigilantes broke strikes and argued that only a planned economy could deliver abundance. Indeed, a planned economy would allow the realisation of "the American Dream". He discussed, somewhat reluctantly, the Communist Party's support for the Soviet Union, acknowledging that there are some restrictions on civil liberties in Russia, but most people "have more freedom than they have ever had before". But there is no reason "to believe that the introduction of Socialism in the United States would follow the same course that it has in Russia". Indeed, "I do not propose to do away with capitalism right now and all of a sudden. Instead, I merely advocate that we do what we can within the capitalist framework, to get our productive machinery working and to distribute its output to those who need it." The Communist Party was only advocating reforms, "wages and hours bills, social security legislation, protection of civil liberties and especially the right to organise", that most right-thinking people could agree on.[687] The book sold some 50,000 copies. Hicks, who was to leave the party over the Nazi-Soviet Pact the following year, later remembered that what had won him over had been the party's "emphasis on American traditions, its willingness to cooperate with all anti-fascists". At the time he wrote the book, "the party seemed to me more than ever the great hope for the United States". Its policies were, he argued, "acceptable to most liberals".[688]

We have already considered the impact of the Popular Front on the CP trade union policy. The attempt to build rank and file movements in the unions was replaced by a policy of capturing positions in the trade union bureaucracy. Increasingly, those occupying these positions never admitted to being CP members or actually denied membership. The party's strategy was not to wage class war on the shop floor, but was to use the unions to pass resolutions endorsing Popular Front policies and furthering the interests of Soviet foreign policy. The key to this was their alliance with John L Lewis. Whereas in the 1920s Lewis "had been the chief enemy of the Communists", he became "their patron saint" in the late 1930s.[689] And the Communists were very successful in entrenching themselves in leadership positions in a number of CIO unions. Foster proclaimed that the Communists were "no longer an opposition force", that they now held "many official posts" and "shared the responsibility of carrying on the movement".[690]

There were two areas where the party did criticise the Roosevelt administration: the cutbacks in the administration's relief programmes, and the policy of non-intervention in Spain. The party campaigned strongly in support of the Republican cause and raised a volunteer force, the Abraham Lincoln Brigade, to fight as a contingent of the International Brigades in Spain. The heroism of these volunteers, mostly party members, was to ennoble the party. Over 700 men died fighting for the Republic. It was one of the greatest displays of international solidarity of the 20th century. The Spanish war became a centrepiece of the anti-fascist alliance that the party was dedicated to building.[691]

At the very same time as the party took a stand over Spain it was also celebrating the Soviet Union and its achievements, not least the Russian success in hunting down and eliminating the fascist fifth column inside Russia. In 1937 William Z Foster found time to write a 79-page pamphlet defending, indeed celebrating, the Second Moscow Trial, *Questions and Answers on the Piatkov-Radek Trial*. He told of how the defendants, one after another, gave evidence "of Trotsky's plot to smash the Soviet government with the help of the fascists". Trotsky, he wrote, had agreed to cede the Ukraine to Germany and to turn Russia into a German client state, restoring capitalism in the process. The Soviet government was to be overthrown "by fascist troops and Trotsky assassins". Fortunately the plot had been foiled. Foster eulogised the Soviet system in the most fulsome terms:

> The Soviet government...is founded on the liberty of the masses. Despite the lies of international capitalist mouthpieces, in no country in the world is there so much real democracy as in the Soviet Union... The new Soviet Constitution raises this fundamental and growing liberty to a higher stage. This document is, as Stalin says, "the only thoroughly democratic constitution in all the world"... The Russian workers and farmers are building the first real classless democracy in the history of the world.

The little problem of the Soviet Union being a one-party state was got over in a dazzling display of dialectics, courtesy of Comrade Stalin: political parties represent different social classes and as in Russia there are only the workers and the farmers, who are united, and no capitalist class, there "are grounds for only one party, the Communist Party". Stalin, Foster insisted, was "not a dictator, but the freely chosen leader of a great democracy". As for the country being overrun by the secret police, this was "a tissue of lies". Trotsky's denunciation of the trials as a "frame-up" was countered with an invitation to "return to Moscow and face the courts of the Russian Revolution". He could be sure of a fair trial because "Soviet courts always give all prisoners an honest hearing". And he warned that while the "American Trotskyites are only a handful... they have shown a capacity to do much harm". They were "a diseased growth that must be cut away from the body of the working class".[692]

The Comintern regarded the defence of the trials as of considerable importance. Indeed, it actually specified in "hundreds of documents and messages—memos, reports, letters, cables—how the trials should be understood, and how their verdicts should be presented to the American public". This was not something Communist Party members were allowed to be agnostic on. They were required to actively celebrate the Great Terror as a victory over the fascist fifth column inside Russia. This was at a time when Stalin's regime far exceeded Hitler's in murderous brutality. Before the outbreak of the Second World War the Nazis had killed some 10,000 Germans; the Russian government was responsible for the deaths of millions of Russians. Indeed, the Stalin regime killed more German Communists (they had fled to Russia for safety), than the Nazis killed in this period. This culminated, of course, in the Russians handing German Communists over to the Gestapo at the time of the Nazi-Soviet Pact.[693]

The unpleasant truth is that Foster, who had spent his life fighting for the liberation of the working class, became an apologist for one of the most brutal murderous regimes in history. He was not alone in this, of course. Communists throughout the world, men and women, who made incredible sacrifices in the fight against oppression and exploitation, celebrated the Russian tyrant, condemned his victims and denied his crimes. This subservience has never been adequately explained. But it was not just Russians who suffered under the Stalin regime. There are also American victims who deserve to be memorialised. Indeed, a good case can be made that Stalin was responsible for the deaths of considerably more American Communists and Communist sympathisers than the US government was in the 1930s. To its shame, the American Communist Party leadership made no effort to discover the fate of those Americans who had emigrated to the Soviet Union in the 1920s and 1930s and disappeared into the gulags, let alone made any protest against their imprisonment, torture and execution. The US government, it has to be said, showed a similar lack of interest in the fate of what one diplomat callously described as "merely flotsam and jetsam on the sea of life".[694]

The adulation of Stalin was an international phenomenon, a compulsory requirement for Communists everywhere. It has considerably more in common with the religious trappings of absolute monarchy than with any notion of socialism that existed before the rise of Stalinism. Earl Browder, who cultivated his own cult of the personality, provides a classic example of Stalin worship:

> And with regard to Joseph Stalin, who has shown the way to the peoples of the world, as to how our enemies can be decisively defeated, how the eternal crisis and starvation of the capitalist world can be overcome, how a life of growing prosperity, well-being, culture and happiness can be won for the broad millions of the whole population, we declare before the whole world, with the deepest pride, that we have been brought to admire, to love, to respect, and to learn from, the greatest leader of democracy that mankind has ever produced, the greatest helper and guide of the common people of every land, the symbol of the united strength of the toiling masses in victory over their oppressors, none other than the man who is the object of the concentrated hatred of every exploiter in the world, Joseph Stalin.[695]

The Nazi-Soviet Pact

The Popular Front came to a sudden and abrupt end on 23 August 1939 when the Nazi-Soviet Non-Aggression Pact was concluded. In the most brutal and unequivocal manner possible Soviet foreign policy changed the political strategy of Communist Parties throughout the world overnight. The American party leadership were not, of course, at any stage consulted about the pact and the change in strategy that it was to occasion. It came as a complete surprise to them. All that they were required to do was to endorse it, regardless of the domestic consequences—and endorse it they did.

For many party members the news was devastating. Peggy Dennis remembered collapsing on the floor. Hatred of fascism had been at the heart of Communist politics and now "came the pact between the Soviet Union and the arch-enemy of all humanity". After the shock of the pact:

> came startling statements by Soviet Foreign Minister Molotov. He now claimed that Hitler fascism was "just another ideology"; that "one may accept or reject the ideology of Hitlerism as well as any other ideological system"; that it had become "not only senseless but criminal to wage a war camouflaged as a fight for 'democracy.'" He chided "short-sighted people" who had gotten carried away by "over-simplified, anti-fascist propaganda". He said the very existence of the Soviet-German pact attested to a change in German foreign policy.[696]

She was not alone. Steve Nelson remembered feeling "like I had been hit by a bolt of lightning" when he heard the news. As he acknowledged, in response to the pact, the party was soon to relegate anti-fascism "to the back burners. We called off our campaign to boycott Nazi goods, disbanded the Anti-Nazi League in Hollywood and watered down our educational efforts to alert people to the dangers of fascism." The party effectively abdicated its leadership "in the fight against fascism" and "people saw us as mechanical pawns of Soviet foreign policy". What was astonishing was that despite the shock, there was only "minimal disagreement within the party over these policies... people either quickly fell into the groove or left... There was scarcely any debate within the party either on a local or national level".[697]

John Gates, a future editor of the *Daily Worker*, described the pact as coming "like a thunderclap" and throwing both party leaders and the rank and file membership into "utter confusion". Once it became clear what the line was, as he acknowledges, "our main attack was against the West. We did not support fascism, but our sharpest criticism was reserved for the Western democracies". The new turn "cost us heavily". As he puts it, "the entire democratic current denounced us. New epithets were coined at our expense: 'red fascists' and 'Communazis.'" The Popular Front was "shattered". From the outside Communist policy looked inconsistent, but there "was one consistency: we supported Soviet policies whatever they might be".[698] For George Cherney, the pact was "a complete shock". The party had been "totally committed to the anti-fascist struggle" and everyone had "an implacable hatred of Hitlerism". Now they were all left "limp and confused... We literally prayed for guidance." The pact left "an ache of uncertainty that continued for years to torment me and many of the comrades". Like Peggy Dennis, he particularly remembered that:

> the one incident that may have proved most revelatory was when Molotov remarked to Ribbentrop that "ideology was a matter of taste". Suddenly the ideology of fascism had become a matter of individual preference, of taste, of "de gustibus". I was never able to forget this revolting episode or the manner in which we hushed it up and ignored it as though we instinctively feared to analyse its implications. And yet, in spite of these shattering experiences our faith held. The Soviet Union could not be wrong. It was still the socialist fatherland.[699]

Although the pact cost the party members, Peggy Dennis, Steve Nelson and George Charney were not among those who left. Indeed, both Peggy Dennis and Steve Nelson were soon to go underground, helping establish a secret organisation ready to continue the struggle if the party should be banned and its members interned.

How did the party explain away its clear subordination to Moscow? William Z Foster provided an ingenious explanation by way of a somewhat strained comparison between Marxism-Leninism and Darwinism. Just as scientists "had no need of instructions from London in order to appreciate the validity of Darwin's great works", so Communists had no need of orders from Moscow to support "the socialist policy of the Soviet Union, world leader of the oppressed masses; it wins support by virtue of its intrinsic merit".[700] Of course this comparison only works if Darwin's theory had been regularly changed to fit the twists and turns of British foreign policy so that one day humanity was descended from apes, another day apes were descended from humanity and on other occasions humanity was descended from other species altogether!

Initially, and quite understandably, the party leadership had trouble catching up with the implications of the pact. To begin with it was welcomed as a blow for peace and against fascism. Then when the Nazis invaded Poland on 1 September the *Daily Worker*, unaware that this was the beginning of a secretly agreed Nazi-Soviet partition of the country, supported Polish resistance. On 3 September it pledged "full moral, diplomatic and economic help for the Polish people and those who help Poland defend its national independence". As late as 11 September the *Daily Worker* proclaimed on its front page, "All Aid to the Heroic Polish People", condemned "this wanton fascist attack" and carried an editorial celebrating Warsaw's "heroic resistance". The Comintern quickly corrected this misunderstanding. Poland, it was suddenly discovered, was "that prison-house of nations...which was emerging as a smaller edition of Hitler's Reich".[701] Its disappearance was to be celebrated, not lamented. And when the Red Army itself invaded Poland they came as liberators, "met with joy by Poles, Byelorussians, Ukrainians and other minorities".[702] Poland now became "fascist Poland" and "White Guard Poland". As for the pact, Browder actually argued that it was a model agreement that other peace-loving countries should seek to emulate! "The Soviet-German agreement", he insisted, "is thus the best example of the way to peace".[703]

By October, with Europe embroiled in war, the differences between the New Deal and anti New Deal camps were losing their significance for the party leadership. What united Roosevelt with the reactionary right was now considerably more important than what divided them.[704] Opposition to the "Second Imperialist War" became the watchword—the party believed that the British and the French were determined to change the war from a war against Germany to an attack on the Soviet Union and that Roosevelt supported this. Roosevelt was transformed from the much-loved leader of the US Popular Front into an arch-imperialist warmonger, who was determined to involve the US in an attack on the Soviet Union. In October 1940 Browder argued that the "Roosevelt course is essentially for America the same direction which Hitler gave for Germany in 1933". Roosevelt was becoming "an unlimited military dictator" and Congress was America's "Hitler Reichstag". Roosevelt, according to Browder, was "adopting the techniques of Hitler".[705]

While the Nazi-Soviet Pact was damaging enough, this damage was seriously compounded by the Russian attack on Finland in the winter of 1939-40. In *The War Crisis: Questions and Answers*, published in January 1940, Foster, at his most robotically Stalinist, attempted to put the Finnish crisis in some sort of context for the party membership. The Roosevelt administration had "adjusted its previous superficial quarrels with the great capitalist interests" and "become an instrument for carrying out their imperialist war policy". American policy was now "the organisation of a general war of the capitalist powers against the Soviet Union". The administration had "lapsed back into the anti-Soviet attitude characteristic of the Hoover-Coolidge days". Foster did his best to defend the indefensible, condemning US trade with Japan on one page and defending Soviet trade with Japan on another. He inevitably defended the Russian invasion of Finland. He tried to explain why it was that in July 1939 the *Daily Worker* had welcomed the election of a Finnish coalition government of "socialists, farmers and liberals" with an "economic and social reform policy", but now that the Russians have invaded that same government was denounced as a dictatorship. Finnish democracy, he patiently explained, "was only a facade, obscuring the true features of the brutal capitalist system, the tool of foreign imperialism". This, of course, had only become apparent once the Popular Front turn came to an end.

What was the impact of the pact and the Finnish War on the party membership? There were a few high profile resignations, most notably Granville Hicks. He remembered hearing the announcement of the pact on the radio news and saying to his wife, Dorothy, "Jesus Christ, that knocks the bottom out of everything." Even so, he did not actually resign until after the Russian invasion of Poland. The party was in such "a state of confusion" that a period of "free discussion" was allowed in which members could speak their minds. Discussion was free, only in the sense that you could say what you "thought without being immediately denounced as a Trotskyist or a fascist". If you were not persuaded of the line, however, you either left or were expelled. Hicks left.[706] Estimates of the actual number of members who left vary widely. The most recent account estimates that only 13 percent of the membership left over the pact.[707]

Whatever the impact on members, the impact on supporters and sympathisers was absolutely devastating. The party's periphery had to a considerable extent been built up on the basis of its militant anti-fascism. Moreover, many party sympathisers had only tolerated the Moscow Trials and the Great Terror because of the Soviet Union's anti-fascism. Now that Russia was allied with Nazi Germany allegations that the trials were a gigantic frame-up suddenly seemed more credible, especially as the accused had all confessed to and been shot for working for Stalin's new friends.

One particularly difficult problem the party faced was explaining the pact to its Jewish members and sympathisers. Melech Epstein remembered the impact among Jewish workers as "volcanic". In the New York clothing factories Communists were greeted by their Jewish workmates "with the Nazi salute and a 'Heil Hitler'. There were fist fights in the garment centre." Jewish party members had "a look of shock and simple disbelief". Epstein remembered being told to "have trust in Stalin". Once he resigned (he had been a member since 1921), he was denounced as a Trotskyist who had sold the party to the HUAC.[708] Browder attempted to explain the new situation to Jewish party members in a pamphlet, *The Jewish People and the War*, published in May 1940. He set about demolishing the myth that Britain and France were "a lesser evil for the Jewish masses" than Nazi Germany. He showed a sudden enthusiasm for Zionism, condemning "Chamberlain's betrayal of the Jews in Palestine". The British had unleashed "a reign of terror" against the Jews. Indeed, "British soldiers have murdered Jews for daring to protest against the establishment of a ghetto in the land which English imperialism cynically promised as a Jewish homeland". There was, he insisted, "no lesser evil for the Jewish people". And as for Roosevelt, he had now allied himself with domestic anti-Semites! Only the Soviet Union stood as a beacon of freedom for the Jewish people.[709] None of this, one suspects, was intended to convince the non-believer, but was merely to provide party members with some cynical arguments they could use until the next time the line changed.

Red scare 1940

The Communist Party actively prepared itself for US involvement in a war against the Soviet Union and its inevitable accompaniment by internal repression and the crushing of dissent. Steps were taken to prepare for the banning of the party and the internment of its members. A secret underground apparatus was set up to continue the struggle in conditions of illegality. Steve Nelson and his wife Margaret were among those who went "on the shelf". They disappeared, changed their names and moved to isolated houses in the countryside where they kept a deliberately low profile, while they waited to take over when the party was banned and its leadership arrested. "Ink, mimeograph machines, and reams of paper and stencils were hidden away in the woods", Nelson remembered. Some of them are probably still there.[710] Peggy Dennis and her husband Gene also went underground. One morning Gene left their apartment as usual but never came back, and three weeks later she went out shopping and never returned. They walked away from everything, spending the next 17 months "living in various backwoods cottages". Eventually they were ordered to Russia, smuggled out of the country, and arrived in Moscow only weeks before the German attack.[711]

If Hitler had not invaded the Soviet Union before the US became involved in the war there is every likelihood that the party would have been banned. Although this never came to pass, there was still a red scare unleashed against the Communists in 1940-41. Earl Browder himself was imprisoned in April 1941 for having travelled on a false passport. He was sentenced to four years in prison. This was clearly a politically motivated sentence. Serious consideration was given to prosecuting veterans of the Lincoln Brigade for violating the 1818 statute prohibiting recruitment for foreign armies. The FBI carried out arrests, but in the end the decision was taken not to prosecute.[712] Harold Ickes noted in his diary that while the administration was not moving against Communists because they were Communists, as "it was not illegal to belong to that party", nevertheless, "every possible effort is being made to indict any Communist who has violated the criminal laws in any respect".[713] That could change, however. In June 1940 Roosevelt signed the Smith Act, which, among other things, effectively criminalised revolutionary politics. The House of Representatives passed the bill by 382 to four votes.

The red scare was carried into the CIO and onto the shop floor. The most dramatic instance of this was provided during the UAW strike at North American Aviation in southern California that began on 5 June 1941. Longstanding grievances led to the walkout and the union put "a massive picket line of several thousand workers, perhaps the longest picket line in Los Angeles history" around the plant.[714] From the beginning the strike was denounced by the administration, the press and sections of the CIO leadership as a Communist conspiracy against US defence preparations. Philip Murray, now CIO president in place of

John L Lewis, ordered the strikers back to work and the UAW sent Richard Frankensteen to bring this about. Wyndham Mortimer, by now one of the UAW organisers in the aircraft industry, was asked where he stood with regard to the strike. He replied, "Well, I am with the rank and file," and was promptly fired.[715] Roosevelt determined on military intervention if union officials could not get the workers back to work. At the cabinet meeting on 8 June, Ickes noted that everyone agreed "that there are active communistic influences at work". "There was", he went on, "very earnest discussion of some means to get rid of these labour agitators. There was even talk of asking for authority to build concentration camps".[716]

The officials completely failed to get the strike called off and on 9 June the police attempted to disperse the picket line by force. They were driven off. In response 2,500 federal troops were sent in to disperse the picket line at bayonet point. They arrived equipped with machine guns, anti-tank and anti-aircraft guns. The pickets were driven a mile from the gates. The *Los Angeles Times* crowed about how "it took no more than a single prick of a bayonet to deflate the bubble of defiance".[717] The strikers voted to return to work with the intention of marching back en masse, a demonstration of their continued solidarity and determination. The army prohibited the demonstration and ruled that the strikers had to individually reapply for their jobs. Mortimer provides a graphic account of the military intervention and subsequent de facto regime of martial law that was imposed:

> The forceful smashing of all picket lines; the illegal arrest of 16 strike captains by the troops and their detention in an army camp where they were stripped, fingerprinted, mugged and third degreed at great length; the subjecting of all neighbourhoods in which NAA workers lived to an armed patrol by army trucks loaded with machine guns; patrolling of the meetings of NAA workers even after they had formally decided to return to work. Most serious of all were the actions of the troops inside the plant. They were posted everywhere, bristling with arms and marching up and down all the aisles. Numerous workers were forced to tear up their union cards and to remove their union buttons. The officer in charge of the plant, Colonel Branshaw, posted a notice calling for an unlimited speed-up in production. Workers were subject to dismissal without possibility of redress.

The union negotiating committee members were all fired "and these men have remained blacklisted ever since".[718]

While most accounts of the North American Aviation strike do blame the Communist Party for instigating it, James Prickett has argued convincingly that while there was plenty of talk at the time of a Communist plot, there is no actual evidence to support this red scare. As he points out, between the summer of 1940 and December 1941 there were 159 strikes in plants "of primary defence importance" and in only four was Communist leadership even alleged. Whatever the talk at the time, there is no evidence of unions where the CP had a strong influence trying to foment strikes. The red scare did not, of course, require evidence.

On 22 June 1941 the Nazis invaded the Soviet Union and once again the Communist Party's position changed overnight. Only the day before the *Daily Worker* had ridiculed the very idea of such an attack being possible. Now the party abandoned its opposition to US involvement in the Second Imperialist War and instead demanded immediate US involvement in the People's War against Fascism. This changeover was to eventually involve the Communists calling for a no-strike policy in industry, for speed-up on the shop floor, for the suppression of opponents of the war and even for social peace once the war was over. Browder was to actually argue in 1944 that Marxists had to "subordinate their socialist convictions in all practical issues" to the interests of national unity, and after the war, "for a long period", they had to be ready "to cooperate in making capitalism work in America for the benefit of our people and the world". The Communist Party had already set "a magnificent example" by its support for the no-strike policy.[719] Some in the party leadership even suggested that the no-strike policy could continue after the war.

The American Trotskyists

While the Communist Party prospered in the late 1930s the small group of Trotskyists led by James Cannon, who had broken away and formed the Communist League in May 1929, remained marginalised. They were never to achieve the critical mass that would have enabled them to move centre stage. The Communist League had around 100 members when it was formed. It could not afford to have a phone installed in its headquarters until 1933. By 1935, following a merger with Abraham Muste's American Workers Party to form the Workers Party, it had about 700 members. By 1938 membership had increased to some 1,500. Even at its height, the American Trotskyist movement had less members than the Communist Party had paid full-timers. What we will attempt here is not a history of American Trotskyism, of its mistakes and successes,[720] but rather a brief discussion of some of the factors that kept it marginalised during a period of massive class struggle.

One major obstacle that Cannon and his comrades confronted was the Communist Party. From day one the Trotskyists were under sustained, unrelenting attack from:

> a party with a membership of tens of thousands of people, with not one daily but no less than ten daily newspapers in their arsenal, with innumerable weeklies and monthlies, with money and a huge apparatus of professional workers. This relatively formidable power was arrayed against a mere handful of people without means, without connections... They slandered us, they ostracised us, and when that failed to break us, they tried to beat us down physically.

In his history of the Trotskyist movement Cannon details the attempts that the Communists made, not to debate with their critics, but to deprive them of the right to be heard. The Communists routinely tried to break up Trotskyist meetings. The IWW helped them defend themselves from these attacks.[721] The Communists treated the Trotskyists as if they were a major threat. This had nothing to do with the situation in the US but was another policy imposed by the Comintern. The Comintern was determined to eliminate independent revolutionary politics and, as far as possible, to bring the international left under Communist control. The left was to become a tool of Russian foreign policy. The Trotskyists, although they were few in number, were a threat to that project. They called into question Stalin's fraudulent claim to the legacy of the Russian Revolution. Trotskyist exposés of the Moscow Trials were of tremendous importance. And although Trotskyist organisations never became mass parties anywhere in the world, they were nevertheless a potential alternative to the politics of Stalinism. It is important to remember that Stalin's domination over the international Communist movement was based on lies, on proclaiming that tyranny was freedom, that mass murder was justice and that exploitation and slavery were socialism. Any voice from the left contradicting these lies, especially the voice of one of the leaders of the Russian Revolution, was seen as a danger to be eliminated. This necessitated not just the systematic slandering of the Trotskyists as fascist agents but, where possible, their assassination, culminating in the murder of Trotsky himself on 20 August 1940, in which members of the American Communist Party were implicated.[722]

Considerable resources were devoted to slandering the Trotskyists. In Browder's *The People's Front*, the party's main theoretical statement of the Popular Front turn, some 10 percent of a 349-page book was devoted to abusing the few hundred American Trotskyists. He condemned "the sinister character of counter-revolutionary Trotskyism...it is nothing but an agent of fascism in the working class...the vanguard of world counter-revolution". These people, Browder insisted, had made "treachery...a science". Tolerating them was "nothing short of a crime against the working class". They might be few in number, but they work "with the deadliness of cholera germs". Just to make clear how much was at stake, Browder was adamant that without the elimination of Trotskyism the defeat of fascism "is impossible".[723] Just as the victims of the Moscow Trials were condemned as a fascist fifth column inside the Soviet Union, so American Trotskyists were a fascist fifth column inside the US labour movement. One reason for the ferocity of this assault was, without any doubt, to deter Communist Party members from engaging in any debate with the Trotskyists. They were expected to break with both friends and relations who became Trotskyists or (a much larger group) were accused of Trotskyism.

In an attempt to Americanise this attack Browder published a pamphlet in 1938, *Traitors in American History: The Lessons of the Moscow Trials*. Here he set out to show that American revolutionary history had been beset by traitors similar to those unmasked in the Soviet Union, although the Russians had been more effective at dealing with them. Where it had taken the US 38 years to root out the traitors to the American Revolution, the Soviet Union had "dug out and liquidated its treasonable sects in only about half that time". Clearly, there had not been enough executions in the aftermath of the American Revolution. He positively boasted of the success, in comparison, with which Russia had "cleansed itself of these vermin". What particularly upset him was the way the Trotskyists slandered Joseph Stalin, something which showed "the putrid essence of their murderous souls".[724] Of course, for the analogy with the American Revolution to really work, Washington's successor as president, John Adams, would have had to have executed all the surviving leaders of the revolution, with the likes of Thomas Jefferson, James Madison and others confessing to working for the British.

Not only was this sustained campaign intended to put the Trotskyists beyond the pale, but more generally it was intended to discredit any revolutionary critique of the Popular Front turn. The fact that the Communists were prepared to reinforce words with deeds was demonstrated by the suppression of the POUM in Spain in 1937. The known involvement of American Communists, such as George Mink, in this repression was a healthy reminder, if one were needed, of the seriousness of the Communist attacks. The Trotskyists in the US were themselves targeted by the Soviet secret police, with phones tapped, offices burgled and agents planted in their ranks. James Cannon's trusted secretary, Sylvia Franklin, was a Soviet agent.[725]

The Trotskyists inevitably found themselves having to devote much of their limited resources to trying to defend the tradition of revolutionary Marxism from the attacks of the Communist Party, exposing the Moscow Trials and helping provide security for Trotsky in exile in Mexico. In 1936 Max Shachtman published *Behind The Moscow Trials: The Greatest Frame-up in History*, a devastating critique of the first trial that still repays reading, unlike the various Stalinist apologies.[726]

At a time of massive working class struggle, they found themselves confronted with an unprecedented situation—the Communist Party was almost universally regarded as the organisation of the revolutionary left. It had behind it the enormous prestige of the Russian Revolution and the support of the world's only "Socialist" state, considerable resources, and its membership included many of the best and bravest militants and activists in the country. And towards the end of the 1930s the Communist Party was advocating, as the latest thing in Marxist thinking, support for the Democratic Party's milk and water brand of reformism. These were tremendous obstacles to developing genuine revolutionary politics. Looking back James Cannon was to describe Roosevelt as "the best political leader crisis-wracked American capitalism could possibly have found" and the Communist Party as "his indispensable helper". The Communist Party helped Roosevelt "domesticate" the working class revolt, "blunt its radical-revolutionary edge".[727] As we have seen, this is an assessment that Earl Browder came to share, although he regarded it as praise rather than criticism.

It is difficult, a generation after the collapse of the Soviet Union, to appreciate how enormous an obstacle Stalinism was to the development of revolutionary politics. If the resources of the Communist Party had been devoted to building a revolutionary party rather than to the service of Stalin's dictatorship, the story would have been very different. As it was, the Communists were able to successfully marginalise the Trotskyists.

One consequence of this was that the Trotskyist movement became plagued by factionalism and splits, its already weak forces dividing and dividing again. While the Communists had the certainty of their faith in Joseph Stalin and the Soviet Union, the Trotskyists had the considerably more difficult task of trying to understand the fate that had befallen the Russian Revolution and the nature of the tyranny that ruled in the Soviet Union. This crystallised towards the end of the 1930s around a bitter debate as to whether or not the Soviet Union remained in any way a workers' state. Paradoxically, the partition of Poland and the invasion of Finland were to do more damage to the Trotskyists than they did to the Communists. Trotsky argued from exile that Marxists should support the Soviet takeover in these two countries as defeats for world capitalism and extensions of workers' power. The Socialist Workers Party (SWP), which the US Trotskyists had established on 1 January 1938, was to split over the issue. For the Communists it was much simpler—you put your faith in Moscow or you left.

The one part of the country where the Trotskyists had succeeded in establishing a strong position in the local trade union movement was in the Teamsters in Minneapolis.[728] This position came under determined attack from Daniel Tobin, the Teamsters' leader, in the spring of 1941. Tobin took steps to remove the Trotskyists from office and, in response, the 5,000-strong Local 544 broke away and affiliated to the CIO. Tobin appealed to Roosevelt for assistance from the federal government. Instead of private detectives infiltrating Local 544, their job was now done by FBI agents.[729] As a direct response to Tobin's appeal the Minneapolis Trotskyists were indicted for their revolutionary politics and anti-war stand under the Smith Act. This prosecution was cheered on by the Communist Party, which had by now become strongly pro-war. Indeed, the party actually provided the FBI with "an important collection of documents to help prove the guilt of the Socialist Workers Party". These documents were accompanied by a 24-page account of the Trotskyist movement, "The Fifth Column Role of the Trotskyists in the United States", proving that they were "a strong fascist weapon in America".[730] On 16 August 1941 the *Daily Worker* pledged its support "in the fight to exterminate the Trotskyite Fifth Column from the life of our nation".[731] Eventually 18 Trotskyists were sentenced to prison; 12 received 16 months and six received a year and a day.[732] One of the accused, Grant Dunne, committed suicide while the trial was under way. The Communists thought their sentences disgracefully lenient. Albert Lannon remembered thinking they should have been shot.[733]

The irony of this was that in 1949 the leadership of the Communist Party were to be prosecuted and imprisoned under the same act. They were to receive harsh sentences after an openly political trial. Judge Harold Medina sentenced ten of the party's leaders to five years imprisonment and the eleventh, Robert Thompson, to three years because he was a war hero.[734] Even at this late stage the Communist Party still endorsed the conviction of the Trotskyists in 1941. At a Bill of Rights Conference in New York in July 1949 a resolution condemning the imprisonment of the Trotskyists was defeated with the black Communist Paul Robeson condemning them as "the allies of fascism... the enemies of the working class" and asking the delegates, "Would you give civil rights to the Ku Klux Klan?"[735]

Conclusion

The experience of the US working class during the 1930s offers both inspiration and example for us today. The scale of the crisis in the 1930s—social, economic and political—instead of completely crushing a weak labour movement, had a radicalising effect.

In 1934 the great strikes in Toledo, Minneapolis and San Francisco, led by assorted Socialists, Communists, Wobblies and Trotskyists, shifted the balance of class forces. This rank and file revolt precipitated a split in the trade union bureaucracy. A number of union leaders, led by John L Lewis of the UMW, broke away from the reactionary AFL to put themselves at the head of this working class insurgency. This brought the movement increased strength but also confronted it with new dangers. What followed was the great 1937 wave of sit-down strikes at GM, Chrysler and hundreds of other workplaces. These struggles again transformed the industrial landscape in the US.

While union organisation was dramatically extended, it was in the hands of a section of the union bureaucracy. Instead of resisting this official takeover of the labour revolt, the largest and most influential organisation on the left, the Communist Party, became complicit in it. Instead of building independent rank and file organisations, the CP set about becoming a part of the union bureaucracy. Not only did the Communists give up the attempt to build rank and file organisation, but their subordination to the interests of Soviet foreign policy led them to embrace Roosevelt's New Deal as the American Popular Front. When, with the conclusion of the Nazi-Soviet Pact in August 1939, Russian foreign policy required a revolution in domestic policy, the US Communist Party obliged regardless of the damage inflicted on the labour movement. And when the interests of Russian foreign policy were dramatically changed from alliance with the Nazis to bloody enmity by the German invasion of June 1941, the American Communist Party changed its stance literally overnight. To all but the most obtuse and determined observers, Communist Party policy with regard to all the great strategic issues was decided by the Stalin dictatorship in Moscow rather than by any engagement with the interests of the American working class.

This inescapable reality was to wreak havoc on the American left, leaving it exposed and vulnerable to the post-war red scare. While the ferocity of the post-war red scare is well known, the Communist Party played into the hands of its enemies with disastrous consequences for the US labour movement. The supporters of and apologists for Stalinist tyranny were never going to be the best defenders of civil liberties or workers' rights. It remains a tragedy for both the American and the international labour movement that many of the best and bravest militants and activists—men and women of great courage and dedication who were prepared to sacrifice everything for the struggle against tyranny and injustice—nevertheless freely subordinated themselves to the Stalin dictatorship.

The history of the US working class does not, of course, end with the history of the Communist Party. During the Second World War, while the CP enthusiastically supported the no-strike pledge, 6.77 million workers in the US went on strike. Once the war was over working class revolt erupted on the shop floor on an unprecedented scale. The years 1945 and 1946 saw the largest strike wave in US history. In 1945 3.5 million workers were on strike for a total of 38 million days and in 1946 4.6 million workers were on strike for a total of 116 million days. These struggles were to ensure that American workers participated in the prosperity that the US arms economy was to produce in the 1950s. For the left, however, the class war was to be swallowed up by the Cold War, and this is, of course, another story.

Nevertheless, the great wave of sit-down strikes in 1937 provides a tremendous example for the labour movement throughout the world today. At a time when the US ruling class seemed to have the whip hand, bolstered both by its huge wealth and by the effects of mass unemployment, socialist and communist militants seized the initiative and forced the most powerful corporations in the world into retreat. The physical seizure and occupation of the workplace put the employers on the defensive and decisively revitalised the US labour movement. Overwhelmingly these struggles that changed the face of America were led by young men and women fighting for the future.

Their fight is an inspiration for working people throughout the world today when we are once again confronted with an attempt to solve a grave economic crisis at the expense of the working class. At a time when politicians from all major parties in country after country stand revealed as wholeheartedly committed to protecting the interests of the rich and the super-rich, the experience of American workers in the 1930s shows both a way forward and the pitfalls to avoid. In the battle for the future there is much we can learn from the workers who sat down in GM and Woolworth's. The question is, will the future be determined by the rich and super-rich or will it be determined by the working class? This is the battle that faces us today.

Notes

1   William Forbath, *Law and the Shaping of the American Working Class*, Cambridge, Mass 1991, p98.

2   William Z Foster, *From Bryan to Stalin*, London 1937, pp108, 111-112.

3   William Z Foster, *The Great Steel Strike and Its Lessons*, New York 1920, pp62, 96, 111-112, 121, 134-135. See also David Brody, *Labor in Crisis*, Philadelphia 1965, for an academic study of the strike.

4   Mary Heaton Vorse, *Men and Steel*, London 1922, pp61-62.

5   George Soule, *Prosperity Decade: From War to Depression 1917-1929*, New York 1962, p200.

6   Colin Davis, *Power at Odds: The 1922 National Railroad Shopmen's Strike*, Urbana 1997, pp83, 131.

7   Davis, as above, pp154-155. See also Charles Alexander, *The Ku Klux Klan in the Southwest*, Norman 1995, p62.

8   Melvyn Dubofsky, *The State and Labor in Modern America*, Chapel Hill 1994, p97.

9   Bernard Mandel, *Samuel Gompers*, Yellow Springs 1963, pp444-446.

10 Philip S Foner, *The TUEL to the End of the Gompers Era*, New York 1991, p167. Dunne had been one of the leaders of the insurgent labour movement in Butte, Montana. After the kidnapping of the IWW organiser, Frank Little, by company gunmen in 1917, an attempt was made to kidnap him. "I had a .32 Colt in my coat pocket—with my hand on it— and I shot twice. Two of the men dropped and the third ran." The next day he searched the press for a report of the shooting, but found instead "headlines announcing that W F Dunne had disappeared" (from Sidney Howard, *The Labor Spy*, New York 1924, pp192-193). At this time Dunne believed that the Workers Party had played into the bureaucrats' hands by isolating themselves from the working class.

11 David McDonald, *Union Man*, New York 1969, pp44-45. McDonald was soon to become ferociously anti-Communist himself.

12 Irving Bernstein, *The Lean Years 1920-1933*, Boston 1960, pp127, 131.

13 Joyce Shaw Peterson, *American Automobile Workers 1900-1933*, Albany 1987, pp113, 126.

14 Sidney Fine, *"Without Blare of Trumpets": Walter Drew, the National Erectors' Association and the Open Shop Movement 1903-57*, Ann Arbor 1995, p203.

15 For Bill Hutcheson see Maxwell Raddock, *Portrait of an American Labor Leader: William C Hutcheson*, New York 1955.

16 Robert Zieger, *Republicans and Labor 1919-1929*, Lexington 1969, p250.

17 For the IWW see in particular Fred Thompson and Jon Bekken, *The Industrial Workers of the World*, Cincinnati 2006; Melvyn Dubofsky, *We Shall Be All*, Chicago 1969; and Philip S Foner, *The Industrial Workers of the World*, New York 1991.

18 For the Socialist Party at this time see James Weinstein, *The Decline of Socialism in America 1912-1925*, New York 1967; David Shannon, *The Socialist Party of America*, New York 1955; and Ernest Freeberg, *Democracy's Prisoner: Debs, the Great War and the Right to Dissent*, Cambridge, Mass 2008.

19 For the Red Scare see H C Peterson and Gilbert C Fite, *Opponents of War 1917-1918*, Madison 1957; Robert Murray, *Red Scare*, New York 1964; and Julian Jaffe, *Crusade Against Radicalism: New York during the Red Scare*, Port Washington 1972.

20 Elaine Elinson and Stan Yogi, *Wherever There'e A Fight*, Berkeley 2009, pp213-215. For contemporary indictments of the "Red Flag" episode see Upton Sinclair's 1929 article, "The Land of Orange Groves and Jails", which is reprinted in Lauren Coodley, *The Land of Orange Groves and Jails: Upton Sinclair's California*, Santa Clara 2004, and ACLU, *The California Red Flag Case*, New York 1930.

21 See in particular Paul Avrich, *Sacco and Vanzetti: The Anarchist Background*, Princeton 1991, and Moshik Temkin, *The Sacco-Vanzetti Affair*, New Haven 2009. See also for a contemporary indictment of the miscarriage of justice Felix Frankfurter, *The Case of Sacco and Vanzetti*, New York 1927.

22 David Goldberg, *Discontented America: The United States in the 1920s*, Baltimore 1999, p178.

23 Soule, as above, p123.

24 David Shannon, *Between the Wars: America 1919-1941*, Boston 1979, p178.

25 Mike Gold quoted in Page Smith, *Redeeming the Time: A People's History of the 1920s and the New Deal*, New York 1986, p187.

26 Peter Fearon, *War, Prosperity and Depression*, Deddington 1987, pp55, 67; Ronald Edsforth, *The New Deal*, Oxford 2000, pp21-22.

27 Oswald Garrison Villard, *Fighting Years: Memoirs of a Liberal Editor*, New York 1939, p498.

28 Villard, as above.

29 H M Gitelman, "Welfare Capitalism Reconsidered", *Labor History* 33 (1999), p23.

30 According to Frederick Lewis Allen, writing in 1931, "the Harding administration was responsible in its short two years and five months for more concentrated robbery and rascality than any other in the whole history of the Federal Government"—from his *Only Yesterday*, New York 1931, p128. For a more recent account of the corruption of the Harding administration see Charles Mee,

The Ohio Gang, New York 1981. While the celebrated oil scandal, the so-called Teapot Dome affair, is perhaps the best known of the administration's crimes, Attorney General Harry Daugherty was also for sale. Most astonishing though was the pillage of the Veterans Bureau, which was robbed of some $200 million, with hospitals being built at vastly inflated prices and medical supplies being sold off cheap, all in return for substantial bribes. Charles Forbes, the bureau's director, sold 72,000 bed sheets that cost $1 each for 20 cents, over a million towels that cost 54 cents each for 3 cents and nearly 30,000 pairs of pyjamas donated by the Red Cross for 30 cents each, and so on. And as for Andrew Mellon with his handouts to the rich, graft was "elevated beyond common recognition, transmuted and dignified to the status of policy" (p125).

31 William Leuchtenburg, *The Perils of Prosperity*, Chicago 1958, p89.

32 For a contemporary indictment of Mellon see Harvey O'Connor, *Mellon's Millions*, New York 1933.

33 Edward Robb Ellis, *A Nation in Torment: The Great Depression 1929-1941*, New York 1995, p25.

34 William Harbaugh, *Lawyer's Lawyer: The Life of John W Davis*, New York 1973, p196. Davis boasted that "I have a fine list of clients... I have JP Morgan and Company, the Erie Railroad, the Guaranty Trust company, the Standard Oil Company, and other foremost American concerns on my list. I am proud of them... Big business has made this country what it is." See Albert Kahn, *High Treason*, Croton NJ 1950, p77.

35 Roland Marchand, *Creating The Corporate Soul*, Berkeley 1998, pp140, 162; Leo Ribuffo, "Jesus Christ as Business Statesman: Bruce Barton and the Selling of Corporate Capitalism", in Leo Ribuffo, *Right, Center, Left*, New Brunswick 1992, pp117-119.

36 Richard Duboff, *Accumulation and Power: An Economic History of the United States*, New York 1989, p87; Soule, as above, pp122-127; Shannon, *Between the Wars*, as above, p150; Robb Ellis, as above, p26.

37 Shannon, as above, p45.

38 Ron Chernow, *The House of Morgan*, New York 1990, p322.

39　Sanford Jacoby, "American Exceptionalism Revisited", in Sanford Jacoby, *Masters to Managers: Historical and Comparative Perspectives on American Employers*, New York 1991, p174.

40　David Brian Robertson, *Capital, Labor and State*, New York 2000, p23.

41　Patricia Cayo Sexton, *The War on Labor and the Left*, Boulder 1991, pp1, 92. According to Philip Taft and Philip Ross, the United States "has had the bloodiest and most violent labour history of any industrial nation in the world". See their "American Labor Violence: Its Causes, Character and Outcome", in Hugh Davis Graham and Ted Robert Gurr, eds, *The History of Violence in America*, New York 1969, p281.

42　David Cannadine, *Mellon*, New York 2006, p361.

43　Stanley Vittoz, *New Deal Labor Policy and the American Industrial Economy*, Chapel Hill 1987, p57.

44　Bernstein, as above, p130.

45　Carl Meyerhuber, *Less Than Forever: The Rise and Decline of Union Solidarity in Western Pennsylvania 1914-1948*, Selingrove 1987, p82.

46　J Joseph Huthmacher, *Senator Robert Wagner and the Rise of Urban Liberalism*, New York 1971, p64.

47　Barry Michrina, *Pennsylvania Mining Families: The Search for Dignity in the Coalfields*, Lexington 2004, pp20, 21, 24.

48　Meyerhuber, as above, p143.

49　Cannadine, as above, pp528-529.

50　See Samuel Gompers, *Seventy Years of Life and Labour*, vol 1, New York 1925.

51　Forbath, as above, p158.

52　David Montgomery, *Workers' Control in America*, Cambridge 1980, p160.

53　Henry Pringle, *The Life and Times of William Howard Taft* 1, Hamden 1964, p128.

54　Bernstein, as above, pp193-194.

55　Zieger, as above, p261.

56　Joel Seidman, *The Needle Trades*, New York 1942, pp307-309.

57　Dayton David McKean, *The Boss: The Hague Machine in Action*, Boston 1940, p189.

58　Forbath, as above, p117.

59　David Kennedy, *Freedom From Fear: The American People in Depression and War 1929-1945*, New York 1999, p26.

60　Accounts of Fannie Sellins's death differ in detail, something which reflects the authorities' determination not to inquire too deeply. See, however, James Cassedy, "A Bond of Sympathy: The Life and Death of Fannie Sellins", *Labor's Heritage* 4 (1992), and Meyerhuber, as above, pp42-59.

61　Vorse, as above, p69.

62　J David Greenstone, *Labor in American Politics*, New York 1969, p19.

63　See Jerold Auerbach, *Labor and Liberty: The La Follette Committee and the New Deal*, Indianapolis 1966. For an excellent local study of the labour spy see Darryl Holter, "Labor Spies and Union-Busting in Wisconsin 1890-1940", *The Wisconsin Magazine of History*, 68, 4 (1985).

64　Leo Huberman, *The Labor Spy Racket*, New York 1937; Irving Bernstein, *The New Deal Collective Bargaining Policy*, New York 1975, pp9-10.

65　John Abt, *Advocate and Activist*, Urbana 1995, p64.

66　Auerbach, as above, p112; William Millikan, *A Union Against Unions*, St Paul 2001, pp223-224; Sidney Fine, as above, p63; Norman Ware, *Labor in Modern Industrial Society*, Boston 1935, pp367-368.

67　Stephen Norwood, *Strike-Breaking and Intimidation*, Chapel Hill 2002, pp171-193, and Robert Lacey, *Ford*, London 1986, p345. Lacey writes that "one of the saddest files in the Ford archive at Dearborn is labelled 'Labor Relations-Es'. The 'Es' stands for espionage, and the box is filled with the intelligence dossiers of the spies—known as 'spotters'—who worked on the assembly line, but whose real job was to keep a careful note of their fellow workers' badge numbers, and then to tittle-tattle on them in detailed reports: '11.03 I noticed all the men in this Dpt washing their hands in oil getting ready for lunch, which we eat at 11.15. 11.09 I saw E-4282 leave the Dpt and purchased two sausage sandwiches.'" And so on.

68　Heber Blankenhorn, *The Strike For Union*, London 1924, pp70-71.

69　Hosea Hudson, *Black Worker in the Deep South*, New York 1972, p43.

70　A J Muste, "Sketches for an Autobiography", in Nat Hentoff, ed, *The Essays of A J Muste*, New York 1970, pp65-66.

71   Thomas Brooks, *Clint: A Biography of a Labor Intellectual*, New York 1978, pp51-52.
72   William Z Foster, *Pages from a Worker's Life*, New York 1939, pp209-211.
73   John Fitch, *The Causes of Industrial Unrest*, New York 1924, p182.
74   John Gates, *The Story of an American Communist*, New York 1958, p34.
75   The phrase is taken from Joseph Page and Mary-Win O'Brien, *Bitter Wages*, New York 1973, p47.
76   Melvyn Dubofsky, *Industrialism and the American Working Class 1865-1920*, Arlington Heights 1975, p19; J K Corn, *Response to Occupational Health Hazards*, New York 1992, p4. For the 1936 and 1937 figures for fatalities see Granville Hicks, *I Like America*, New York 1938, p59.
77   Page and O'Brien, as above, p61.
78   Michael Cherniak, *The Hawk's Nest Incident*, New Haven 1986, pp20, 95-96; David Rosner and Gerald Markowitz, "Workers' Health and Safety: Some Historical Notes", in David Rosner and Gerald Markowitz, eds, *Dying For Work: Health and Safety in Twentieth Century America*, Bloomington 1987, ppxvi-xvii.
79   Cherniak, as above, pp105-106.
80   Page and O'Brien, as above, p63.
81   Testimony to the power and influence of big business is provided by the career of Democrat politician Homer Holt. First as West Virginia's Attorney General (1932-1937) and then as governor (1937-1941), he did his best to protect Union Carbide. When he stepped down as governor in 1941, he somewhat predictably became the company's chief legal representative!
82   One important exception occurred in Bogalusa, Louisiana, on 22 November 1919, when white trade unionists fought a lynch mob to protect Sol Dacus, a black union organiser. Lem Williams, J Bouchillon and Thomas Gaines were killed in the shootout and Stanley O'Rourke died later from his wounds. Their bravery allowed Dacus to make good his escape. See Stephen Norwood, "Bogalusa Burning: The War against Biracial Unionism in the Deep South 1919", *The Journal of Southern History*, 63, 3 (1997).
83   See Leon Fink, *Workingmen's Democracy: The Knights of Labor and American Democracy*, Urbana 1985; Melton

McLaurin, *The Knights of Labor in the South*, Westport 1978; and Joseph Gerteis, *Class and the Color Line*, Durham 2007.
84   For the IWW see Philip S Foner, *Organized Labor and the Black Worker 1619-1973*, New York 1976, pp107-119, See also Peter Cole, *Wobblies on the Waterfront*, Urbana 2007.
85   For the standard account of the East St Louis pogrom see Elliott Rudwick, *Race Riot at East St Louis*, Carbondale 1964, and more recently see Charles Lumpkins, *American Pogrom: The East St Louis Race Riot and Black Politics*, Athens, Ohio, 2008.
86   Herbert Shapiro, *White Violence and Black Response*, Amherst 1988, pp149-150. See also William Tuttle, *Race Riot: Chicago in the Red Summer of 1919*, Urbana 1970, and Arthur Waskow, *From Race Riot to Sit-In, 1919 and the 1960s*, Gloucester, Mass, 1975. For the most recent account see Jan Voogd, *Race Riots and Resistance: The Red Summer of 1919*, New York 2007.
87   Shapiro, as above, p63.
88   Hal Steed, *Georgia: Unfinished State*, Atlanta 1976, pp278-285.
89   Barbara Foley, *Spectres of 1919: Class and Nation in the Making of the New Negro*, Urban 2008, pp40-41. In fact, Williams was made a prison trustee, supervising black convicts, but was killed in an accident before any pardon was considered politic.
90   C Eric Lincoln, *Coming Through The Fire: Surviving Race and Place in America*, Durham 1996, pp24-25. Later, during the Second World War, when he was in the US army, he found himself crossing the country on a train where German prisoners of war could use the diner because they were white but black soldiers had to go without food (p5). Lincoln was to go on to become Professor of Religion and Culture at Duke University.
91   Shapiro, as above, p146; Donald L Grant, *The Way It Was In The South: The Black Experience in Georgia*, Athens 1993, pp316-317; Leon F Litwack, *Trouble In Mind: Black Southerners in the Age of Jim Crow*, New York 1998, pp288-289; Philip Dray, *At the Hands of Persons Unknown: The Lynching of Black America*, New York 2003, pp245-246; George Tindall, *The Emergence of the New South 1913-1945*,

Baton Rouge 1999, p172. Lynching was not just a rural or small town phenomenon in the South. In April 1923, for example, students at the University of Missouri lynched a black campus employee, James Scott, for allegedly making "an amorous pass" at a white girl. As W E B Du Bois observed in *The Crisis*, while Southern universities had often defended lynching, the University of Missouri was the first "actually to arrange a mob murder so that the students might see it in detail" and he bitterly congratulated them on their new "course in Applied Lynching". See Dray, as above, pp292-294.

92 See Grif Stockley, *Blood In Their Eyes: The Elaine Race Massacres of 1919*, Fayetteville 2001 and Robert Whitaker, *On the Laps of Gods*, New York 2008. See also Stockley's *Ruled By Race: Black/White Relations in Arkansas from Slavery to the Present*, Fayetteville 2009, pp153-179. And Walter White, *A Man Called White*, New York 1969, p49; Nan Elizabeth Woodruff, *American Congo: The African American Freedom Struggle in the Delta*, Cambridge, Mass 2003, p1.

93 Frank Freidel, *Franklin Roosevelt: The Ordeal*, Boston 1954, p30.

94 Robyn Spencer, "Contested Terrain: The Mississippi Flood of 1927 and the Struggle to Control Black Labour", *Journal of Negro History*, 79, 2, 1994, p172.

95 Pete Daniel, *The Shadow of Slavery: Peonage in the South 1901-1969*, Urbana 1990, pp149-163; John M Barry, *Rising Tide*, New York 1997, pp312-316, 322-323, 330, 378-385; Kenneth Robert Janken, *White*, New York 2001, p81.

96 Lester Chandler, *America's Greatest Depression*, New York 1970, pp4, 27; Rhonda Levine, *Class Struggle and the New Deal*, Lawrence 1988, p50.

97 Roger Biles, *Big City Boss in Depression and War: Mayor Edward J Kelly of Chicago*, DeKalb 1984, p32.

98 Irving Bernstein, *A Caring Society*, Boston 1985, p291.

99 Sidney Lens, *Unrepentant Radical*, Boston 1980, p14.

100 Ronald Edsforth, *The New Deal*, Oxford 2000, p82.

101 Rita James Simons, *As We Saw The Thirties*, Urbana 1967, p120.

102 According to Alan Lawson, the US "was equipped with the worst welfare system in the western world, a patchwork of voluntary institutions and pinch-penny state and local agencies": see Alan Lawson, *A Commonwealth of Hope*, Baltimore 2006, p9.

103 Frank Freidel, *Franklin Roosevelt: Launching the New Deal*, Boston 1973, p12. For Edmund Wilson in the 1930s see Daniel Aaron, "Edmund Wilson's Political Decade", in Ralph Bogardus and Fred Hobson, *Literature at the Barricades: The American Writer in the 1930s*, Alabama 1982.

104 Louis Adamic, *My America*, New York 1938, p113.

105 Lens, *Unrepentant Radical*, as above, p13.

106 Sean Dennis Cashman, *America in the Twenties and Thirties*, New York 1989, p120.

107 John Bauman and Thomas Goode, *In the Eye of the Great Depression: New Deal Reporters and the Agony of the American People*, DeKalb 1988, p97.

108 Edsforth, as above, pp84-85.

109 Steve Babson et al, *Working Detroit*, Detroit 1986, p57.

110 John Anderson, "How I Became Part of the Labor Movement", in Alice Lynd and Staughton Lynd, eds, *Rank and File: Personal Histories of Working Class Organizers*, New York 1988, pp42-43.

111 Bauman and Goode, as above, p102.

112 David Shannon, *The Great Depression*, Eaglewood Cliffs 1960, p27.

113 Nancy Weiss, *Farewell to the Party of Lincoln: Black Politics in the Age of FDR*, Princeton 1983, p15.

114 Raymond Wolters, *Negroes and the Great Depression*, Westport 1970, p91.

115 *The Public Papers and Addresses of Franklin D Roosevelt 1: The Genesis of the New Deal*, New York 1969, pp649, 846.

116 Edward Robb Ellis, *A Nation in Torment*, as above, p240. Of course, he did not mean it. Green remained resolutely opposed to militancy, but even he could see the dangers that were on the horizon.

117 The failure of fascism to become a mass phenomenon in the US is a neglected question but see my unpublished paper "It Did Not Happen Here: The Failure of Fascism in the United States in the 1930s".

118 Mauritz Hallgren, *Seeds of Revolt*, New York 1933, pp13, 132-133, 165-170, 348.

119 Biles, as above, p23.
120 According to Lovestone's biographer, at the meeting in Moscow that imposed the Third Period on the American party Lovestone and his allies, who were confident that they had the support of the great majority of the party's membership, were told by Stalin that they were deluding themselves. As he eloquently put it: "Who do you think you are? Trotsky defied me. Where is he? Zinoviev defied me. Where is he? Bukharin defied me. Where is he? And you! Who are you? Yes, you will go back to America. But when you get there nobody will know you except your wives." Stalin was, of course, absolutely right: the first loyalty of American Communists was to Moscow. See Ted Morgan, *A Covert Life: Jay Lovestone*, New York 1999, p99.
121 Irving Howe and Lewis Coser, *The American Communist Party: A Critical History*, New York 1974, pp187, 188.
122 William Z Foster, *Toward Soviet America*, Chicago 1932, ppv, 177-178, 185, 195, 275.
123 Nathan Glazer, *The Social Basis of American Communism*, New York 1961, p101. According to Glazer, 60,000 people joined the CP between 1930 and 1934, but membership only went up by 16,000.
124 Howe and Coser, as above, pp186-187.
125 According to Harvey Klehr, "From 1930 to 1934 the Communist Party was largely a party of the unemployed. Over 40 percent of the entire party membership was unemployed in 1932. At the Eighth Convention in 1934, Browder noted that 60-70 percent did not have jobs. In some districts 80 percent of new recruits between 1930 and 1934 were looking for work, and one party organ put the figure at 90 percent of the new recruits in 1933." See his *The Heyday of American Communism: The Depression Decade*, New York 184, p161.
126 See in particular James J Lorence, *Organizing the Unemployed*, New York 1996. See also Roy Rosenzweig, "Organizing the Unemployed: The Early Years of the Great Depression 1929-1933", *Radical America*, 10, 4 (1976).
127 Len De Caux, *Labor Radical*, Boston 1970, p162.
128 William Z Foster, *Pages From a Worker's Life*, New York 1939, pp184-187. See also Franklin Folsom, *Impatient Armies of the Poor*, Niwot 1991, pp252-253.
129 Peggy Dennis, *The Autobiography of an American Communist*, Westport 1977, p48.
130 Folsom, as above, p257. The LA police chief, Roy Steckel, had quite bluntly warned the organisers of an unemployed march earlier that year that if they went ahead "then some of your people will be killed. If it takes bloodshed to protect constituted authority then there will be bloodshed." From William Mullins, *The Depression and the Urban West Coast*, Bloomington 1991, p58.
131 Steve Nelson, with James Barrett and Rob Ruck, *Steve Nelson, American Radical*, Pittsburgh 1981, pp82-83. When the black Communist Harry Haywood, "the new nigger red from New York", was picked up by the Chicago police in 1934 as part of their attempted intimidation, they asked him how Harold Williamson was doing. See Harry Haywood, *Black Bolshevik*, Chicago 1978, p445.
132 See Richard Leo, *Police Interrogation and American Justice*, Cambridge 2008. He catalogues what was known at the time as "the Chicago treatment" in police departments across the country: "Suspects were beaten and kicked all over their bodies. They were hit with nightsticks and blackjacks, pistol butts, leather saps loaded with lead, slabs of wood, chairs and baseball bats. They were whipped with rubber hoses and leather straps, beaten on the soles of their feet with copper-bound rulers, and punched in the face, most commonly with clenched fists, sometimes with brass knuckles." He notes the use of "lighted cigars, matches, or red-hot pokers...and in at least one instance, enlisting a dentist to drill into the nerves of a suspect's molars". Prisoners were hung out of windows, subjected to water torture and, on occasions, to electric shock treatment. One Chicago speciality was beating suspects about the head with a telephone book (pp49-50).
133 John Williamson, *Dangerous Scot*, New York 1969, p81.
134 Randi Storch, *Red Chicago: American Communism at its Grassroots 1928-1935*, Urbana 2007, pp100-102.

135 St Clair Drake and Horace Clayton, *Black Metropolis: A Study of Negro Life in a Northern City*, New York 1945, p87.

136 Kimberley Philips, *Alabama North: African American Migrants, Community and Working Class Activism 1915-1945*, Urbana 1999, p202. According to John Williamson, altogether "five comrades were killed in local battles" with the Cleveland police, including a young black woman. See Williamson, as above, p97.

137 For the Ford Hunger March see Keith Sward, *The Legend of Henry Ford*, New York 1968, pp231-239. See also Babson et al, as above, p59.

138 Maurice Sugar, *The Ford Hunger March*, Berkeley 1980, p55.

139 B J Widick, *Detroit: City of Race and Class Violence*, Detroit 1989, pp49-50. For Ford's relations with the Soviet Union see Peter Filene, *Americans and the Soviet Experiment 1917-1933*, Cambridge, Mass 1967, pp120-121. See also Alex Goodall, "The Battle of Detroit and Anti-Communism in the Depression Era", *The Historical Journal*, 51, 2 (2008). Goodall quotes from Ford's *Dearborn Independent* newspaper, where, in November 1926, Russia was praised for "leaving behind the doctrines of world revolution and pure Marxism" and Stalin was praised for having "thrust aside at least temporarily the Jewish ideal of world revolution" (p465).

140 Sugar, as above, p54.

141 Hallgren, as above, p178.

142 Williamson, as above, p100.

143 Al Richmond, *A Long View From The Left*, Boston 1973, pp176-177. Richmond is almost the only person to have a good word for George Mink, who went on to work for the GPU, earning the nickname "The Butcher". He was involved in the destruction of the revolutionary left in Barcelona in 1937 and was "publicly charged by the anarchists as the organiser of the murder of Camillo Berneri and his friend Barbieri": see Hugo Dewar, *Assassins At Large*, London 1951, pp100-101.

144 De Caux, as above, p163.

145 Angelo Herndon, *Let Me Live*, Ann Arbor 2007, pp81, 228. See also Charles Martin, *The Angelo Herndon Case and Southern Justice*, Baton Rouge 1976. For

William Dunne and "the Negro question" see Mark Solomon, *The Cry Was Unity: Communists and African Americans*, Jackson 1998, pp45-46. For the ILD see Charles Martin, "The International Labor Defense and Black America", *Labor History* 26 (spring 1985).

146 Sidney Hook, *Out of Step*, New York 1987, p184.

147 John Spivak, *A Man In His Time*, New York 1967, pp229-230. Spivak reported the case and notes the ferocity of the anti-Semitism whipped up by the prosecution. It was his opinion that if the jury at the boys' second trial had found them innocent then both they and their lawyers would certainly have been lynched, "soldiers or no soldiers", such was the feeling at the time.

148 For the Scottsboro Boys see Dan T Carter, *Scottsboro: An American Tragedy*, Baton Rouge 1976, and Walter T Howard, *Black Communists Speak on Scottsboro*, Philadelphia 2008. This miscarriage of justice resulted in one remarkable volume, originally published in 1935, that is worth noticing: Lin Shi Chan and Tony Perez, *Scottsbro Alabama: A Story in Linoleum Cuts*, New York 2002.

149 Herndon, as above, pp158, 159, 164. According to Robin Kelley in his *Hammer and Hoe: Alabama Communists during the Great Depression*, Chapel Hill 1990, there were "dozens of young men killed or wounded" in this pogrom (p82).

150 Kelley, as above, p88.

151 Hallgren, as above, pp176-177.

152 Howe and Coser, as above, p229.

153 Howe and Coser, as above, p225.

154 Lens, *Unrepentant Radical*, as above.

155 Max Shachtman, "Radicalism in the Thirties: The Trotskyist View", in Rita James Simon, ed, *As We Saw The Thirties*, Urbana 1967, p19.

156 Franklin Rosemont, *Joe Hill: The IWW and the Making of a Revolutionary Working Class Counterculture*, Chicago 2003, pp371-371. Rosemont makes the point that "despite the fact that the party's rank and file barely knew of their existence, and that they are almost never mentioned in books on US radicalism, these Stalinist hit-men were a brutal fact of life for independent and revolutionary minded workers". As he puts it, these CP

"goon-squads" have succeeded in "eluding the attention of historians".

157 Lens, *Unrepentant Radical*, as above.

158 Albert Romasco, *The Poverty of Abundance*, London 1965, p25.

159 David Farber, *Sloan Rules: Alfred P. Sloan and the Triumph of General Motors*, Chicago 2002, p140. Perhaps inevitably the yacht became a tax scam.

160 James Stuart Olson, *Herbert Hoover and the Reconstruction Finance Corporation 1931-1933*, Ames 1977, p59.

161 Don Mitchell, *The Lie of the Land*, Minneapolis 1996, p79.

162 Edward Robb Ellis, *A Nation in Torment*, as above, pp193-194.

163 Jesse Jones, *Fifty Billion Dollars*, New York 1951, p3.

164 Glen Jeansonne, *Transformation and Reaction: America 1921-1941*, New York 1994, p129.

165 Jones, as above, p5.

166 Roger Daniels, *The Bonus March*, Westport 1991, pp49-50.

167 Nancy Beck Young, *Wright Patman: Populism, Liberalism and the American Dream*, Dallas 2000, p44.

168 Daniels, as above, p185; D Clayton James, *The Years of McArthur 1880-1941*, London 1970, pp401, 403-404.

169 Donald Lisio, *The President and Protest*, Columbia 1974, p285.

170 James Johnson, *The Politics of Soft Coal*, Urbana 1979, p177.

171 Mauritz Hallgren, *The Gay Reformer*, New York 1935, pp12, 16; Jean Edward Smith, *FDR*, New York 2008, p27. See also Richard Hofstadter, *The American Political Tradition and the Men Who Made It*, New York 1989.

172 Frank Freidel, *Franklin D Roosevelt: The Apprenticeship*, New York 1952, p121.

173 Smith, *FDR*, as above, p82.

174 Robert Dallek, *Franklin D Roosevelt and American Foreign Policy*, New York 1979, pp8, 12.

175 Kenneth O'Reilly, *Nixon's Piano: Presidents and Racial Politics from Washington to Clinton*, New York 1995, p110.

176 See in particular Ralph Chaplin, *The Centralia Conspiracy*, New York 2007, and Tom Copeland, *The Centralia Tragedy: Elmer Smith and the Wobblies*, Seattle 1993.

177 Freidel, as above, pp81, 84.

178 James MacGregor Burns, *Roosevelt: The Lion and the Fox*, New York 1956, pp83-84.

179 Nathan Miller, *FDR: An Intimate History*, New York 1983, pp192, 207, 211.

180 Frederick Lewis Allen, *Only Yesterday*, New York 1931, p251.

181 Kenneth Davis, *FDR: The New York Years 1928-1933*, New York 1994, pp128-129.

182 Martin Fausold, *The Presidency of Herbert C Hoover*, Lexington 1985, p197.

183 David Burner, *The Politics of Provincialism: The Democratic Party in Transition 1918-1932*, New York 1967, p245.

184 Davis, as above, p239.

185 Folsom, as above, p257.

186 H W Brands, *Traitor to his Class: The Privileged Life and Radical Presidency of Franklin Delano Roosevelt*, New York 2009, p238.

187 For the regime of corruption that operated in New York see Norman Thomas and Paul Blanshard, *What's The Matter With New York*, New York 1932.

188 For Hearst's role as president-maker see Ben Procter, *William Randolph Hearst: The Later Years 1911-1951*, Oxford 2007, pp166-173. In 1936 Hearst was to give extremely well-paid, many said overpaid, jobs to Roosevelt's son in law John Boettiger (editor of the *Seattle Post-Intelligencer* on $30,000) and to his son Elliott (put in charge of Hearst's radio interests on $50,000). This was a pretty barefaced attempt at influence buying.

189 M S Venkataramani, "Some Aspects of Life and Politics in the United States of America in 1932", *International Review of Social History*, 3 (1958), p367.

190 Bascom Timmons, *Garner of Texas*, New York 1948, p168.

191 Frank Freidel, "Election of 1932", in Arthur Schlesinger Jr, ed, *History of American Presidential Elections*, vol 3, New York 1971, pp2734-2735.

192 Frances Perkins, *The Franklin Roosevelt I Knew*, London 1948, pp67, 135, 256.

193 Burns, as above, p143.

194 Venkataramani, as above, pp367-368.

195 *The Public Papers and Addresses*, as above, pp679, 761, 772, 797, 806, 807.

196 Jordan Schwarz, *The Speculator: Bernard M Baruch in Washington 1917-1965*, Chapel Hill 1981, pp258, 274. Baruch did

not just "cultivate" American politicians. He also covered Winston Churchill's substantial speculative losses that threatened to ruin him in 1929. See William Manchester, *The Glory and the Dream*, Boston 1974.

197 One feature of the campaign that is too often ignored is the fact that Hoover, Nixon-style, authorised the burglary of the Democratic Party offices in New York by the Office of Naval Intelligence. Apparently, he feared they had a dossier on him "so damaging that if made public it would destroy both his reputation and his entire administration". Nothing was found. See Jeffery Dorwart, *Conflict of Duty: The US Navy's Intelligence Dilemma*, Annapolis 1983, pp3-4.

198 Wendy Wall, *Inventing the American Way*, Oxford 2008, p19.

199 Robert Brown, *Teachers and Power: The Story of the American Federation of Teachers*, New York 1972, p41.

200 See David Ziskind, *One Thousand Strikes of Government Employees*, New York 1971, pp73-74, 76-77.

201 Teachers were not the only city employees to go unpaid. One city worker, James O'Reilly, actually had his home auctioned off to pay the $34 he owed in city taxes, at a time when the city owed him $850 in back pay! See Ellis, as above, p233.

202 Studs Terkel, *Hard Times: An Oral History of the Great Depression*, New York 1970, p388.

203 John F Lyons, *Teachers and Reform: Chicago Public Education*, Urbana 2008, pp40-41.

204 William Manchester, as above, p56.

205 Brown, as above, p47.

206 Jones, as above, p177.

207 Harold Ickes always suspected that Cermak was actually the intended target and in his autobiography he points out that Cermak was wearing a "bulletproof vest" when he was shot, "which was some indication that he stood in fear of an attempt on his life". See Harold Ickes, *The Autobiography of a Curmudgeon*, Chicago 1969, p256.

208 James Merriner, *Grafters and Goo Goos: Corruption and Reform in Chicago*, Carbondale 2004, p129.

209 Biles, as above, pp28, 107. According to Biles, the Kelly machine's annual income from corruption was anything between $12 million and $20 million, principally from illegal gambling.

210 Julia Wrigley, *Class Politics and Public Schools: Chicago 1900-1950*, New Brunswick 1982, pp222-223.

211 William Leuchtenburg, *Franklin D Roosevelt and the New Deal*, New York 1963, p18.

212 Ronald Edsforth, *The New Deal*, Oxford 2000, p68.

213 Arthur M Schlesinger, *The Coming of the New Deal*, London 1960, p3.

214 Kenneth Davis, *FDR: The New Deal Years 1933-1937*, New York 1986, p146. At this time Roosevelt was very taken with Douglas, describing him as presidential material, but eventually Roosevelt's embrace of relief for the unemployed prompted his resignation, accompanied by complaints of "Hebraic influences" at the White House. He was the millionaire heir to the Phelps Dodge copper mining fortune and his father had been one of the organisers of the Bisbee Deportation of 1917. See Robert Paul Browder and Thomas G Smith, *Independent: A Biography of Lewis W Douglas*, New York 1986, pp85, 111.

215 Richard Lowitt, *Bronson M Cutting: Progressive Politician*, Albuquerque 1992, p235.

216 Sharon Hartman Strom, "Woman's Place: Feminism, the Left and Industrial Unionism in the 1930s", *Feminist Studies*, 9, 2 (1983), p361.

217 Rexford Tugwell, *In Search of Roosevelt*, Cambridge, Mass 1972, pp160, 161.

218 Frank Freidel, *Franklin D Roosevelt: Launching the New Deal*, Boston 1973, p237.

219 Julian Zelizer, "The Forgotten Legacy of the New Deal: Fiscal Conservatism and the Roosevelt Administration", *Presidential Studies Quarterly*, 30, 2 (June 2000), pp332, 335. See also James Sargent, "Roosevelt's Economy Act: Fiscal Conservatism and the Early New Deal", *Congressional Studies* 7 (1980).

220 See Gary Dean Best, *FDR and the Bonus Marchers*, New York 1992, and Jay Barnes, *Florida's Hurricane History*, Chapel Hill 2007.

221 Abt, as above, pp49-50. Abt was a covert member of the Communist Party.

222 The piece is reprinted in George Murphy, ed, *The Key West Reader*, Key West 1989, pp112-117. See also Phil Scott, *Hemingway's Hurricane: The Great Florida Keys Storm of 1935*, New York 2006.

223 James Farley, *Behind the Ballots*, New York 1938, pp347-348.

224 Page Smith, *Redeeming the Time: A People's History of the 1920s and the New Deal*, New York 1987, p448.

225 Ferdinand Pecora, *Wall Street Under Oath*, London 1939, p189. See also Donald Ritchie, "The Pecora Wall Street Expose 1934", in Arthur Schlesinger Jr and Roger Burns, *Congress Investigates*, vol 4, New York 1975.

226 John Douglas Forbes, *JP Morgan 1867-1943*, Charlottesville 1981, p116. Morgan was not prejudiced against all Italians— he had a great liking for Mussolini; indeed he had been in Rome at the time of his taking power and wrote of his "great satisfaction of seeing Mr Mussolini's Revolution". In return for the Morgan bank's financial services, Mussolini was to award him the Royal Order of the Crown of Italy in 1927(pp126, 157).

227 Edward Lamont, *The Ambassador from Wall Street: The Story of Thomas W Lamont*, Lanham 1994, p339. Lamont, a senior Morgan partner, told Roosevelt that if Pecora were not removed there was a danger of "breaking Jack's heart".

228 Morgan's discomfort was nothing in the scale of things: the unfortunate Lya Graf, a German Jew, returned to Germany in 1935 and was to die in a concentration camp. See John Brooks, *Once In Golconda*, London 1970, p182.

229 William Harbaugh, *Lawyer's Lawyer: The Life of John W Davis*, New York 1973, p330.

230 Wall Street was expected to clean up its act, but Roosevelt had no intention of countenancing any reform that Pecora favoured. He did much the same with the Senate Munitions Inquiry headed by Senator Gerald Nye. Devastating evidence was heard, but Roosevelt appointed a committee headed by Bernard Baruch to consider legislation, absolutely confident that nothing would emerge that could possibly embarrass or inconvenience the arms industry. For the Nye Committee see Matthew Ware Coulter, *The Senate Munitions Inquiry of the 1930s*, Westport 1997.

231 Stuart Weiss, *The President's Man: Leo Crowley and President Roosevelt in Peace and War*, Carbondale 1996, pp33-64.

232 Michael Katz, *In the Shadow of the Poorhouse: A Social History of Welfare in America*, New York 1986, pp217, 218.

233 Nancy Rose, *Put To Work: Relief Programs in the Great Depression*, New York 1986, pp47, 53.

234 Elliott Rosen, *Roosevelt, the Great Depression and the Economics of Recovery*, Charlottesville 2005, p152.

235 Ferdinand Lundberg, *America's Sixty Families*, New York 1938, pp459-460.

236 Norman Thomas, *After The New Deal What?*, New York 1936, p16. Thomas emphasised that state ownership must not be confused with socialism. It depends "on who owns the government, and for what purpose the government owns industry: for war and militarism, for greater security of banking as a better instrument of the profit system, or for the sake of planned abundance for all" (p17).

237 Sidney Lens, *Left, Right and Center*, Hinsdale, Ill, 1949, p272.

238 Irving Bernstein, *Turbulent Years 1933-1941*, Boston 1970, p34. One aspect of Section 7a that is often ignored is its impact on black workers. Attempts by black organisations to have anti-discrimination written into the codes, banning unions from barring black workers, were shamefully opposed by the AFL and dropped. See Raymond Wolters, "Section 7a and the Black Worker", *Labor History*, 10 (1969). See also Michael Holmes, "The Blue Eagle as Jim Crow: The NRA and Georgia's Black Workers", *Journal of Negro History*, 57, 3 (1972)

239 Tugwell, as above, p242.

240 Saul Alinsky, *John L Lewis: An Unauthorized Biography*, New York 1949, p70.

241 T H Watkins, *The Great Depression*, New York 1999, p218.

242 Joseph Finley, *The Corrupt Kingdom*, New York 1972, p80.

243 John Brophy, *A Miner's Life*, Madison 1964, p236.

244 Robert Zieger, *John L Lewis: Labor Leader*, Boston 1988, p65.

245 James Johnson, *The Politics of Soft Coal*, Urbana 1979, p169.
246 F Ray Marshall, *Labor in the South*, Cambridge, Mass 1967, pp139-140. For the Alabama coalfield see Peter Alexander, "Rising from the Ashes: Alabama Coal Miners 1921-1941" in Edwin Brown and Colin Davis, eds, *It Is Union And Liberty: Alabama Coal Miners and the UMW*, Tuscaloosa 1999.
247 Benjamin Stolberg, *Tailor's Progress*, New York 1944, p211.
248 Edward Levinson, *Labor on the March*, New York 1938, p52.
249 Robert Zeiger, *American Workers, American Unions*, Baltimore 1994, p42.
250 John W Anderson, "How I Became Part of the Labor Movement", in Alice Lynd and Staughton Lynd, eds, *Rank and File: Personal Histories of Working Class Organizers*, New York 1988, p57. He emphasises the fact that "left-wing groups, the Communists, Socialists, the IWW and other groups of the left were the inspiration and leaders of the strikes" (p57).
251 Art Preis, *Labor's Giant Step*, New York 1972, p17.
252 Bernard Bellush, *The Failure of the NRA*, New York 1975, p56.
253 John Kennedy Ohl, *Hugh Johnson and the New Deal*, DeKalb 1985, p198; Bellush, as above, p94.
254 Bellush, as above, p114.
255 As David Shannon puts it, Roosevelt was "an extraordinarily gifted political broker... He did not design the New Deal; he 'brokered' it." See David Shannon, *Between the Wars: 1919-1941*, New York 1979, p178.
256 Mauritz Hallgren, *The Gay Reformer*, New York 1935, p218.
257 McAlister Coleman, *Men and Coal*, Toronto 1943, p83.
258 Craig Phelan, "William Green and the Ideal of Christian Cooperation", in Melvin Dubofsky and Warren Van Tine, eds, *Labor Leaders in America*, Urbana 1987, p135.
259 Robert Dunn and Jack Hardy, *Labor and Textiles*, New York 1931, p192.
260 Gary Dean Best, *Harold Laski and American Liberalism*, New Brunswick 2005, p94.
261 Bellush, as above, pp55, 79-80.

262 James Wechsler, *Labor Baron*, Westport 1972 (originally published in 1944), p57.
263 Lens, *Unrepentent Radical*, as above, pp62-63.
264 Carey McWilliams, *Factories in the Field*, Boston 1935, p211.
265 Devra Weber, *Dark Sweat, White Gold: California Farm Workers, Cotton and the New Deal*, Berkeley 1994, p79.
266 Cletus Daniels, *Bitter Harvest: A History of California Farmworkers*, Berkeley 1981, pp183, 219.
267 Don Mitchell, as above, p144.
268 For the nutpickers' strike see Rosemary Feurer, "The Nutpickers' Union 1933-1934", in Staughton Lynd, ed, *"We Are All Leaders": The Alternative Unionism of the Early 1930s*, Urbana 1996, and Myrna Fichtenbaum, *The Funsten Nut Strike*, New York 1992.
269 Roger Horowitz, *Negro and White Unite and Fight! A Social History of Industrial Unionism in Meatpacking 1930-1990*, Urbana 1997, p35.
270 See Larry Engelman, "'We Were The Poor People': The Hormel Strike of 1933", *Labor History*, 15 (1974); Peter Rachleff, "Organizing 'Wall to Wall': The Independent Union of All Workers 1933-1937", in Staughton Lynd, ed, *"We Are All Leaders": The Alternative Unionism of the Early 1930s*, Urbana 1996; and Peter Rachleff, *Hard-Pressed in the Heartland: The Hormel Strike and the Future of the Labor Movement*, Boston 1993, pp31.
271 Bellush, as above, p178.
272 For Muste see in particular Jo Ann Ooiman Robinson, *Abraham Went Out: A Biography of AJ Muste*, Philadelphia 1988.
273 Thomas Coode and John Bauman, *People, Poverty and Politics: Pennsylvanians during the Great Depression*, Lewisburg 1981, p54.
274 See Gene Grabiner, "Conservative Labor Leaders Clean House: The Case of Brookwood Labor College", *Educational Theory*, 29, 3 (1979), and Jonathan Bloom, "Brookwood Labor College: The Final Years", *Labor's Heritage*, 2, 2 (1990).
275 John A Salmond, *Southern Struggles*, University Press of Florida 2004, pp7-8, 22-23, 63-64, and Herbert Harris, *American Labor*, New Haven 1938, p340.
276 See Roy Rosenzweig, "Radicals and the Jobless: The Musteites and the

Unemployed Leagues 1932-1936", *Labor History*, 16 (1975).

277 In his memoirs Hook describes the AWP as "an authentic American party rooted in the American revolutionary tradition, prepared to meet the problems created by a breakdown of the capitalist economy with a plan for a cooperative commonwealth expressed in a native idiom intelligible to blue collar and white collar workers, miners, sharecroppers and farmers". It was greeted with ferocious hostility by the Communist Party that "unleashed a propaganda barrage against us as the most dangerous of all the social fascists in America. We were denounced as American National Socialists." Looking back, he remembered his time on the AWP's Political Committee as "a rewarding and humbling experience", not a sentiment that he was particularly prone to. Party members had 'sacrificed opportunities...for lives heavy with risk of violent injury and imprisonment". See Sidney Hook, *Out of Step: An Unquiet Life in the Twentieth Century*, New York 1983, pp191, 193, 195. For an interesting discussion of Sidney Hook's involvement with the AWP see Christopher Phelps, *Young Sidney Hook*, Ithaca 1997, pp109-123.

278 A J Muste, "My Experience in the Labor and Radical Struggles of the Thirties", in Rita James Simon, ed, *As We Saw The Thirties*, Urbana 1967, p142. Budenz had an interesting, if depressing, trajectory. He subsequently joined the Communist Party, became a dedicated Stalinist, a senior party official and eventually the managing editor of the *Daily Worker*. In 1945 he announced his return to the Catholic church and his excommunication (for marrying a divorcee) was rescinded in a well-publicised ceremony at St Patrick's Cathedral in New York. He was given an academic post at Notre Dame University courtesy of the church. Budenz went on to become a key FBI informant and an important professional witness in the McCarthyite witch-hunts. In his memoirs, published in 1947, he still retains one Stalinist trait: a ferocious hatred of Trotskyism. He writes that "Hitler used Trotskyites as guards... That is the Trotskyite style." He positively boasts that

when a CP member, he had handed over information about the Trotskyists to the Russian secret police. Even after this depressing political trajectory, however, Budenz was still, in his own words, "justly proud" of his part in the Auto-Lite strike, helping turn "a lost strike into a tremendous victory". See Louis Budenz, *This Is My Story*, New York 1947, pp96, 110, 244-247. Budenz actually gave one of his daughters the middle name "Toledo".

279 Bernstein, *Turbulent Years*, as above, pp222-223.

280 Fine, as above, p279.

281 John Spivak, *America Faces the Barricades*, New York 1935, p272-273.

282 Hentoff, as above, p157.

283 Craig Phelan, *William Green*, Albany 1989, pp86-87.

284 Edward Lamb, *No Lamb For Slaughter*, New York 1963, p42. Lamb was the lawyer representing the Auto-Lite strikers. Many years later when an FBI informer, Budenz, whose release Lamb had secured from jail in 1934, was to name him as a Communist. For Lamb's devastating indictment of what Budenz had become see pp141-142.

285 William Millikan, *A Union Against Unions*, Minneapolis 2001, p219. See also Lois Quam and Peter Rachleff, "Keeping Minneapolis an Open-Shop Town: The Citizens' Alliance in the 1930s", *Minneapolis History*, 50, 3 (1986).

286 Elizabeth Faue, *Community of Suffering and Struggle: Women, Men and the Labor Movement in Minneapolis 1915-1945*, Chapel Hill 1991, p56.

287 Charles Rumsford Walker, *American City: A Rank and File History of Minneapolis*, Minneapolis 2005, p90.

288 Farrell Dobbs, *Teamster Rebellion*, New York 1972, p103.

289 Walker, as above, p272.

290 Millikan, as above, p272.

291 Dobbs, as above, p91.

292 Dobbs, as above, p94. Subsequently an attempt was made to prosecute two workers, Emanuel Holstein and Phillip Scott, for killing Lyman. The prosecution case was made particularly difficult because in bars across the city, especially after a few drinks, many workers claimed to have killed him. Dobbs describes their successful defence in the second volume

of his memoirs, *Teamster Power*, New York 1973, pp20-23.

293 In his biography of Floyd Olson, George Mayer writes of this incident that the Local 574 leadership "played an equally reprehensible role as the police". He claims that "the strike leaders sought the shedding of blood to reinforce working class solidarity", and deliberately sent pickets into an ambush where they knew men would be killed— George Mayer, *The Political Career of Floyd B Olson*, St Paul 1987, pp209-210. This is taken up by Bernstein in his widely read *Turbulent Years* where he writes that Dunne and Dobbs deliberately sent "unsuspecting pickets into the rain of police gunfire". He puts it down to the "Marxist doctrine of class warfare, with its inversion of ordinary ends and means" (p243). The problem with this is that the only evidence for it is the author's distaste for Trotskyism. The slander seems to have originated with people on Olson's staff, who had their own reformist political agenda. Harry DeBoer, the picket captain involved, provides his own account in Bud Schultz and Ruth Schultz, eds, *The Price of Dissent: Testimonies to Political Repression in America*, Berkeley 2001, pp39-40. He was badly wounded himself and nearly lost a leg.

294 Dobbs, as above, p156.

295 Dobbs, as above, p157.

296 Walker, as above, p198.

297 Dobbs, as above, pp170-171.

298 James Cannon, *The History of American Trotskyism*, New York 1944, p161.

299 Mayer, as above, p221.

300 The May and July strikes provoked the publication of a minor Stalinist classic— William Dunne and Morris Childs, *Permanent Counter-Revolution: The Role of the Trotzkyites in the Minneapolis Strikes*, New York 1934. Here they condemned the Trotskyists' "defeatist strategy and tactics", accused them of "strikebreaking", of writing "another miserable page in the history of class collaboration", of being "spineless and unprincipled leaders", and of following "a counter-revolutionary and, therefore, anti-working class policy". According to Dunne and Childs "the four Marx brothers would have done a better job for

the strikers". The result in July "was one of the most serious recent setbacks suffered by the working class" (pp3, 21, 22, 23, 47). Ironically, when Bill Dunne was expelled from the CP in 1946, one of the charges against him was his failure to fight Trotskyism! Morris Childs went on to become an FBI agent in the early 1950s and was awarded the Presidential Medal of Freedom by Ronald Reagan in 1987.

301 According to one account there were between three and six accidents every eight-hour shift on the San Francisco docks. See Robert Cherny, "The Making of a Labor Radical: Harry Bridges 1901-1933", *Pacific Historical Review*, 64, 3 (1995), p379.

302 Charles Larrowe, *Harry Bridges: The Rise and Fall of Radical Labor in the US*, Westport 1977, p13.

303 David Selvin, *The Terrible Anger: The 1934 Waterfront and General Strikes in San Francisco*, Detroit 1996, p57. The best account of the strike along the whole Pacific coast is Ottilie Markholt's *Maritime Solidarity: Pacific Coast Unionism 1929-1938*, Tacoma 1988. See also, for the strike in the union stronghold of Tacoma, Ronald Magden and A D Martinson, *The Working Waterfront: The Story of Tacoma's Ships and Men*, Tacoma 1982. For a Trotskyist account of the rise of union organisation on the Pacific coast see Andrew Bonthius, "Origins of the International Longshoremen's and Warehousemen's Union", *Southern California Quarterly*, 59 (1977).

304 The party organiser in California, Sam Darcy, had little time for dual unionism. On one occasion, when he was being berated by an emissary from party general secretary Earl Browder for rightist deviations, he threw the man out of the window. See Howard Kimeldorf, *Reds or Rackets: The Making of Radical and Conservative Unions on the Waterfront*, Berkeley 1992, p8.

305 During the 1934 strike the party organiser in Seattle, Michael Rapapport, actually complained to Earl Browder that the San Francisco party under Darcy was attacking the employers instead of the "social fascists" and a delegation was sent from New York to bring Darcy into line. See Robert Cherny, "Prelude to the

Popular Front: The Communist Party in California 1931-1935", *American Communist History*, 1, 1 (2002). Ironically, Darcy was to be expelled from the Communist Party for opposing Browder's dissolution of the CP in 1944, arguably carrying the Popular Front to its logical conclusion, and its reconstitution as the Communist Political Association.

306 Larrowe, as above, p21.
307 Harvey Schwartz, *Solidarity Stories: An Oral History of the ILWU*, Seattle 2009, p27.
308 Selvin, as above, p75.
309 Ronald Magden, *A History of the Seattle Waterfront Workers 1884-1934*, Seattle 1991, p199.
310 Bruce Nelson, "The Big Strike", in Daniel Cornford, ed, *Working People of California*, Berkeley 1995, p240.
311 Albert Gunns, *Civil Liberties in the Pacific Northwest 1917-1940*, New York 1983, p159; Schwartz, as above, p106.
312 Michael Woodiwiss, *Organized Crime and American Power*, Toronto 2001, p160.
313 Ryan was a friend to employers, gangsters, priests and bishops, and politicians, including Roosevelt, when he was Governor of New York State. In fact, he was a friend to just about everyone except his members. Incredibly, his political friends made him head of the New York State Parole Board, which was very useful to his gangster friends. Many of the ILA's New York officials were gang members, most notably the head of the union in Brooklyn, Albert Anastasia, whose brother, Tony, ran Murder Incorporated for the New York mob. In the aftermath of the Pacific strike a rank and file opposition developed in New York, led by Peter Panto. He built up widespread support but then suddenly disappeared in 1939. His body was eventually found in a secret mob cemetery in 1947; he had been strangled. Investigation into Panto's murder was effectively sabotaged by the New York district attorney, a former policeman with mob connections, Bill O'Dwyer. He had been elected as the man to clean up the gangs! One potential witness to Panto's murder, Abraham Reles, a mob gunman, was thrown from a sixth floor window while being guarded by five of New York's "finest" under the command of Frank Bals, one of O'Dwyer's close friends from his days on the force. Bals later claimed they were all asleep when Reles fell to his death. Bals was promoted. O'Dwyer went on to become the Democrat Mayor of New York from 1946 until 1950 when President Truman appointed him ambassador to Mexico. See Kimeldorf, as above, p124; James Fisher, *On The Irish Waterfront*, Ithaca 2009, p60; and for O'Dwyer see Edward Robb Ellis, *The Epic of New York City*, New York 1966, pp565-578.
314 For a graphic account see Bernstein, *Turbulent Years*, as above, pp272-279. For Nick Bordoise see Daniel Frontino Elash, "Greek American Communists and the San Francisco General strike of 1934", *Journal of the Hellenic Diaspora*, 33 (2007). See also Kenneth Casebeer, "Distinctly American Radicals: The Rank & File and the Coastwise Longshore and General Strike of 1934", http://wiki.law.miami.edu/facdev/images/5/56/Distinctly_American_Radicals.pdf, pp20-24.
315 Wilfred Crook, *Communism and the General Strike*, Hamden, Conn 1960, p123.
316 Bruce Nelson, *Workers on the Waterfront*, Urbana 1990, pp149.
317 Nelson, "The Big Strike", as above, p240.
318 Selvin, as above, p178.
319 George Whitney Martin, *Madame Secretary, Frances Perkins*, New York 1976, p320.
320 In California the American Legion urged the state legislature to "enact a law punishing radical agitation by death or a hundred years in jail". Some posts, in San Francisco and Portland, however, sided with the union. Indeed, one of the two men shot dead by the police in San Francisco on 5 July, Howard Sperry, was a Legion member and his post defied the state leadership and marched in his funeral procession. See William Pencak, *For God and Country: The American Legion 1919-1941*, Boston 1989, p224.
321 See David Selvin, "An Exercise in Hysteria: San Francisco's Red Raids of 1934", *Pacific Historical Review*, 58, 3 (1989).
322 Eventually, after what was then the longest trial in the history of California, eight of the CAWIU defendants in the Sacramento Conspiracy Trial were found

guilty with six of them, including Pat Chambers and Caroline Decker, receiving sentences of one to 14 years. Two of them, including the only Trotskyist in their ranks, Norman Mini, were placed on probation, but both refused this and remained in jail with the others. The three women served a year and the men were not released until October 1937 when their convictions were overturned. Meanwhile the union was successfully smashed. See Kevin Starr, *Endangered Dreams: The Great Depression in California*, New York 1996, pp165-174.

323 Larrowe, as above, p99-100.

324 Nelson, *Workers on the Waterfront*, as above, pp156-162.

325 The strike created problems for the CP leadership in New York because members of the "fascist" AFL had actually conducted a successful strike of historic significance. This could not be ignored and the strike leaders just be subjected to a torrent of slander as was the case in Minneapolis, because the local CP, led by Sam Darcy, was so heavily involved in helping win the strike. This difficulty is reflected in William Dunne's pamphlet on the strike, which desperately tries to find a role for the CP's revolutionary trade union, the Marine Workers' Industrial Union (MWIU), in the conflict but without any success. See William Dunne, *The Great San Francisco General Strike*, New York 1934. The Communist Party was still absolutely committed to the Third Period, however, and when Darcy wanted to support the left reformist Upton Sinclair in his EPIC campaign for Governor of California later that year, he was actually ordered to stand against the "fascist" Sinclair, as far as he was concerned, as a test of loyalty to the party line and leadership. And, of course, he did.

326 Nathan Glazer, *The Social Basis of American Communism*, New York 1961, p110.

327 See Daniel Nelson, "The Beginning of the Sit-Down Era: The Reminiscences of Rex Murray", *Labor History*, 15 (1974).

328 Bryant Simon, *A Fabric of Defeat*, Chapel Hill 1998, p111.

329 Jacquelyn Dowd Hall, James LeLoudis, Richard Korstad, Mary Murphy, Lu Ann Jones and Christopher Daly, *Like A Family: The Making of a Southern Cotton Mill World*, Chapel Hill 1987, p325.

330 Dowd Hall et al, as above, p296.

331 Bryant Simon, as above, p113.

332 George Tindall, *The Emergence of the New South 1913-1945*, Baton Rouge 1999, p527.

333 For Talmadge's role see John Allen, "Eugene Talmadge and the Great Textile Strike in Georgia, September 1934", in Gary Fink and Merl Reed, eds, *Essays in Southern Labor History*, Greenwood 1987. Talmadge was, of course, a brutal white supremacist and in his early days had kept black sharecroppers in their place by personally flogging them. See William Anderson, *The Wild Man from Sugar Creek: The Political Career of Eugene Talmadge*, Baton Rouge 1975, p21. James Cox, who had been the Democratic Party's presidential candidate in 1920, wrote of Talmadge's administration in Georgia that "I doubt whether in all the history of our American commonwealths there was ever a more dangerous and disgraceful regime than that of Eugene Talmadge"—see James Cox, *Journey Through My Years*, New York 1946, p394.

334 John A Salmond, *Southern Struggles: The Southern Labor Movement and Civil Rights*, Gainsville 2004, p19. The owner of the Chiquola Mill, Dan Beecham, was also the town's mayor and chief of police.

335 John A Salmond, as above, p117; Jack Irby Hayes, *South Carolina and the New Deal*, Columbia 2001, p105. For Myers's remarkable career as a supporter of the US labour movement see Elizabeth Fones-Wolf and Ken Fones-Wolf, "Lending a Hand to Labor: James Myers and the Federal Council of Churches 1926-1947", *Church History*, 68, 1 (1999).

336 Janet Irons, *Testing the New Deal: The General Textile Strike of 1934 in the American South*, Urbana 2000, pp148-150. For a comprehensive nationwide account of the strike see John Salmond, *The General Textile Strike of 1934: From Maine to Alabama*, Columbia, Missouri, 2002.

337 Leuchtenburg, *Franklin D Roosevelt*, as above, p113.

338 Davis, as above, pp410-411. Davis provides an interesting account of Roosevelt's thinking whereby he was worried about the political cost of his stance during the textile strike: "He feared

that what it cost him in goodwill on the left was offset by no equivalent gain in goodwill on the right" (p412).

339 Norman Thomas, *After The New Deal What?*, New York 1936, p47.

340 James Hodges, *New Deal Labor Policy and the Southern Cotton Textile Industry 1933-1941*, Knoxville 1986, p117.

341 James Hodges, as above, p146.

342 Caroline Moorehead, *Martha Gellhorn*, London 2004, pp93, 98. She was working as an investigator for Harry Hopkins and the Federal Emergency Relief Administration (FERA), one of a team of journalists providing "soft data". She was to be fired after telling men in Idaho that the best way to get attention was to break a few windows (p99).

343 Irons, as above, p163.

344 According to Philip Taft and Philip Ross there were many violent incidents resulting in fatalities in 1935. Among them were: "In Omaha a clash between striking streetcar men and strikebreakers was responsible for the death of two strike sympathisers and the wounding of a number of others. Governor R L Cochran immediately sent troops into the city. Other communities which reported deaths resulting from violence in labour disputes were Rossville, Ga, during a textile walkout, and a strike at the Callaway mills in La Grange, Ga. Two fruit and vegetable strikers were killed in El Centro, Cali. A striking clay worker was killed in Toronto, Ohio, and a brewery picket in Stockton, Cali. The police in Eureka, Cali, killed four pickets in a lumber strike, and a picketing ornamental iron worker was shot to death in Minneapolis. Striking maritime workers in New Orleans, Houston and Port Arthur, Tex, were killed, as were two striking iron miners in Alabama. Finally a coal miner in Pikeville, Ky, and a striker at the Motor Products Corp in Detroit lost their lives while picketing." And there were more! See Philip Taft and Philip Ross, "American Labor Violence: Its Causes, Character and Outcome", in Hugh Davis Graham and Ted Robert Gurr, eds, *The History of Violence in America*, New York 1969, pp356-357.

345 See Gary Bailey, "The Terre Haute, Indiana, General Strike, 1935", *Indiana Magazine of History*, LXXX (September 1984).

346 See Staughton Lynd, "The Possibility of Radicalism in the Early 1930s: The Case of Steel", *Radical America*, 6, 6 (1972). Edward Levinson, *Labor On The March*, New York 1938, p72.

347 Sidney and Beatrice Webb, *The History of Trade Unionism*, London 1894, pp456-457, 462. See also Ralph Darlington, *Syndicalism and the Transition to Communism*, Aldershot 2008, pp219-232.

348 For a good introduction to this subject see David Witwer, *Shadow of the Racketeer*, Urbana 2009. He makes the very good point that mob involvement in the trade union movement was a very real phenomenon, but that organised crime had even more extensive connections with business, the police and the courts, and, of course, the politicians. These connections were ignored while trade union connections were seen as a very good stick to beat the labour movement with. Union officials who tried to resist the mob by and large got no help from police, courts or politicians. When George McLane of the Chicago Bartenders Association was preparing to give evidence against Frank Nitti in 1939, it was the chief investigator of the state attorney's office, Captain Dan Gilbert, who told him that if he did, his wife would be kidnapped and tortured to death. Both Gilbert and the state attorney who was prosecuting the case, Thomas Courtney, had strong mob connections (pp54-55). Courtney was Democratic Party candidate for Governor of Illinois in 1944 and when he lost was appointed a judge. He remained on the bench until 1970.

349 Gary Dean Best, *Harold Laski and American Liberalism*, New Brunswick 2005, p94. Laski thought that Lewis underwent an "emotional revolution" in the 1930s, transformed by the impact of the Great Depression.

350 Saul Alinsky, *John L Lewis: An Unauthorized Biography*, New York 1949, p64.

351 William Z Foster, *Misleaders of Labor*, New York 1927, pp133-134.

352 John Brophy, *A Miner's Life*, Madison 1964, pp213, 218.

353 Foster, *Misleaders of Labor*, as above, pp290, 294.

354 For Powers Hapgood see Robert Bussel, *From Harvard to the Ranks of Labor: Powers Hapgood and the American Working Class*, University Park, Penn, 1999.

355 Walter Galenson, *The CIO Challenge to the AFL*, Cambridge, Mass, 1960, p195.

356 Alan Singer, "'Something of a Man': John L Lewis, the UMWA and the CIO 1919-1943", in John H M Laslett, ed, *The United Mine Workers of America: A Model of Industrial Solidarity*, University Park, Penn, 1996, p111.

357 Melvyn Dubofsky and Warren Van Tine, *John L Lewis*, New York 1977, pp96, 109.

358 Alinsky, as above, p70.

359 Benjamin Stolberg, *The Story of the CIO*, New York 1938, p34.

360 De Caux, *Labor Radical*, as above, pp241-242.

361 David Selvin, *The Thundering Voice of John L Lewis*, New York 1969, p91.

362 Dubofsky and Van Tine, as above, p239.

363 Robert Zieger, *John L Lewis: Labor Leader*, New York 1988, pp81-82.

364 For an over-sympathetic biography of the appalling Bill Hutcheson see Maxwell Craddock, *Portrait of an American Labor Leader: William L Hutcheson*, New York 1955. Hutcheson was one of the most right wing and dictatorial of American trade union leaders, and there was a lot of competition. He tolerated no opposition to his control of the union and only the forms of democracy. There were no union conventions between 1928 and 1936, and he dealt with any votes cast against him by not counting them. He installed his son, Maurice, as his successor when he finally stepped down in 1952, after leading the union for 37 years. Most notoriously in 1916, on behalf of the employers, he had vetoed a pay rise negotiated by the New York carpenters. When, after an overwhelming vote repudiating his actions (11,745 to 119), they went on strike to keep the rise, he expelled all 65 New York locals from the union and helped the employers break the strike. It was believed that he was paid over $40,000 for this service. See Herbert Harris, *American Labor*, New Haven 1938, p116.

365 Victor Reuther, *The Brothers Reuther and the Story of the UAW*, Boston 1976, p125.

366 Alinsky, as above, p78.

367 Robert Parmet, *The Master of Seventh Avenue: David Dubinsky and the American Labor Movement*, New York 2005, p168.

368 See Philip S Foner, *The TUEL to the End of the Gompers Era*, New York 1991, pp269-286 and Philip S Foner, *The TUEL 1925-1929*, New York 1994. See also Stanley Nadel, "Reds Versus Pinks: a Civil War in the International Ladies Garment Workers Union", *New York History*, 66, 1 (1985).

369 James Ryan, *Earl Browder*, Tuscaloosa 1997, p90.

370 Bert Cochran, *Labor and Communism*, Princeton 1977, p97.

371 Ruth Mckenney, *Industrial Valley*, New York 1939, pp249-250, 261-262.

372 Jim Pope, "Worker Lawmaking, Sit-Down strikes and the Shaping of American Industrial Relations 1935-1938", *Law and History Review*, 24, 1 (2006), p8.

373 Edward Levinson, *Labor on the March*, Ithaca 1995, p144.

374 Robert Zieger, *The CIO 1935-1955*, Chapel Hill 1997, p32.

375 For Hapgood and Pesotta see Robert Bussel, "'A Love of Unionism and Democracy': Rose Pesotta, Powers Hapgood and the Industrial Union Movement 1933-1949", *Labor History*, 38, 4 (1997).

376 Levinson, as above, p146.

377 Mary Bethune Mcleod, "My Secret Talks with FDR", in Bernard Sternsher, *The Negro in Depression and War*, Chicago 1969, p58.

378 Roy Wilkins, *Standing Fast*, New York 1982, pp127, 131-132.

379 Nancy Weiss, *Farewell to the Party of Lincoln: Black Politics in the Age of FDR*, Princeton 1983, p100.

380 For the lynching of Claude Neal see James McGovern, *Anatomy of a Lynching: The Killing of Claude Neal*, Baton Rouge 1992, pp80-82, 85-91, 138. See also Walter T Howard, *Lynchings: Extralegal Violence in Florida during the 1930s*, New York 1995. See also Joshua Youngblood, "'Haven't Quite Shaken the Horror': Howard Kester, the Lynching of Claude Neal, and Social Activism in the South During the 1930s", *Florida Historical Quarterly*, 8, 1, (2007).

381 Philip Dray, *At the Hands of Persons Unknown: The Lynching of Black America*, New York 2003, p344.

382 Johnpeter Horst Grill and Robert Jenkins, "The Nazis and the American South in the 1930s: A Mirror Image?", *The Journal of Southern History*, 58, 4 (1992), p676. The NAACP actually asked how it was that American politicians could protest about developments in Germany and yet "do nothing about lynchings". Even the Nazis had "not yet sunk to our own level of burning human beings at the stake". See Dray, as above, p338.

383 David Eugene Conrad, *The Forgotten Farmers: The Story of the Sharecroppers in the New Deal*, Urbana 1965, pp163-164. For the Communist Party's organising of sharecroppers in Alabama see Robin D G Kelley, *Hammer and Hoe: Alabama Communists during the Great Depression*, Chapel Hill 1990.

384 Naomi Mitchison, *You May Well Ask*, London 1986, p199.

385 Raymond Gregory, *Norman Thomas: The Great Dissenter*, New York 2008, p118.

386 Harry Fleischman, *Norman Thomas*, New York 1964, p148.

387 Gregory, as above, p120-121.

388 Fleischman, as above, p149.

389 Conrad, as above, pp92-93.

390 H L Mitchell, *Mean Things Happening In This Land*, Montclair, NJ 1979, pp70-71.

391 Gregory, as above, p129. See also Donald Grubbs, *Cry From The Cotton*, Chapel Hill 1971, pp99, 107.

392 Gregory, as above, p130.

393 Howard Kester, *Revolt Among The Sharecroppers*, New York 1936, pp27-28. Kester was a member of the Socialist Party executive and had been an investigator for the NAACP. He had produced their report on the Claude Neal lynching.

394 Bernard Johnpoll, *Pacifist's Progress: Norman Thomas and the Decline of American Socialism*, Chicago 1970, p150.

395 See Lawrence Nelson, "The Art of the Possible: Another look at the 'Purge' of the AAA Liberals in 1935", *Agricultural History*, 57 (October 1983). For the STFU's later troubled relations with the CIO see Mark Naison, "The Southern Tenant Farmers Union and the CIO", *Radical History*, 2, 5 (1968).

396 H G Wells, *The New America*, London 1935, pp41-42.

397 The remarkable Clara Lemlich Shavelson had, as a young woman, proposed the general strike resolution that had launched the great historic shirtwaist makers' strike of 1909, the "revolt of the 30,000". As a married woman, she played a leading role in rent strikes and food protests during the First World War and in the 1930s. Even when she was living out her last years in a nursing home, she organised the staff into the union. See Annelise Orleck, "'We Are That Mythical Thing They Called The Public': Militant Housewives during the Great Depression", *Feminist Studies*, 19, 1 (1993), and also Annelise Orleck, *Commonsense and a Little Fire: Women and Working Class Politics 1900-1965*, Chapel Hill 1995. See also Denise Lynn, "United We Spend: Communist Women and the 1935 Meat Boycott", *American Communist History*, 10, 1 (2011).

398 See Georg Schrode, "Mary Zuk and the Detroit Meat Strike of 1935", *Polish American Studies*, 11 (1985).

399 For the EPIC campaign see Greg Mitchell, *The Campaign of the Century*, New York 1992. For Sinclair's own account see his *I, Candidate for Governor and How I Got Licked*, Berkeley 1994.

400 Harvey Klehr, *The Heyday of American Communism*, New York 1984, p174. In the election of governor, Sinclair received 850,000 votes and Sam Darcy, the CP candidate, received 8,799.

401 See Alan Brinkley, *Voices of Protest: Huey Long, Father Coughlin and the Great Depression*, New York 1982. In 1938 Coughlin was to embrace fascism and anti-Semitism, establishing the Christian Front.

402 Glen Jeansonne, *Messiah of the Masses: Huey Long and the Great Depression*, New York 1993, p120.

403 William Ivy Hair, *The Kingfish and His Realm*, Baton Rouge 1991, p272.

404 Allan Sindler, *Huey Long's Louisiana: State Politics*, Baltimore 1956, p86.

405 Edward Haas, "Huey Long and the Communists", *Louisiana History*, 32 (1991), p36. In 1935 the party published two pamphlets attacking Long and his Share Our Wealth movement—*The Real Huey Long* and *How Can We Share The Wealth? The Communist Way Versus Huey Long*.

406 George Tindall, *The Emergence of the New South 1913-1945*, Baton Rouge 1999, p614.

407 Brinkley, as above, p43.

408 Edward Robb Ellis, *A Nation In Torment*, as above, p396.

409 Sindler, as above, p105. According to Sindler and others, Long also invited the Mafia in the shape of Frank Costello to move gambling operations to Louisiana, but T Harry Williams argues that this was, in fact, the work of Long's "respectable" political opponents in New Orleans. See T Harry Williams, *Huey Long*, New York 1969, pp824-825.

410 Jeansonne, p158-159.

411 Williams, as above, pp703, 706.

412 See Glen Jeansonne, "Huey Long and Racism", *Louisiana History*, 33, 3 (1992).

413 Jeansonne, *Messiah*, as above, p149.

414 Sindler, as above, pp86-87. See also Robert Snyder, "Huey Long and the Presidential Election of 1936", *Louisiana History*, 16, 2 (1975).

415 Hair, as above, p288. Once Long was dead and his successors were reconciled with the White House, investigation into their tax affairs ended in what was described at the time as a "new Louisiana Purchase".

416 Raymond Moley, *After Seven Years*, New York 1939, p305.

417 Rexford Tugwell, *The Democratic Roosevelt*, New York 1957, pp98, 350.

418 Brinkley, as above, p80.

419 Warren F Kimball, *The Juggler: Franklin Roosevelt as Wartime Statesman*, Princeton 1991, p7.

420 Harold Ickes, *The Secret Diary of Harold L Ickes: The First Thousand Days 1933-1936*, New York 1953, pp195-196.

421 See Daniel J Leab, *A Union of Individuals: The Formation of the American Newspaper Guild 1933-1936*, New York 1970, pp193-194.

422 Ickes, as above, p354.

423 David Nasaw, *The Chief: The Life of William Randolph Hearst*, London 2003, p512.

424 Edmund Coblentz, ed, *William Randolph Hearst: A Portrait In His Own Words*, New York 1952, pp176-179.

425 Charles Noble, *Welfare As We Knew It: A Political History of the American Welfare State*, New York 1997, p66.

426 Leuchtenburg, *Franklin D Roosevelt*, as above, p132.

427 See Jaap Kooijman, "'Just Forget About It': FDR's Ambivalence towards National Health Insurance", in Robert Garson and Stuart Kidd, eds, *The Roosevelt Years*, Edinburgh 1999.

428 James Patterson, *America's Struggle Against Poverty 1900-1994*, Cambridge, Mass 1994, p73.

429 Michael Katz, *In the Shadow of the Poorhouse: A Social History of Welfare in America*, New York 1996.

430 Leuchtenburg, *Franklin D Roosevelt*, as above, p166.

431 Alonzo Hamby, "High Tide: Roosevelt, Truman and the Democratic Party 1932-1952", in William Chafe, ed, *The Achievement of American Liberalism*, New York 2003, p32.

432 Peter Fearon, *War, Prosperity and Depression*, Deddington 1987, p251.

433 Jason Scott Smith, *Building New Deal Liberalism: The Political Economy of Public Works 1933-1956*, Cambridge 2006, p135.

434 Noble, as above, p75.

435 David Milton, *The Politics of US Labor: From the Great Depression to the New Deal*, New York 1982, p174.

436 Kevin McMahon, *Reconsidering Roosevelt On Race*, Chicago 2004, p52. Similarly, attempts to extend the protections offered in the act to farm workers failed.

437 James Pope and Rebecca Zietlow, "The Toledo Auto-Lite Strike and the Fight against Wage Slavery", *University of Toledo Law Review*, 839 (2007), pp114-115. See also Michael Goldfield, "Worker Insurgency, Radical Organization and New Deal Labor Legislation", *The American Political Science Review*, 83, 4 (1989).

438 Thomas Greer, *What Roosevelt Thought: The Social and Political Ideas of Franklin D Roosevelt*, East Lansing 1958, pp210-211.

439 George Wolfskill, *The Revolt of the Conservatives*, Boston 1962, pp106-107. He wrote, "From Newport to Miami, from Wall Street to Park Avenue...the broad stories: Roosevelt was an inveterate liar, immoral (hadn't you heard about his affair with Frances Perkins?), a syphilitic, a tool of Negroes and Jews, a madman given to unprovoked gales of immoderate laughter, an alcoholic, a megalomaniac dreaming his dreams of dictatorship". He was even supposed to have had his smile fixed in place by plastic surgery!

440 Moley, as above, p313.

441 *The Public Papers and Addresses of Franklin D Roosevelt: The People Approve 1936*, New York 1969, p385.

442 Marriner Eccles, *Beckoning Frontiers*, New York 1966, p102.

443 William O Douglas, *Go East Young Man*, New York 1974, pp361-362, 363.

444 Francis Biddle, *In Brief Authority*, New York 1962, p18.

445 James Olson, *Saving Capitalism: The Reconstruction Finance Corporation and the New Deal 1933-1940*, Princeton 1988, p57, 68.

446 Ickes, as above, p652.

447 Gerard Colby, *DuPont Dynasty*, Secaucus 1984, pp278, 323. See also Robert F Burk, *The Corporate State and the Broker State: The Du Ponts and American National Politics*, Cambridge, Mass 1990.

448 Between 1928 and 1932 the Du Ponts had collectively donated $400,000 to the campaign to repeal prohibition. See Burk, as above, p107. In 1936 they collectively donated $620,000 to the Republican Party. See John Allswang, *The New Deal and American Politics*, New York 1978, p60.

449 Pap Ndiaye, *Nylon and Bombs: DuPont and the March of Modern America*, Baltimore 2007, p122.

450 See Wolfskill, as above, pp62-67.

451 Wolfskill, as above, pp177-178.

452 William Anderson, *The Wild Man from Sugar Creek: The Political Career of Eugene Talmadge*, Baton Rouge 1975, p139.

453 See Colby, as above, pp328-329. See also Jules Archer, *The Plot To Seize The White House*, New York 1973, and John Spivak, *A Man In His Time*, New York 1967, pp294-331. Roosevelt was advised of the plot by the FBI—see Athan Theoharis, *Spying on Americans*, Philadelphia 1978, p68.

454 Emil Ludwig, *Roosevelt*, London 1938, pp15, 155, 156, 214, 314, 316. Ludwig had already interviewed Stalin in April 1932 and published a biography of him that is not without interest—*Stalin*, New York 1942.

455 Donald McCoy, *Landon of Kansas*, Lincoln 1966, p342.

456 *The Public Papers and Addresses: The People Approve*, as above, pp232, 233, 235, 384, 486, 487.

457 John MacGregor Burns, *Roosevelt: The Lion and the Fox*, New York 1956, pp281-282.

458 *The Public Papers and Addresses of Franklin Roosevelt: The Constitution Prevails*, 1937 , New York 1969, pp4-5.

459 The "Sit-Down" song was written by the socialist lawyer Maurice Sugar for the UAW in 1937. See Christopher Johnson, *Maurice Sugar: Law, Labor and the Left in Detroit*, Wayne State 1988, pp212-213.

460 Joyce Shaw Peterson, *American Automobile Workers 1900-1935*, New York 1987, pp130-131.

461 Wyndham Mortimer, *Organize!*, Boston 1971, p51.

462 John Bernard, *American Vanguard: The United Auto Workers During the Reuther Years 1935-1970*, Wayne State 2004, p45.

463 Sidney Fine, *The Automobile Under The Blue Eagle*, Michigan 1963, p148.

464 One admiring contemporary, Frank Marquart, wrote of Matt Smith, "Socialist, atheist and iconoclast, Matt refused to become a citizen of the United States on principle: 'I'm an internationalist, a citizen of the human race.'" As far as he was concerned MESA had to "act as a revolutionary industrial organization which set its sights on the common ownership of the means of production". See his *An Auto Workers Journal: The UAW from Crusade to One-Party State*, University Park 1975, p56.

465 Steve Babson, "British and Irish Militants in the Detroit UAW in the 1930s", in Robert Asher and Charles Stephenson, *Labor Divided: Race and Ethnicity in United States Labor Struggles 1835-1960*, Albany 1990, p227.

466 Marquart, as above, p57.

467 Irving Bernstein, *Turbulent Years*, as above, p98.

468 Irving Bernstein, *Turbulent Years*, as above, p182.

469 Lens, *Left, Right and Center*, as above, p295.

470 Irving Howe and B J Widick, *The UAW and Walter Reuther*, Cambridge, Mass 1973, p50.

471 Mortimer, as above, pp87-88.

472 Sidney Fine, *Sit Down: The General Motors Strike of 1936-1937*, Michigan 1969, p38.

473 Ronald Edsforth, *Class Conflict and Cultural Consensus: The Making of a Mass Consumer Society in Flint Michigan*, New Brunswick 1987, pp163-164.

474 Mortimer, as above, pp104, 112; BJ Widick, *Detroit: City of Race and Class*

Violence, Detroit 1989, p66. The Black Legion without any doubt had connections with GM. Many foremen were members and on 1 June 1936 Harry Anderson, GM's labour relations director, actually wrote to Edward Cowdrick that "you could use a little Black Legion down in your country". There is also evidence that the organisation was planning the assassination of Maurice Sugar, the UAW attorney, who played a major role in exposing their activities—see Johnson, as above pp170-171, 181-182. More particularly, see Peter Amann, "Vigilante Fascism: The Black Legion as an American Hybrid", *Comparative Studies in Society and History*, 25 (1983), and Stephen Norwood, *Strike-breaking and Intimidation: Mercenaries and Masculinity in Twentieth Century America*, Chapel Hill 2002, pp196-200.

475 Fine, *Sit Down*, as above, p128.
476 Ronald Edsforth and Robert Asher, "The Speedup: The Focal Point of Workers' Greivances 1919-1941", in Ronald Edsforth and Robert Asher, eds, *Autowork*, New York 1995, p78. See also Kenneth West, "'On The Line': Rank and File Reminiscences of Working conditions and the General Motors Sit-Down strike of 1937", *Michigan Historical Review*, 12, 1 (1986).
477 Mortimer, as above, pp123-124.
478 Edsforth, as above, p169.
479 Steve Babson et al, *Working Detroit*, Detroit 1986, p72. A third of the workforce were black and the occupation was a notable exercise in black and white workers fighting together.
480 Reuther, as above, pp134-141.
481 For an oral history account of the Atlanta strike, which began with a sit-down see Neill Herring and Sue Thrasher, "UAW Sit-down Strike: Atlanta 1939", in Marc Miller, ed, *Working Lives*, New York 1980, pp172-183.
482 It is worth noting that on that same day over 100 workers at the Standard Cotton Products Company, a small independent firm manufacturing uphostelry for GM, also occupied, a forgotten occupation that lasted five days longer than the GM occupation, before victory was achieved. See Kenneth West, "Standard Cotton Products and the General Motors Sit-

down Strike: Some 'Forgotten Men' Remembered", *Michigan Historical Review*, 14, 1 (1988).
483 De Caux, *Labor Radical*, as above, p228.
484 Edsforth, *Class Conflict*, as above, p171.
485 C L Sulzberger, *Sit Down With John L Lewis*, New York 1938, p71.
486 Henry Kraus, *The Many and the Few: A Chronicle of the Dynamic Auto Workers*, Chicago 1985, pp90-105. See also Kirk Fuoss, *Striking Performances/Performing Strikes*, Jackson 1997, and Timothy Lynch, *Strike Songs of the Depression*, Jackson 2001, pp85-123. For an academic rendering of the CP version of these events see Roger Keeran, *The Communist Party and the Auto Workers Unions*, Bloomington 1980.
487 Sidney Fine, "John L Lewis Discusses the General Motors Sit-Down Strike: A Document", *Labor History*, 15 (1974), p567.
488 William Weinstone, *The Great Sit-Down Strike*, New York 1937, p23. Weinstone actually acknowledges the contribution of individual Socialist Party members, those, that is, "who were not infected with the poison of Trotskyism" (p40).
489 Fine, *Sit Down*, as above, p200.
490 Sol Dollinger and Genora Johnson Dollinger, *Not Automatic: Women and the Left in the Forging of the Auto Workers' Union*, New York 2000, pp135-136. This book is an important corrective to the Kraus account, *The Many and the Few*, which minimises the contribution of non-Communists to the struggle as well as the part played by women. See also Carlton Jackson, *Child of the Sit-Downs: The Revolutionary Life of Genora Dollinger*, Kent, OH, 2008. And for the Women's Emergency Brigade itself see Patricia Yoghissian, *Emergence of the Red Berets*. Ann Arbor 1980, pp11-12.
491 Reuther, as above, p157.
492 Sidney Fine, *Frank Murphy: The New Deal Years*, Chicago 1979, pp316-317.
493 See Claude Hoffman, *Sit-Down In Anderson: UAW Local 663 Anderson, Indiana*, Detroit 1968. Once the sit-down strike was over, the UAW sent hundreds of volunteers into Anderson where they visited the bars frequented by the Black Legion and the Klan. As Victor Reuther rather mildly puts it, "scuffles and shootings occurred"—Reuther, as above, p181.

494 David Farber, *Sloan Rules*, Chicago 2002, p205.

495 In his account of this decisive episode, Henry Kraus gives credit for the plan to fellow Communist Bob Travis and goes out of his way to slander Kermit Johnson as "this scared kid" with "a case of funk" (Kraus, as above, p200). This is part of his attempt to diminish the contribution of Socialist Party members in the struggle, particularly when like the Johnsons they were to become Trotskyists.

496 Levinson, as above, p163.

497 Sulzberger, as above, p84.

498 Sulzberger, as above, pp164-165.

499 Fine, *Frank Murphy*, as above, p318.

500 De Caux, as above, p254.

501 De Caux, as above, p317.

502 Frances Perkins, *The Roosevelt I Knew*, London 1947, pp259-261. She insisted that with regard to the sit-down strike it "has been agreed by nearly all sensible labour leaders that it is a method of excess and should never be used". Even the CIO leaders agreed with this and only supported the GM workers out of "a sense of solidarity".

503 Fine, *Frank Murphy*, as above, p317.

504 J Woodford Howard, "Frank Murphy and the Sit-Down Strikes of 1937", *Labor History*, 1 (1960), p125.

505 When Studs Terkel interviewed Charles Stewart Mott, a member of the GM board from 1913 until 1973, even in his nineties he still complained that Murphy "didn't protect our property". As far as he was concerned, the sit-down strikers "should have been shot". See Studs Terkel, *Hard Times: An Oral History of the Great Depression*, New York 1970, p135.

506 Dee Garrison, ed, *Rebel Pen: The Writings of Mary Heaton Vorse*, New York 1985, pp177, 179-180. Her son, Heaton Vorse, was nearly killed working for the union in Anderson. He was shot in the legs and had 80 shotgun pellets in his wounds.

507 Dubofsky and Van Tine, as above, p270.

508 William Green was, of course, completely opposed to sit-down strikes and on one occasion described them as "sabotage beyond the wildest dreams of the IWW"—see Craig Phelan, *William Green*, New York 1989, p145.

509 West, "Standard Cotton Products", as above, p70.

510 David Milton, *The Politics of US Labor*, New York 1989, p101.

511 John Barnard, *American Vanguard: The United Auto Workers During the Reuther Years 1935-1970*, Detroit 2004, p113.

512 Fine, *Sit Down*, as above, p331.

513 De Caux, as above, p278.

514 Peggy Dennis, as above, p215.

515 Barbara Warne Newell, *Chicago and the Labor Movement*, Urbana 1961, p151-152.

516 Philip Foner, *Women and the American Labor Movement*, New York 1982, p333.

517 Philip Dray, *There Is A Power In A Union*, New York 2010, p487.

518 Ahmed White, "The Depression Era Sit-Down Strikes and the Limits of Liberal Labor Law", *Seton Hall Law Review*, 40, 1 (2010), p17. The history of the sit-down strike remains to be explored, but as White points out, as late as June 1947 the National Maritime Union staged a 700-ship sit-down strike! (p47) See also Ahmed White, "Mutiny, Shipboard Strikes and the Supreme Court's Subversion of New Deal Labor Law", *Berkeley Journal of Labor and Employment Law*, 275 (2004).

519 Darryl Halter, "Sources of CIO Success: The New Deal Years in Milwaukee", in Darryl Halter, ed, *Workers and Unions in Wisconsin*, Madison 1999, p128.

520 Peter Rachleff, *Hard-Pressed in the Heartland: The Hormel Strike and the Future of the Labor Movement*, Boston 1993, pp37-42. Rachleff argues that joining the CIO proved to be a disaster.

521 Rosemary Feurer, *Radical Unionism in the Midwest 1900-1950*, Urbana 2006, pp49-64.

522 See Donald Kennedy, "Hershey, Pennsylvania, Chocolate Workers' Strike of 1937", in Ronald Filippelli, ed, *Labor Conflictin the United States: An Encyclopaedia*, New York 1990.

523 Peggy Dennis, as above, pp86-87; Edward Levinson, *Labor on the March*, New York 1938, pp173-174. See also Ahmed Smith, "The Depression Era Sit-Down Strikes", as above, p28.

524 Feurer, *Radical Unionism*, as above, p93. The Maytag strike went down to defeat, however. The workers evacuated on the promise that the plant would stay shut but the Democrat governor, Nelson Kreschel, sent in the National Guard to open it.

525 Steve Babson, *The Unfinished Struggle*, Lanham 1999, pp98-99.

526 Margaret Collingwood Nowak, *Two Who Were There*, Detroit 1989, p32.

527 Kraus, as above, p279.

528 Nowak, as above, p86.

529 Mary Stolberg, *Bridging the River of Hatred*, Detroit 1998, p54. Edwards was a Socialist Party member at this time, but was to eventually desert to the Democrats and briefly became Detroit's police commissioner in 1962 before going on to become a federal judge.

530 Widick, *Detroit*, as above, p72.

531 Babson, *Working Detroit*, as above, pp77-79; Daniel Opler, *For All White Collar Workers*, Columbus 2007, pp64-66.

532 Marquart, as above, p78. The management obsession with visits to the toilet is not some sort of perversion but a recognition of the fact that a lot of organising can take place in the toilet, a place where the foreman cannot see what is going on!

533 Abt, as above, pp62-63.

534 Steve Jefferys, *Management and Managed: Fifty Years of Crisis at Chrysler*, Cambridge 1986, p73.

535 Babson, *Working Detroit*, as above, p86; Mortimer, as above, p149

536 Sulzberger, as above, p109. There are many stories of Lewis's skill as a negotiator. On one occasion he was called in to try and end an unofficial miners' strike where the contract specified a $1 a day fine for unofficial action and the men had accumulated fines of over $200,000. The owner's representative said that as a gesture of goodwill the company was prepared to write off half the fines owed. Lewis welcomed this gesture and said that in the same spirit of goodwill he was prepared to match it by writing off the other half (pp10-11).

537 Jefferys, as above, p74.

538 Lens, *Left, Right and Center*, as above, pp310-312.

539 George Edwards, *Pioneer-At-Law*, New York 1974, p178.

540 Zieger, *John L Lewis*, as above, p98.

541 According to Jim Pope, "the court was plainly and simply yielding to pressure from the sit-down strikers"—see Pope, as above, p97.

542 Albert Blum and Ira Spar, "The Lansing Labor Holiday", *Michigan History*, 49

(1965), p8. See also Lisa M Fine, *The Story of Reo Joe*, Philadelphia 2004, pp82-90.

543 Reuther, as above, pp201-202.

544 Keith Sward, *The Legend of Henry Ford*, New York 1968, pp392-393.

545 Robert Lacey, *Ford*, London 1986, p357.

546 Neil Baldwin, *Henry Ford and the Jews: The Mass Production of Hate*, New York 2003, pp180-181, 185.

547 See Leo Ribuffo, "Henry Ford and the International Jew", in Leo Ribuffo, *Right, Center, Left*, New Brunswick 1992. According to one account by a Ford executive, Henry Ford had his first stroke, from which he never recovered, in May 1946 while watching a US government documentary about the liberation of the Majdanek concentration camp that revealed at least some of the horror of the Holocaust! See Max Wallace, *The American Axis*, New York 2003, pp358-359.

548 Charles Higham, *Trading with the Enemy*, London 1983, p97.

549 See Reinhold Billstein, Karola Fings, Anita Kugler and Nicholas Levis, *Working for the Enemy: Ford, General Motors and Forced Labour in Germany during the Second World War*, New York 2000. See also Jacques Pauwels, "Profits über Alles! American Corporations and Hitler", Labour/Le Travail 51 (2003).

550 Norwood, as above, p178.

551 Mary Stolberg, as above, pp116-117.

552 Wallace, as above, p137; Albert Kahn, *High Treason*, New York 1951, pp172-173. See also George Seldes, *Facts and Fascism*, New York 1947, pp122-138.

553 Reuther, as above, pp206-209.

554 Elizabeth Fones-Wolf, *Waves of Opposition: Labor and the Struggle for Democratic Radio*, Urbana 2006, p56.

555 George Green, "Discord in Dallas: Auto Workers, City Fathers and the Ford Motor Company 1937-1941", *Labor's Heritage* 1, 3 (1989), p24.

556 Edwards, as above, p168.

557 Sward, as above, p398.

558 Michael Honey, *Southern Labor and Black Civil Rights*, Urbana 1993, pp87-89.

559 Lacey, as above, p371.

560 Martin Halpern, *Unions, Radicals and Democratic Presidents*, Westport 2003, pp47, 50, 51.

561 Harvey Klehr, *The Heyday of American Communism*, New York 1984, pp17, 94.

562 George Wolfskill and John Hudson, *All But The People: Franklin D Roosevelt and His Critics 1933-1939*, London 1969, pp121, 124.

563 Cletus Daniel, *The ACLU and the Wagner Act*, Ithaca 1980, pp71, 119.

564 What is interesting is that this slogan that is often seen as establishing the Communist Party's credentials as an "American" party went too far for the Comintern and was soon abandoned under their instructions! See Harvey Klehr, John Earl Haynes and Kyrill M Anderson, *The Soviet World of American Communism*, New Haven 1998, pp36-40. Georgi Dimitrov, the secretary general of the Comintern and one of the architects of the Popular Front, made it clear that "it would be helpful to explain to Browder the necessity for a greater degree of principled precision in certain party slogans, and concerning the gradual retiring of the popular but non-Marxist slogan 'Communism is twentieth century Americanism.'" See Ivo Banac, ed, *The Diary of Georgi Dimitrov 1933-1949*, New Haven 2003, p81.

565 James G Ryan, *Earl Browder*, Tuscaloosa 1997, pp348-350.

566 William Z Foster, *History of the Communist Party of the United States*, New York 1952, pp348-350.

567 Cochran, as above, p136.

568 Cochran, as above, p138.

569 Nelson Lichtenstein, *Walter Reuther*, Champaign, IL, 1995, pp119-121. Pope describes the Pontiac strike as "a serious defeat for shop-floor activism and worker lawmaking"—see Pope, as above, p102. The significance of the Pontiac strike is, quite incredibly, not discussed in Keeran's book on the CP.

570 Klehr, *The Heyday*, as above, p248.

571 Al Richmond, *A Long View From The Left*, Indianapolis 1973, pp243-244.

572 Robert Zieger, *The CIO 1935-1955*, Chapel Hill 1995, p70.

573 De Caux, *Labor Radical*, as above, p280.

574 For the struggle at Homestead see in particular Paul Krause, *The Battle for Homestead 1880-1892*, Pittsburgh 1992.

575 Horace Davis, *Labor and Steel*, New York 1933, pp163-168.

576 William Z Foster, *Organizing Methods in the Steel Industry*, New York 1936, pp3, 4, 9, 12, 17, 18, 19, 24.

577 William Z Foster, *What Means A Strike In Steel*, New York 1937, pp3, 18, 21-22, 31, 33, 37.

578 Elizabeth Cohen, *Making A New Deal: Industrial Workers in Chicago 1919-1939*, Cambridge 1991, p502.

579 Lens, *Left, Right and Center*, as above, p314.

580 Robert Brooks, *As Steel Goes*, New Haven 1940, p119.

581 Stanley Vittoz, *New Deal Labor Policy and the American Industrial Economy*, Chapel Hill 1987, p162.

582 Jack Metzgar, *Striking Steel: Solidarity Remembered*, Philadelphia 2000, p25.

583 Tom Girdler, *Boot Straps*, New York 1944, pp166, 169-170, 176.

584 Thomas Brooks, *Clint: The Biography of a Labor Intellectual*, New York 1978, pp133-135.

585 Brooks, as above, p112.

586 Kenneth Casebeer, "Aliquippa: The Company Town and Contested Power in the Construction of Law", *Buffalo Law Review*, 43, 3 (1995), p680. See also James Green, "Democracy Comes to Little Siberia: Steel Workers Organize in Aliquippa, Pennsylvania 1933-1937", *Labor's Heritage*, 5, 2 (1993).

587 Brooks, as above, pp123-126, 128, 133-134.

588 For the Mohawk Valley Formula see in particular John Steuben, *Strike Strategy*, New York 1950, pp230-282. US strikebreaking methods were actually imported into Britain in the 1980s by the Thatcher government. They were most in evidence during the 1984-85 Miners' Strike.

589 Steuben, as above, p251.

590 Randy Whittle, *Johnstown, Pennsylvania: A History 1937-1980*, Charleston 2007, p10.

591 Jerold Auerbach, *Labor and Liberty: The La Follette Committee and the New Deal*, Indianapolis 1966, p101.

592 Rhonda Levine, *Class Struggle and the New Deal*, Lawrence 1988, p147.

593 Girdler, as above, pp312, 355, 449-450.

594 Robin D G Kelley, *Hammer and Hoe: Alabama Communists during the Great Depression*, Chapel Hill 1990, p144.

595 Ahmed White, "Industrial Terrorism and the Unmaking of New Deal Labor Law", *Nevada Law Journal*, 11, 3 (2011), p597.

596 Michael Dennis, *The Memorial Day Massacre and the Movement for Industrial Democracy*, New York 2010, p108.

597 Alice Lynd and Staughton Lynd, ed, *Rank and File: Personal Histories of Working Class Organizers*, New York 1988, pp88, 95.

598 Meyer Levin, *In Search*, Paris 1950, p140. His classic novel of the massacre, *Citizens*, was published in 1940.

599 Donald Sofchalk, "The Chicago Memorial Day incident: An Episode of Mass Action", *Labor History*, 6 (1965), p16.

600 Clancy Sigal, *A Woman of Uncertain Character*, New York 2006, p107. In this memoir of his mother, Jenny, he remembers how on one occasion he trailed after his mother who was following a scab who had been threatening the pickets. It was during a strike at Regal Frocks where she was working. He saw her remonstrate with the woman who threatened her with a pair of shears: "She knocked that woman down with a haymaker punch to the jaw... Then, scanning to see if there were any witnesses, she dragged the yelping woman by her hair into scrub bushes and while I watched in astonishment slugged her a couple of times and kicked her in the ribs for good measure." She told him: "You saw nothing, you heard nothing" (pp143-144).

601 Auerbach, as above, p127.

602 Daniel Leab, "The Memorial Day Massacre", *Midcontinent*, 8 (1967), p8.

603 See Carol Quirke, "Reframing Chicago's Memorial day massacre, May 30, 1937", *American Quarterly*, 60, 1 (2008), p140.

604 According to Michael Dennis, "the authorities had good reason to wonder whether or not the incident at Republic Steel would spark a working class insurrection"—see Michael Dennis, as above, p162.

605 Newell, as above, pp184-185.

606 Sofchalk, as above, p29.

607 Levin, as above, p106.

608 Steuben, as above, pp217-218; Dee Garrison, *Rebel Pen: The Writings of Mary Heaton Vorse*, New York 1985, p209.

609 David McDonald, *Union Man*, New York 1969, pp113, 114, 118.

610 Robert Brooks, as above, p143.

611 Steuben, as above, p223.

612 James Gross, *The Reshaping of the National Labor Relations Board 1937-1947*, Albany 1981, p10.

613 Lens, *Left, Right and Center*, as above, p314.

614 McDonald, as above, pp118, 119.

615 Melvyn Dubofsky and Warren Van Tine, *John L Lewis*, New York 1977, p315.

616 Frank Freidel, *Franklin D Roosevelt*, Boston 1990, pp242-244.

617 Lewis's speech is available at americanrhetoric.com

618 Cochran, as above, pp100-101.

619 Foster, *History of the Communist Party*, as above, p351.

620 Clint Golden and Harold Ruttenberg, *The Dynamics of Industrial Democracy*, New York 1942, pp60-61.

621 Robert Brooks, as above, p110.

622 Robert Slayton, "Labor and Urban Politics: District 31, Steel Workers Organizing Committee, and the Chicago Machine", *Journal of Urban History*, 23, 1 (1996), pp53-56.

623 Ray Allen Billington, "Government and the Arts: The WPA Experience", *American Quarterly*, 13, 4 (1961), p468.

624 Jane DeHart Matthews, *The Federal Theatre 1935-1939: Plays, Relief and Politics*, New York 1967, p43.

625 DeHart Matthews, as above, p110.

626 DeHart Matthews, as above, pp67-68.

627 Hallie Flanagan, *Arena: The History of the Federal Theatre*, New York 1940, pp125, 221. Flanagan appeared before the Dies Committee and was asked whether Christopher Marlowe was a Communist! (p342).

628 See Susan Quinn, *Furious Improvisation*, New York 2008, pp112-134. See also John Hunter, "Marc Blitzstein's 'The Cradle Will Rock' as a Document of America in 1937", *American Quarterly*, 18, 2 (1966).

629 Eric Gordon, *Mark the Music: The Life and Music of Marc Blitzstein*, New York 1989, p131.

630 DeHart Matthews, as above, p122.

631 Quinn, as above, p162.

632 Quinn, as above, p174.

633 Flanagan, as above, pp202-203.

634 Quinn, as above, p178.

635 Bonnie Nelson Schwartz, ed, *Voices From The Federal Theatre*, Madison 2003, pp194-195.

636 Gordon, as above, pp143-144.

637 Flanagan, as above, p314.

638 C Ray Marshall, *Labor in the South*, Cambridge, Mass 1967, p17.

639 Barbara Griffith, *The Crisis of American Labor: Operation Dixie and the Defeat of the CIO*, Philadelphia 1988, pp18-19.

640 Steven Fraser, *Labor Will Rule: Sidney Hillman and the Rise of American Labor*, Ithaca 1991, p388.

641 Herbert Harris, *American Labor*, New Haven 1938, pp347-348.

642 Foner, *Organized Labor and the Black Worker*, as above, p230.

643 Benjamin Stolberg, *The Story of the CIO*, New York 1938, pp211-213.

644 Fraser, as above, p420.

645 Michael Honey, *Southern Labor and Black Civil Rights: Organizing Memphis Workers*, Urbana 1993, p59.

646 Foner, *Organized Labor and the Black Worker*, as above, p235.

647 Henry Kraus, *Heroes of Unwritten Story*, Urbana 1993, p225.

648 Robert Zeiger, *For Jobs and Freedom: Race and Labor in America since 1865*, Lexington 2007, p115. See also Michael Goldfield, "Race and the CIO: the Possibilities for Racial Egalitarianism in the 1930s and 1940s", and the responses by Gary Gerstle, Robert Korstad, Marshall Stevenson and Judith Stein in *International Labor and Working Class History*, 44 (1993).

649 B J Widick, *Detroit: City of Race and Class Violence*, Detroit 1989, p107.

650 Edward Levinson, *Labor on the March*, New York 1935, p135.

651 Lens, *Unrepentant Radical*, as above, p98.

652 Craig Phelan, *William Green*, Albany 1989, pp147-148.

653 Walter Goodman, *The Committee*, London 1969, pp28-34. For an overly sympathetic account of AFL support for the Dies Committee see Jennifer Luff, *Common Sense Anticommunism: Labor and Civil Liberties Between the World Wars*, Chapel Hill 2002, pp166-167, 171-177.

654 See in particular Barry Kritzberg, "An Unfinished Chapter in White-Collar Unionism: The Formative Years of the Chicago Newspaper Guild", *Labor History*, 14, 3 (1973) and Newell, as above, pp190-191.

655 See George Suggs, *Union Busting in the Tri-State: The Oklahoma, Kansas and Missouri Metal Workers' Strike of 1935*, Norman 1986.

656 Gerald Rose, "The Westwood Lumber Strike", *Labor History*, 13, 2 (1972), pp192-193. Merriam's Republican predecessor as governor, James "Sunny Jim" Rolph, had achieved a certain distinction with his public championing of lynching in late 1933. See Philip Dray, *At the Hands of Persons Unknown: The Lynching of Black America*, New York 2002, pp333-335.

657 Jerry Lembcke and William Tattam, *One Union in Wood*, New York 1984, p56.

658 Lens, *Left, Right and Center*, as above, pp331-332. In his memoirs, Lens describes how, "union leaders went in to see employers without a single member and came out after a few hours conference with the right to collect dues from hundreds, sometimes thousands, of working people. The next day company supervisors would walk around the plant and get workers to sign application cards." In the early 1950s, he had organised a Chicago factory, signing up almost every worker in the union, only to be then told by the employer that the workers were already members of the Teamsters. The company had signed a contract with the Teamsters and was paying the union the men's membership dues, but neither the company nor the union had ever told the workers of this convenient arrangement. See his *Unrepentant Radical*, as above, pp98, 212-213.

659 Gross, as above, p11.

660 For an overly sympathetic account of the AFL see Christopher Tomlins, "AFL Unions in the 1930s: Their performance in Historical Perspective", *Journal of American History*, 65, 4 (1979).

661 *The Public Papers and Addresses of Franklin D Roosevelt: The Constitution Prevails 1937*, New York 1969, pp4-5.

662 Kenneth Davis, *FDR: Into the Storm 1937-1940*, New York 1993, p230.

663 James Stuart Olson, *Saving Capitalism: The Reconstruction Finance Corporation and the New Deal 1933-1940*, Princeton 1988, p187.

664 Maurice Spector, "The Collapse of the New Deal", *New International*, 4, 6 (1938), p173.

665 Alan Lawson, *A Commonwealth of Hope*, Baltimore 2006, p183.

666 Marriner Eccles, *Beckoning Frontiers*, New York 1966, p304.

667 Lawson, as above, p190.

668 Lens, *Left, Right and Center*, as above, pp315, 320.

669 See Dominic Tierney, *FDR and the Spanish Civil War*, Durham 2007.

670 Davis, *FDR*, as above, pp123-124.

671 Blanche Wiesen Cook, *Eleanor Roosevelt: The Defining Years 1933-1938*, New York 1999, p325.

672 Henry Feingold, *The Politics of Rescue*, New York 1970, pp41-42.

673 Wiesen Cook, as above, p558.

674 Richard Breitman and Alan Kraut, *American Refugee Policy and European Jewry 1933-1945*, Bloomington 1987, p74.

675 Davis, *FDR*, as above, pp370-371. See also Sarah Ogilvie and Scott Miler, *Refuge Denied: The St Louis Passengers and the Holocaust*, Madison 2006.

676 See in particular Brigid O'Farrell, *She Was One Of Us: Eleanor Roosevelt and the American Worker*, Ithaca 2010.

677 Wiesen Cook, as above, p444.

678 Doris Kearns Goodwin, *No Ordinary Time—Franklin and Eleanor Roosevelt: The Home Front in World War 2*, New York 1994, pp175-176.

679 For different interpretations see Harvey Klehr, *The Heyday of American Communism*, New York 1984, and Fraser Ottanelli, *The Communist Party of the United States: From the Depression to World War 11*, New Brunswick 1991.

680 See Robert Cherny, "Prelude to the Popular Front: The Communist Party in California", *American Communist History*, 1 (2002).

681 Geoffrey Roberts, *The Soviet Union and the Origins of the Second World War*, Basingstoke 1995, pp9-10, 15-16.

682 Earl Browder, "The American Communist Party in the Thirties", Rita James Simon, ed, *As We Saw The Thirties*, Urbana 1967, p237.

683 See Dorothy Borg, "Notes on Roosevelt's 'Quarintine' Speech", *Political Science Quarterly*, 72, 3 (1957). In practical terms, however, the only government to be "quarantined" by Roosevelt was the Spanish Republic that was under fascist attack!

684 David Bennett, "Could the New Deal have taken America to the Left?", in Wilbur Cohen, ed, *The Roosevelt New Deal*, Austin 1986, p38.

685 George Charney, *A Long Journey*, Chicago 1968, pp42-43, 59, 78, 94-95.

686 Peggy Dennis, *The Autobiography of an American Communist*, Westport, Conn, 1977, p128.

687 Granville Hicks, *I Like America*, New York 1938, pp145-146.

688 Granville Hicks, *Part of the Truth*, New York 1965, pp145, 163.

689 Browder, as above, pp230-231.

690 Peggy Dennis, as above, p129.

691 For the Lincoln Brigade see Peter Carroll, *The Odyssey of the Abraham Lincoln Brigade*, Stanford 1994, and Robert Rosenstone, *Crusade in the Left*, New Brunswick 2009. For a Trotskyist memoir see William Herrick, *Jumping The Line*, Madison 1998.

692 William Z Foster, *Questions and Answers on the Piatakov-Radek Trial*, New York 1937, pp3, 5, 36, 37, 72, 75, 77, 7.9

693 See Margarete Buber Neuman, *Under Two Dictators*, London 1948.

694 See Tim Tzouliadis, *The Forsaken: An American Tragedy in Stalin's Russia*, New York 2008, p144. See also pp95-102. There was Victor Tyskewicz-Voskov, a 25 year old New Yorker, who confessed under interrogation that his mother was a "Trotskyist" working for the Nazis. They were both shot on 7 June 1938. There was the Reverend Julius Hecker, a Communist sympathiser, shot for espionage on 28 April 1938. There was the 21 year old violinist, Arthur Talent, shot on 7 June 1938. The Abolins, father James and sons Arthur and Carl, all shot in 1938. And the veteran black Communist, Lovett Fort-Whiteman, who died in a labour camp on 13 June 1939. The majority of Stalin's American victims, however, were Finnish-Americans, who had emigrated to the Soviet Union in the 1920s and 1930s. According to Tzouliadis, an NKVD mass grave near Sandarmorkh in Karelia contained 9,000 corpses, of whom at least 140 were Americans, among them Oscar Corgan and Helen Hill (p354). See also Mayme Sevander, *Red Exodus: Finnish American Emigration to Russia*, Duluth 1996; and Mayme Sevander, *They Took My Father: Finnish Americans in Stalin's Russia*, Minneapolis 2004.

695 Earl Browder, *Traitors in American History: Lessons of the Moscow Trials*, New York 1938, pp27-28.

696 Peggy Dennis, as above, pp133, 136.

697 Steve Nelson with James Barrett and Rob Ruck, *Steve Nelson, American Radical*, Pittsburgh 1981, pp247, 248-249.

698 John Gates, *The Story of an American Communist*, New York 1958, pp74-76.

699 Charney, as above, pp123, 125.

700 William Z Foster, *The War Crisis: Questions and Answers*, New York 1940, p42.

701 Earl Browder, *The Jewish People and the War*, New York 1940, pp10-11.

702 Harvey Klehr, *The Communist Experience in America*, New Brunswick 2010, p194; Klehr, *The Heyday*, as above, p389; Melech Epstein, *The Jew and Communism 1919-1941*, New York 1959, pp352, 354.

703 Earl Browder, *The Second Imperialist War*, New York 1940, pp37, 99.

704 Peggy Dennis, as above, p135.

705 Klehr, *The Heyday*, as above, p397.

706 Hicks, *Part of the Truth*, as above, p176; Granville Hicks, *Where We Came Out*, New York 1954, p73.

707 Harvey Klehr, John Earl Haynes and Kyrill Anderson, *The Soviet World of American Communism*, New Haven 1998, pp72-73.

708 Epstein, as above, pp351, 366, 367.

709 Browder, *The Jewish People*, as above, pp7, 8, 15, 16, 19-20.

710 Steve Nelson, as above, p252.

711 Peggy Dennis, as above, p158. This was not her first visit to the Soviet Union. She had lived there in the early 1930s. Her memoir provides an interesting account of the mores of the new Communist middle class. She was very reluctant to employ a maid: "Never, I vowed. A maid! In Moscow?" (p62). She did, of course. Similarly, she was reluctant to use the Foreign Specialists' Store where you could buy goods not available to ordinary Russians. Inevitably, she did (p64). And most disturbingly, she writes of a Russian comrade, Bob, and his American wife, Valerie, who had brought her father, mother, and two brothers and their families to live in Russia. They were good friends. In 1941 she saw Valerie in the street, but Valerie ignored her greeting and walked by without any acknowledgement. When she asked comrades why she had behaved like this, she was told "that Bob had been executed and that Valerie, only recently released from prison, carefully stayed away from all foreign comrades. I was told for her sake to leave her alone" (pp64-65). Looking back she admits that American Communists obviously knew of the Show Trials, but they never realised that they were "but the tip of the iceberg... We knew that the Comintern had been decimated. We read of the public trials...but we read the accounts and accepted them. We saw it as part of the brutal realities of making revolution, of building an oasis of socialism in a sea of enemies" (p117).

712 Carroll, as above, pp230-231.

713 Harold Ickes, *The Secret Diary of Harold Ickes* vol 3, New York 1954, p97.

714 James Prickett, "Communist Conspiracy or Wage Dispute?: The 1941 Strike at North American Aviation", *Pacific Historical Quarterly*, 50, 2 (1981), p224.

715 Barnard, as above, p174.

716 Ickes, vol 3, as above, p536.

717 Prickett, as above, p229.

718 Mortimer, as above, p185.

719 Earl Browder, *Teheran: Our Path in War and Peace*, New York 1944, pp67-68, 71, 86.

720 For histories of American Trotskyism see James Cannon, *The History of American Trotskyism*, New York 1944; George Breitman, Paul Le Blanc and Alan Wald, eds, *Trotskyism in the United States: Historical Essays and Reconsiderations*, New Jersey 1996; Constance Ashton Myers, *The Prophet's Army*, Westport, Conn, 1977. See also M S Venkataramani, "Leon Trotsky's Adventure in American Radical Politics", *International Review of Social History*, 9, 1 (1964).

721 Cannon, as above, p65.

722 Louis Budenz, *Men Without Faces*, New York 1950, pp126-129. He claims that those involved were told they were foiling a Trotskyist attempt to assassinate Stalin, rather than helping assassinate Trotsky.

723 Earl Browder, *The People's Front*, New York 1938, pp276-318.

724 Earl Browder, *Traitors in American History: The Lessons of the Moscow Trials*, New York 1938, pp14, 25, 31.

725 Louis Budenz, *Men Without Faces*, as above, p126. Budenz claims to have been behind the infiltration of the American Trotskyists. With his tutoring, Sylvia Franklin "so ingratiated herself with the leading Trotskyites that she became a close friend of James Cannon, American Trotskyite chief, and his wife, Rose Karsner. She had full run of the Trotskyite offices, became Cannon's secretary, and

made available to the Soviet secret police all the correspondence with Trotsky in Mexico City and with other Trotskyites throughout the world."

726 Max Shachtman, *Behind the Moscow Trial: The Greatest Frame-up in History*, New York 1936. For Shachtman see Peter Drucker, *Max Shachtman and His Left*, New Jersey 1994.

727 James Cannon, *The First Ten Years of American Communism*, New York 1961, pp39-40.

728 For the Trotskyists in the UAW see Victor Devinatz, "The Role of the Trotskyists in the United Auto Workers 1939-1949", *Left History*, 10, 2 (2005).

729 As John Abt, the Communist lawyer, put it, "corporate espionage...was socialised when J Edgar Hoover took it over". See John Abt, as above, p68.

730 Philip Jaffe, *The Rise and Fall of American Communism*, New York 1975, pp50-51.

731 Art Preis, *Labor's Giant Step*, New York 1972, p141.

732 See Thomas Pahl, "G-String Conspiracy, Political Reprisal or Armed Revolt?: The Minneapolis Trotskyite Trial", *Labor History*, 8, 1 (1967). See also Barry Eidlin, "'Upon this (Foundering) Rock': Minneapolis Teamsters and the Transformation of Business Unionism 1934-1941", *Labor History*, 50, 3 (2009). For the SWP's contemporary assessment see Felix Morrow, "The Minneapolis 'Sedition' Trial", *Fourth International*, 3, 1 (1942).

733 Albert Lannon, *Second String Red*, Lanham 1999, p93. John Abt, looking back after the prosecution of the CP leadership in 1949, recognised the party's failure to defend the SWP as "a terrible mistake". See John Abt, as above, p89.

734 See Michael Belknap, *Cold War Political Justice*, Westport, Conn, 1977, and Scott Martelle, *The Fear Within: Spies, Commies and American Democracy on Trial*, New Brunswick 2011.

735 Martin Duberman, *Paul Robeson*, New York 1989, p382.

Index

Abt, John 26, 71, 254 n, 274 n
Aliquippa 188-190, 191, 193, 201
Amalgamated Association of Iron, Steel and
    Tin Workers 104, 108, 112, 182
Amalgamated Clothing Workers (ACW)
    24-25, 77, 10, 113, 206,209
Amalgamated Iron, Steel and Tin Workers 77
Amalgamated Meat Packers Union 166
American Civil Liberties Union (ACLU) 78,
    137, 214
American Federation of Hosiery Workers 26
American Federation of Labor (AFL) 8-14, 18,
    23, 27, 33, 34, 43, 46, 71, 75-80, 85, 86,
    88-89, 91, 94-95, 98, 103, 105-108, 111-117,
    133, 143, 145-147, 153, 160, 162, 165-166,
    169, 171, 175-178, 183, 186, 196, 206, 209,
    211-215, 222, 243, 255 n, 260 n
American Plan 11-14
American Workers Party 8, 86-87, 145, 238,
    257 n, see also Abraham Muste
Anarchists 16, 53, 56, 62, 116
anti-Semitism 49, 53, 137, 172-173, 220-222, 234
Auto-Lite strike 85-89, 133, 145

Back to Work marches 165, 190-191
Battle of Deputies Run 92
Battle of the Running Bulls 155
Black Legion 137, 148, 265-266 n
black workers 8, 31-32, 33-38, 46, 50-55,
    183-184, 192, 209-211, 255 n
Bridges, Harry 96-100
Brophy, John 76, 108, 114, 178
Browder, Earl 114, 177-180, 183, 200, 224-225,
    229, 232, 234-237, 239, 241, 258-259 n

Cannery and Agricultural Workers Industrial
    Union (CAWIU) 81-82
Cannon, James 94, 237-240
Cermak, Anton 45, 58, 69, 254 n

Chaplin, Charlie 154
Chicago massacre 193-196, 199
Chicago schoolteachers' protest, 1932 67-69
Chrysler Corporation 142, 157, 158, 167-168,
    171, 172, 179, 220, 243
Citizens' Alliance (CA) 27, 89, 92-94
Civil Works Administration (CWA) 74
Civilian Conservation Corps (CCC) 71, 74
Comintern 9, 55, 177, 222-224, 228, 232, 238,
    269 n, 273 n
Committee for Industrial Organization (CIO)
    9, 106, 111-117, 129, 133, 147, 153, 156, 159,
    161, 162, 164-165, 168-169, 176-180, 182,
    185, 186-188, 190-192, 196, 196, 198-205,
    206-215, 218, 224, 227, 235, 241
Communist League 8, 89, 237-238
Communist Party 8, 46-56, 81-82, 95-96,
    99-100, 113-114, 124, 140, 147, 149-150, 153,
    154, 162, 164, 171, 171-181, 183-184, 188,
    192, 200, 202, 203, 212, 243-244;
    anti-racism 52-55; Hitler-Stalin Pact
    229-237; Popular Front 177-179, 222-229;
    Third Period 45-47, 52, 55, 124, 177, 178;
    and Trotskyists 238-242
Conference for Progressive Labor Action
    (CPLA) 86-87
Congress of Industrial Organizations (CIO)
    see Committee for Industrial
    Organization
Cradle Will Rock, The 203-204

Daily Worker 125, 177, 180, 230, 232-233, 237, 241
Dawes, Charles 12, 57-58, 68
De Caux, Len 48, 52, 111, 114, 151, 162, 183
Debs, Eugene 15
Democratic Party 8, 19, 37, 42, 48, 60-67, 69,
    70, 73, 78, 81, 102, 105, 109-110, 120,
    122-124, 126, 127, 131, 136-137, 139, 140, 156,
    188, 206-207, 212, 218, 240

Dennis, Peggy 49, 225, 230-231, 235
Dobbs, Farrell 89-90, 93-94
Dockers 85, 95-100, 222
Dubinsky, David 113-114, 211
Dunne, Grant 89, 242
Dunne, Miles 89
Dunne, Ray 89, 93
Dunne, William 13, 52

Economy Act, 1933 70-71
Elaine Massacre 36-37
End Poverty In California (EPIC) 123-124, 222

Farmer-Labor Party 83, 92, 184
Federal Arts Project 202
Federal Bureau of Investigation (FBI) 174, 235, 241-242
Federal Emergency Relief Administration (FERA) 74
Federal Labor Unions (FLU) 77, 85-86, 105-106, 115, 143, 145
Federal Music Project 202
Federal Theatre Project 202-205
Federal Writers' Project 202
First World War 7, 10, 14, 23, 34, 59, 61, 86, 144
Flint Auto Worker 150
Food Workers Industrial Union 82
Ford Company 27, 50-51, 142-143, 152, 158, 171-176, 217, 230
Ford, Henry 18, 27, 158, 175, 176-177, 220; anti-Semitism 172-173
Foster, William Z 10-11, 29, 46-49, 55, 108-109, 178, 184-188, 195-196, 200, 203, 227-228, 231, 232-233

General Motors (GM) 9, 19, 27, 57, 63, 141, 143, 146-149, 151-161, 165, 171, 179, 185-187, 191, 220, 243, 245
Germany 8, 20, 47, 147, 173, 177, 178, 203, 220-221, 224, 227, 232-233
Gompers, Samuel 13, 23
Gorman, Francis 100-103
Great Depression 8, 39-45, 55, 58, 63, 107, 109-110, 114, 142, 209
Green, William 13, 17, 43, 71, 79-80, 86, 89, 106, 111, 115, 117, 143, 146, 159, 196, 211-212

Hallgren, Mauritz 43-45, 51, 79
Hapgood, Powers 109, 114, 116
Harding, Warren 12, 18, 24, 62
Hearst, William Randolph 65, 129-131, 212
Hemingway, Ernest 71
Herndon, Angelo 52, 54
Hicks, Granville 226, 233
Hillman, Sidney 113, 177-178, 180, 206-209, 211

Hitler, Adolf 47, 172-173, 177, 228, 230-232, 235 see also Nazis (Germany)
Hitler-Stalin Pact see under Communist Party
Hook, Sidney 53, 87
Hoover, Herbert 16, 18, 37, 38, 46, 57-60, 62-66, 68, 71, 72, 109, 110, 134, 217, 219, 233
House Un-American Activities Committee (HUAC) 211-212, 234
hunger marches 50-51, 64
Hutcheson, Bill 14, 113, 115, 147, 213

Independent Union of All Workers (IUAW) 83-84, 163-164
industrial accidents 30-33
Industrial Employees Union (IEU) 213
Industrial Woodworkers of America (IWA) 213
Industrial Workers of the World (IWW) 14-15, 28, 34, 47, 56, 62, 80, 83, 95, 108, 141, 172, 213, 238, 243
International Labor Defense (ILD) 53-54
International Ladies Garment Workers Union (ILGWU) 77, 106, 113, 209
International Longshoremen's Association (ILA) 95-97, 222

Japan 224, 233
Jewish workers 234
Jim Crow 33-34, 37, 184
Johnson, General Hugh 78-79
Johnson, Genora 155-157

Kraus, Henry 150, 153, 157, 166, 209, 210
Ku Klux Klan 12, 127, 136-137, 207, 242

labour spies 26-30, 78, 148 see also Pinkerton Agency, Service Department
La Follette Committee 26, 194-195, 212
Lemlich Shavelson, Clara 123
Lens, Sidney 40, 41, 55, 75, 85, 146, 168-169, 198, 214, 218
Lewis, John L 8-9, 22, 27, 75-76, 107, 108-117, 153, 154, 156, 159-161, 168-169, 175, 177, 178, 182, 183, 186-187, 192, 199-201, 211, 226, 236, 243
Little Steel strike 9, 190-193, 196-198, 200, 204
Long, Huey 65, 124-129, 130-131, 137
Lynching 12, 34-37, 54, 62, 118-119, 127, 219, 222

Machinists' union 28-29, 147, 211
Mechanics Educational Society of America (MESA) 143-147, 150
Mellon, Andrew 18-23, 57, 59
Mine, Mill and Smelter Workers Union (MMSWU) 213
Mink, George 52, 240

Minneapolis 8, 17, 85, 89-95, 100, 112, 214, 241, 243
Minute Men 12
Morgan, J P 18, 20, 72-73, 80
Mortimer, Wyndham 142, 146-150, 168, 179, 180, 236
Moscow trials 233, 238, 239, 240
Murray, Philip 13, 117, 180, 182-183, 188, 192, 200, 201, 235
Mussolini, Benito 13, 109, 173
Muste, Abraham 28, 47, 80, 86-89, 108, 116, 146, 238
Musteites see Muste

National Association for the Advancement of Colored People (NAACP) 34, 36, 37, 118-119, 127
National Guard 38, 83, 88, 93, 98, 102, 103, 105, 156, 158, 160, 191, 196, 207
National Industrial Recovery Act (NIRA) 74-75, 77, 79, 85, 89, 95, 101, 110, 115, 136, 143, 145
National Labor Board (NLB) 79, 145
National Labor Relations Board (NLRB) 133
National Recovery Administration (NRA) 78-80, 96, 101, 110
Nazis (Germany) 8, 119, 173, 178, 221, 223, 226, 228, 229-234, 237, 243-244
Nazis (US) 173, 220 see also Ku Klux Klan, Black Legion
Neal, Claude 119
New Deal 58, 63, 65, 71, 74, 99-100, 110, 120, 122, 123-124, 129, 131-137, 177-178, 202, 217-218, 222-225, 232, 243

Ollman, Joe 83
Olson, Governor Floyd 83, 92-94
open shop 10-14, 21, 27, 76, 86, 88-95, 98, 103, 108, 143, 144, 147, 166, 169, 182, 187, 191, 207
Organizer, The 92

Perkins, Frances 65, 98, 99, 102, 149, 156-157, 159
Pesotta, Rose 116
Pinkerton Agency 26-27, 148, 160, 198
Pogroms 34, 54, 210-211, 220
Poland 232-233, 241
police 28, 36-37, 40, 43-45, 48-51, 54, 59, 68, 69, 86-88, 91, 92-93, 97-99, 101, 103, 106, 123, 135, 143, 145, 148, 152, 154-160, 162, 163, 164, 166, 167, 168, 169, 170, 171, 176, 190-197, 200, 201, 211, 236
Polish workers 150-151, 165, 175
Popular Front see under Communist Party
POUM (Spain) 87, 240

racism 33-38, 46, 52-55, 209-211
Reconstruction Finance Corporation (RFC) 57-58, 68-69, 94, 134-135, 217
red scares 7, 11, 14-16, 45, 91, 212, 234-237, 244
Reuther, Victor 113, 143, 150-151, 155, 156, 157
Reuther, Walter 143, 157, 169, 171, 175, 179
Revolutionary Workers League 168
Roosevelt Depression 9, 206-208, 218, 222
Roosevelt, Eleanor 60, 71, 137, 220, 221-222
Roosevelt, Franklin Delano 8-9, 15, 37, 42-43, 55, 58, 59, 60-66, 69, 70-75, 78-81, 85, 94, 96, 98-103, 105, 106, 110, 114, 118-120, 122-141, 143, 145, 156, 159, 176, 177, 185, 187, 195, 198, 199, 200, 201, 204, 206, 208, 214, 216-222, 224-225, 227, 232-233, 235, 236, 240, 241, 243
Ryan, Joseph 96, 97

Scottsboro Boys 53-54
Second World War 9, 173, 181, 210, 218, 219, 228, 244
Section 7a 75, 77, 79, 85, 89, 101, 110, 115, 136, 143, 145
Sellins, Fannie 25
Service Department (Ford's) 27, 50, 171-172, 173-175
Shachtman, Max 56, 92, 240
Share Our Wealth campaign 125-127
Sinclair, Upton 123-124, 175, 203, 222-223
sit-down strikes 7, 9, 84, 100, 115-116, 150-161, 162-166, 168-170, 179, 186, 190, 192, 193, 205, 209, 214, 243, 244
Skogland, Carl 89-90
Sloan, Alfred 57, 147, 157-158
Small Home and Landowners Federation 51
Socialist Party 8, 14-15, 45, 47, 56, 75, 113, 120-121, 123, 124, 143, 153, 155, 179
Socialist Workers Party (SWP) 241-242
Southern Tenant Farmers' Union (STFU) 120-122
Soviet Union 46, 51, 55, 178, 224-241
Spanish Civil War 219-220, 222, 227, 240
Spector, Maurice 217
Stalin 9, 177, 181, 223, 227, 228-229, 238, 239, 241
Stalinism see Communist Party
Starvation 14, 22, 40-42, 68, 74, 229
Steel Workers' Organising Committee (SWOC) 117, 169, 178, 182-184, 187-193, 195-197, 200-201

Taft, William Howard 24
Teamsters Union 26, 77, 85, 89-100, 208, 214-215, 241
Temporary Emergency Relief Administration (TERA) 64

Textile Workers Organising Committee (TWOC) 206-209
Third Period Communism see under Communist Party
Tobin, Daniel 77, 92, 241
Toledo 8, 85-89, 145-147, 153, 154, 159, 243
Travis, Bob 146, 150, 153, 157, 158, 160
Triangle factory fire 31, 60-61
Trotsky, Leon 227, 228, 239, 240, 241
Trotskyists 47, 55-56, 80-84, 89, 92, 93-94, 108, 168, 214, 217, 237-242, 243; see also Muste, Musteites, Cannon, Socialist Workers Party, American Workers Party, Workers Party

Unemployed Councils 47, 51
union bureaucracy 105-108, 113-114, 178-180, 183, 200, 226-227, 243
Union Carbide 31-33
United Auto Workers 26, 146-153, 156-161, 165-176, 179-180, 187, 191, 209, 218, 235-236
United Brotherhood of Carpenters 14
United Council of Working Class Women 123
United Electrical Workers (UE) 163-164
United Mine Workers (UMW) 13, 17, 21-25, 27, 34, 76, 105, 106, 108-110, 112-114, 117, 133, 153, 182-183, 189, 195, 198, 201, 209-210, 243

United Rubber Workers 115
United Textile Workers (UTW) 80, 86, 101, 103, 206
US Steel 29, 39-40, 72, 169, 183, 187-188, 191, 192, 200

Volunteer Emergency Committee (VEC) 68

Wagner, Senator Robert 22, 58, 130, 133, 138, 169-170, 177, 221
Waterfront Worker 95-96
Webb, Beatrice and Sidney 106
Welles, Orson 203-204
Wobblies see Industrial Workers of the World
Women's Auxiliary groups 91, 154-155, 171, 185
Women's Emergency Brigade 155, 158, 160
Women's Trade Union League 221
Woolworth's 7, 162-163, 166-167, 245
Workers Party 238
Works Progress Administration (WPA) 132, 202-204, 217

Young Communist League (YCL) 51
Young People's Socialist League 220

Zuk, Mary 123